The Learning Centre Library
236-250 Holloway Road
London N7 6PP
Tel: 020 7133 2371 (Renewals)
            ~200 (Switchboard)
                        ·//opac.unl.ac.uk

CW00750790

SOAP

THE GENDERED POLITICS

OF FANTASY

PN 9203908 1

THE HAMPTON PRESS COMMUNICATION SERIES
Popular Culture
John A. Lent, series editor

Advertising in Everyday Life
Neil Alperstein

Jewish Jesters: A Study in American Popular Comedy
Arthur Asa Berger

Agent in the Agency: Media, Popular Culture, and Everyday
Life in America
Arthur Asa Berger

Indian Popular Cinema: Industry, Ideology, and Consciousness
Manjunath Pendakur

Serial Monogamy: Soap Opera, Lifespan, and the Gendered
Politics of Fantasy
Christine Scodari

forthcoming

Cartooning in Africa
John A. Lent (ed.)

Cartooning in Latin America
John A. Lent (ed.)

SERIAL MONOGAMY

SOAP OPERA, LIFESPAN, AND
THE GENDERED POLITICS
OF FANTASY

The Learning Centre
Library
236-250 Holloway Road
London N7 6PP

LONDON
metropolitan
university

Christine Scodari
Florida Atlantic University

HAMPTON PRESS, INC.
CRESSKILL, NEW JERSEY

Copyright © 2004 by Hampton Press, Inc.

All rights reserved. No part of this publication may be reproduced, stored in a retrieval system, or transmitted in any form or by any means, electronic, mechanical, photocopying, microfilming, recording, or otherwise, without permission of the publisher.

Printed in the United States of America

Library of Congress Cataloging-in-Publication Data

Scodari, Christine.
   Serial monogamy : soap opera, lifespan, and the gendered politics of fantasy / Christine Scodari.
      p. cm. -- (Hampton Press communications series)
   Includes bibliographical references and index.
   ISBN 1-57273-555-4 -- ISBN 1-57273-556-2 (alk. paper)
      1. Soap Operas--United States--History and criticism. 2. Television and women--United States. I. Title. II. Series.

   PN1992.8.S4S36 2003
   791.45'6--dc22
                                                2003061252

WITHDRAWN

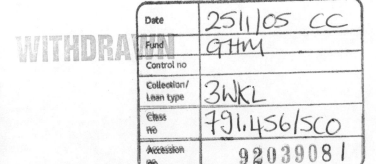

Date	25/1/05 CC
Fund	GTHM
Control no	
Collection/ Loan type	3WKL
Class no	791.456/SCO
Accession no	92039081

Hampton Press, Inc.
23 Broadway
Cresskill, NJ 07626

In memory of my grandparents

LONDON metropolitan university
LIBRARY SERVICES

CONTENTS

ACKNOWLEDGMENTS   xi

INTRODUCTION: MEANING AS CONTEST   xiii

    Production and Meaning   xvi
    Content and Meaning   xvii
    Consumption and Meaning   xx
    Notes   xxviii

1

MARKETING DESIRE: FANTASY, SOAP OPERA,
    AND THE PREFERRED AUDIENCE   1

    Desire, Fantasy, and Pleasure   1
    Identity and Interpellation   3
    Affect and Currency   4
    Soap Production: Blueprinting Consumption   6
       Anonymity Unlimited?   6
       Are You Demographically Correct?   8
       Give Us Your Daughters 'Til They Are Sixteen. . . .   9
       Baby Boom or Bust/The "X" Factor   11
    Notes   13

2

IMAGINED SUBJECTS AND THE GENDERED TEXT   15

    Soap Text: Prefabricated Construction   16
       A Flexibly Feminine Format?   16
       The Case of the Well-Married Heroine   17
       The Case of the Retroactively Redeemed Rapist   18
       What's Behind Door # 3?   22

Soap Text: Parcelled Passion   24
    Hunks, Babes, Divas, Vixens, and Harridans   25
    Satellites, Supervillains, and Supercouples   28
    Tethering Time   31
    Triangulation Station   34
    Front Burner, Back Burner, and Ye Olde Chopping Block   35
    The DOOLification of Soap Opera   36

3

**ACTIVE INTERPRETERS AND THE
SOCIAL AUDIENCE**   41

Soap Audience: Unavoidable Disruption   41
    Collective Bargaining   41
    Tabloid Talk/Tabloid Soap   43
    Why Would a Campy Gay Man Keep a Lady in a Cage?"   46
Soap Audience: Negotiating Currency   50
Notes   59

4

**HE'S MAY, SHE'S SEPTEMBER, BUT ARE THEY
BOTH FROM *ANOTHER WORLD*?**   61

Sauce for the Gander   62
Mrs. Robinson in Soapland   64
The "Chemistry You Don't Often See"   66
Geese Unite! "No Status Quo"   69
    Mind Your Own Genre   69
    Reducing Ambiguity   72
    "We Can Dream, Can't We?"   76
"Real Men" Don't Mind Menopause   79
It's a Wonderful Midlife   83
Notes   88

5

**OVER THE RAINBOW... DREAMS BECOME
NIGHTMARES**   89

Nostalgia Versus P.C.   89
Arresting Resistance   92
    "It Doesn't Matter How Old You Are"   92
    "It Matters How Much You Love"   93
Notes   110

6
PLAYING (WITH) FAVORITES 111
Conditions of Love 112
Reality Checks 114
Future Projections 117
Alienations of Affection 119
Feasts of Burden 120
Poached Pleasures 122
There's No Place Like Home 127
Notes 130

7
PLEASURE PRINCIPLES 131
All the Network Allows 131
Love and the "Geritol" Soap 131
Serealities 136
Meta-text and Medium Matter 138
I'm Not an Older Woman But I Play One on TV 138
Lies, Damned Lies, and "Cybergossip" 141
No Politics Here 145
Notes 152

CONCLUSION: END IN HINDSIGHT 155
Ego-Tripping on the Information Superhighway 155
The Plot Thickens: A Synopsis 158
Notes 171

APPENDIX: METHODOLOGY 173
Data Sources 173
Data Selection 176
Data Collection 176
Data Analysis 179

REFERENCES 181
AUTHOR INDEX 195
SUBJECT INDEX 199

ACKNOWLEDGMENTS

A project of this magnitude cannot come to fruition without a blend of sound advice, provocative subject matter and subjects, practical help, and kind gestures of support to fortify the investigator in her endeavors. Special thanks go to former graduate students Ronald Antonin and Sue Holt for their crucial assistance in the collection and management of relevant Internet and video data, and to Amy Oxner for the photographs taken from TV and peppered throughout the book. Celeste Condit and Bonnie Dow of the University of Georgia provided key commentary on material from the project prior to its publication as an article in *Women's Studies in Communication*. Colleagues and students from the Communication and Women's Studies programs at Florida Atlantic University helped pave the way to publication by offering both feedback and enthusiasm in response to in-house and in-class presentations of the work. Anonymous reviewers encountered along the way and Hampton's own John Lent and Barbara Bernstein also deserve recognition. Finally, I could not have achieved this goal without family and friends, whose unrelenting encouragement bolstered my research and publication efforts, and countless fans, whose participation and fervor are reflected on the pages to follow.

Material from this book was previously published by its author as a journal article entitled, "'No Politics Here': Age and Gender in Soap Opera 'Cyberfandom,'" in *Women's Studies in Communication*, Volume 21, Fall 1998, pages 168–187.

Introduction

Meaning as Contest

A 19-year-old environmental science major named Kerry has hit a slump. Her grades are suffering, and her plan to do political work for a conservation group has been put on hold. While her sorority sisters have snagged older, professional guys who seem to appreciate their girlfriends' intelligence and ambition, she has been tethered to her high school sweetheart— a sports junkie in a state of arrested adolescence. She wants to end it, but is still unsure. Can she appeal to the sort of sophisticated man she truly wants—a man like attorney Slate Garrison, 32, her favorite soap opera hunk? In such a man's eyes, could she compete with women who have lived longer and accomplished more? Slate had been shackled to Jacy Steele, a diva as old as Kerry's mom, who is also self-centered and takes him for granted. Now, finally, he has seen the light, and has fallen for spunky graduate student, Taryn Burke. Kerry is emboldened; she will dump junior varsity and set her sites higher before it's too late.

Meanwhile, across town, a successful, 42-year-old architect named Denise has two great kids and a happy marriage. Every other weekend, she volunteers at a women's shelter and campaigns for stiffer laws against domestic violence. Slowly, however, Denise's confidence and ambition begin to wither. She winces upon hearing that her older sister's ex-husband is marrying a woman their daughter's age. She looks the other way as a married male colleague sneaks off for long lunches with a young secretary. She attends the fourth movie in a row in which an actor her age is coupled with an actress who was in kindergarten when she was a high school senior. To top it all off, her favorite soap opera heroine, Jacy Steele, whose life milestones had paralleled her own and whose vitality and professional savvy had always energized her, becomes an insecure, desperate harridan and promptly loses her younger husband to her best pal's spunky daughter. . . .

Although the impact of TV fantasies on the psyche and spirit might be somewhat overstated in these hypothetical cases, the analyses to be reported herein insinuate that they are not far off the mark. The perplexing thing is, however, that an audience ethnographer might interview both soap opera viewers a year later and note only the bursts of empowerment they experienced as a result of their fandom. Or she might concentrate on younger viewers likely to be in Kerry's situation and assume that women, regardless of other aspects of their identity, will react to soaps similarly. In neglecting long-term textual analysis, and in gathering impressions well after the fact, this researcher might also dismiss the evolution of the narrative and its ideological implications for particular groups of viewers at particular junctures. Even if she were to observe Kerry and Denise's disparate reactions, in eschewing study of soap opera's commercial strategies, she might overlook a highly relevant finding—that (someone like) Kerry's pleasure at (someone like) Denise's expense is, logically, anticipated and desired by the show's creators. Absent of these crucial dimensions, her ultimate verdict might be that soaps exhilarate, generate pleasure, lead to solidarity among female fans, and, consequently, encourage resistance to the patriarchal status quo.

In fact, critical/cultural media scholars debate the extent to which audiences interpret and use popular texts in resistive ways. Political economists (see e.g., Garnham, 1995; Kellner, 1992a) have examined this question macroscopically, arguing that the structures, processes, and commercial imperatives of capitalist media institutions determine a range of available content, restrict access and ownership, and reproduce dominant ideologies that help maintain unequal power relations. According to this view, the power to direct meaning rests *primarily* with cultural producers for whom any commitment to diversity and free speech halts at the doorstep of their own class interests.

Scholars of the British cultural studies tradition (see e.g., McRobbie, 1981; Morley, 1980) problematized the issues of power and meaning-making beyond the economic. They argued that lived culture is elemental, texts are fluid, and their interpretation is dependent on the identities of those who encounter them and the contexts in which they are encountered. Dominant meanings may prevail, but they can be negotiated and/or opposed. Power inequities must be continuously reproduced through a complex process that Gramsci (1971) labeled *hegemony*, whereby a consensus evolves in favor of those cultural understandings that mesh with the interests of the powerful. The focus shifts to the microscopic, localized consumption of media audiences in efforts to discover whether and in what ways hegemony is achieved or frustrated. Marginal identities of class, race, sexuality, and/or gender are often scrutinized in this regard because it is the complicity or opposition of the disempowered that is pivotal.

Scholars of a third strain, dubbed U.S. cultural studies (see e.g. Brown, 1994, Fiske, 1987; Jenkins, 1992), insisted that the power to make meaning rests squarely with consumers who become producers in their own right as they interpret and use available cultural products in ways that are often both pleasurable and empowering. These defenders of a postmodern, semiotic democracy argue that texts are pregnant with potential meanings and a repertoire of appropriative strategies regularly confound the forces of domination, particularly in the hands of those whose marginal status cultivates such ingenuity. Some scrutinize fan subcultures, maintaining that collective audience engagement facilitates resistive activity. These studies endeavor to rescue audiences from the charge that they are easily manipulated "cultural dopes" (see Grossberg, 1992, p. 65). Such claims often stimulate or emanate from ethnographic audience study generally via focus groups, interviews, and/or observation.

Debates among these perspectives are legion, particularly between the production-oriented view of political economists and active audience theorists of the U.S. cultural studies mode,[1] and have often centered on whether class or other markers of identity such as gender or race should be viewed as central to questions of hegemony and power. Political economists contend that class supersedes all else, whereas feminist and critical race theorists, among others, may see other aspects as pre-eminent. Postmodernism is also central in this regard because active audience adherents assert that and others debate whether postmodern polysemy—the openness of texts—facilitates readers' ability to extract empowering messages (see Grossberg, 1995; Harms & Dickens, 1996). Lately, however, many participants in these conversations have called for studies that assess more than one locus of difference and combine examinations of production, text, and consumption in a multiperspectival approach (see Harms & Dickens, 1996; Kellner, 1992b), which considers meaning-making at all levels and avoids extremes of economic determinism or what McGuigan (1992) referred to as *cultural populism*.

The study I elaborate in succeeding chapters endeavors to answer this call. It investigates commercial TV and the soap opera genre with an eye toward understanding intersections of gender, lifespan, and power in the discourses of fantasy and romance and in terms of economically determined production practices, texts, and the consumptive activities of fans. It considers generic conventions, specific narratives, creative decision making, meta-textual commentary, and audience responses as they develop and change over time. Thus, it is sensitive to actual circumstances such as those reflected in the hypothetical cases rendered at the beginning of this introduction.

Moreover, the study explores particular facets of soap opera fantasy, assessing their potential to empower fans and motivate them to political awareness, and the degree to which they are keyed to various viewer subjectivities, perhaps setting one marginal group against another. It gauges the extent to which creators can reproduce hegemonic meanings through textual manipulation and the boundaries of and conflicts arising from viewer negotiations of the narratives they provide. It also appraises whether fan interactivity online animates and/or hinders counter-hegemonic opposition to soap opera content. As this review of relevant theory and scholarship proceeds, additional issues surrounding audience pleasure and resistance as supposed results of engagement with romantic fantasies, and the need to contextualize such study in terms of producer aims, the storylines they do and do not choose to create as a consequence, and the multiple identities of viewers—particularly, the gender/age nexus—become increasingly manifest.

Accordingly, the literature review is organized in terms of emphases on production, text, and consumption in the negotiation of meaning. The introduction closes with a discussion of the noteworthy features and method of the study. Along the way, key issues warranting deliberation in the ensuing chapters emerge.

PRODUCTION AND MEANING

When it comes to media production and the various foci of this project, studies assuming that the invigoration of women's participation in the structures of power will automatically translate into improved content are most conspicuous. This stance has been associated with liberal feminism and an *image of women* approach (Walters, 1996) to media studies and is criticized for neglecting the "organizational context in which media production takes place" (van Zoonen, 1994, p. 64). According to Ferguson (1990), "the naive expectation that more women in the media lead to changes in female images ignores conflict between the professional norms and values shared by both sexes and uniquely female experience of structural inequality" (p. 227).

D'Acci's (1994) account of backstage deliberations over definitions of femininity in the production of the 1980s' American TV series *Cagney and Lacey* is one of the few studies to address this deficiency. Among other things, D'Acci illustrated how the notion of targeting a quality audience was negotiated and constructed, and how such an audience could be comparatively small, predominantly female, and somewhat older as long as its loyalty and affluence made it a valuable commodity in the eyes of commercial interests.

Feminist investigations of soap opera have tended to shy away from a production orientation. One exception is McEachern's (1994) analysis of the British rural soap opera *Emmerdale Farm*, which illuminates negotiations of gender representation in the creative process. These negotiations appear strangely independent of the advertiser influence previous studies of American soaps had considered crucial. For instance, Intintoli's (1984) exhaustive, behind-the-scenes case study of the long-running soap opera *Guiding Light* reveals economic and other pressures attendant to its creation and provides insight into soaps' representation of romance in the effort to attract sought-after younger viewers.

Cantor and Pingree (1983) offered a sociological examination of the backstage production process, whereas Hobson (1982), in her analysis of *Crossroads*, and Buckingham (1987), in his study of *EastEnders*, interviewed creators and viewers of these popular British soaps to assess negotiations at both levels. Most abundant among soap opera studies of the discourses and issues of power relations relevant to this inquiry are those that feature content.

CONTENT AND MEANING

Research relating to media content and issues of age and/or gender range from such quantitative appraisals as those based on Gerbner's cultivation hypothesis, to textual analyses of television or film proceeding from feminist, psychoanalytical, narrative, and/or reader-oriented approaches. Cultivation studies (see Gerbner, 1995) demonstrate the relative dearth of women, particularly older women, in featured roles on TV, and link these results to heavy viewers' perceptions of the real world. A content analysis of older women in popular film from the 1940s to the 1980s confirms that they are not only underrepresented, but framed as "unattractive, unfriendly, and unintelligent" (Bazzini, McIntosh, Smith, Cook, & Harris, 1997, p. 531). Content analyses of soap opera compiled and/or performed by Cassata and Skill (1983) and Greenberg and Busselle (1996) continue to assume that the manifest content will be interpreted as reflections of a pre-existing and normative reality. This assumption is consistent with the image of women trend discussed earlier. It does little to ascertain how these texts are negotiated and lived by viewers who may or may not associate them with the real world (see Allen, 1985).

However, studies adopting a woman as image demeanor (Walters, 1996) abound. For instance, Dow's (1996) textual analyses of prime-time

TV shows such as *The Mary Tyler Moore Show, One Day at a Time,* and *Murphy Brown* pinpoint popular representations of single womanhood as articulated to the evolution of the feminist movement in the late 20th century. She found these programs complicit with hegemonies of self-interest as opposed to collective resistance.

Additional feminist studies explore other narrative and generic features of texts, how the audience might be expected to negotiate meanings of texts, and how they are *interpellated* in and by texts. Althusser (1971) borrowed from Lacanian psychoanalytical theory in using the term *interpellation* to describe how actual subjects can be hailed by and ideologically positioned as subject/spectators within the text. The identifications forged by this process are perhaps a key means by which pleasure and empowerment may be realized by TV viewers or other readers/audiences.

Any discussion of gender and visual media must address this related issue of spectatorship—the subjectivities of the text as "constituted in signification" (Kuhn, 1996, p. 65). Mulvey's (1975) concept of the cinematic *male gaze* has been central in this regard, drawing on psychoanalytic theories of scopophilia, voyeurism, and fetishism to consider the positioning of gendered subjects. Mulvey's claim that film interpellates both male and female onlookers to share the masculine gaze of the camera and male subjects in relegating the female to the status of pleasurable object has been vigorously debated. Its applicability to TV has been a bone of contention for some feminist scholars, who hypothesize multiple gazes in postmodern televisual forms such as music video (see Kaplan, 1988) and/or extol the existence of the feminine subject in genres such as soap opera (see Modleski, 1982; Nochimson, 1992).

Still intersections of age, gender, and romance have rarely been considered in textual analyses of TV and soap opera. Feminist scholarship informing the present research on these matters includes Banner's (1992) historical analysis of aging women, their sexuality, and the taboo against older woman/younger man romances as represented in a variety of texts. Woodward's (1999) collection entitled *Figuring Age* includes articles covering the issues of aging as scandalous anachronism (Russo), resisting age-related decline (Gullette), the social inertia of aging (Brennan), and the representation of scary older women in film (Sobchack). Stoddard's (1983) intensive examination of cinematic portrayals of aging women as well as *From Reverence to Rape*, Haskell's (1987) overview of women in film, devote a portion of their introductory material to the gender/age inequity.

Soap opera's serial narrative form, its presumed lack of closure, its focus on the female subject, and its multiple, concurrent plots have been widely studied and linked to a feminine sensibility. Although

Nochimson (1992) celebrated these features without qualification, Modleski (1982) argued that multiple protagonists and never-ending stories preclude the sense of empowerment offered the film subject interpellated as a single, all-powerful, masculine protagonist who masters his fate in a 2-hour narrative. Instead, she theorized a spectator "constituted as sort of an ideal mother . . . whose sympathy is large enough to encompass the conflicting claims of her family . . . and who has no demands or claims of her own (she identifies with no one character exclusively)" (p. 92). Flitterman-Lewis (1992) suggested that soap operas provide pseudo-endings that invoke the cinematic experience. However, Mumford (1995) maintained that individual storylines achieve a definite point of closure, but tend to reproduce and accentuate dominant ideologies of capitalism and patriarchy in so doing—a key perspective of the present investigation. Similarly, Rogers (1991) claimed that the fragmentation of the soap opera narrative provides an opportunity for conservative messages to take hold.

Many narrative/genre studies of soap opera have largely ignored age/gender convergences or have adopted a peculiarly essentialist position regarding them. Both Williams (1992) and Nochimson (1992), for instance, catalogued examples of stock heroines and formulaic plots, but the ages of the female characters they highlighted appear to be of little consequence. However, few of these heroines were older than 30 and virtually none was older than 35 at the time of the analyzed stories. Geraghty's (1991) discussion of soap opera and women's utopian fantasies accounts for class and race in addition to gender, but does not acknowledge age as a possible factor in spectatorship. Indeed, the definition of the term *woman* is at stake.

Age does factor into other, similar investigations of soap opera, but in a manner philosophically at odds with this inquiry. In a textual ethnography of character relationships on British and American soaps, Liebes and Livingstone (1994) criticized the American brand for their "denial of the cycle of life" (pp. 732–733). Because grandmothers and matriarchs on American soaps often remain eligible for romance and mothers and daughters compete for the same men, supposedly biological certainties of the female cycle of life are, according to this assessment, bypassed. This essentialist thinking discounts the possibility that older women's apparent ineligibility for romance is a culturally constructed, rather than a purely natural, phenomenon.

Various configurations of Hall's (1980) *encoding/decoding* model have become standard tools to evaluate interpellated or actual audience positions and frame larger issues in critical media theory and research in terms of encoding (production) and/or decoding (consumption) emphases. The model's classification of the meanings (or readings) of a text into *dominant/preferred*, *negotiated*, and *oppositional* categories has been subjected to multiple readings.

Traditionally, reader-oriented studies of soap opera have attempted to situate the envisioned onlooker without confronting the actual audience—the social audience—in the empirical sense. Geraghty's (1991) examination of prime-time soaps, Brunsdon's (1981) consideration of the British soap opera *Crossroads*, and Allen's (1985) reader-oriented poetics of the genre are noteworthy examples. However, whether it is for philosophical or pragmatic reasons, such studies do not encounter real viewers.

CONSUMPTION AND MEANING

Viewer surveys such as those catalogued by Cassata and Skill (1983) involve the social audience, but they cannot and do not consider it i*n the light* of textual subjectivities. Even when content is also appraised in some general, descriptive fashion, as in soap opera studies performed by Matelski (1988) and Williams (1992), the dearth of open-ended responses impedes meaningful linkages between text and audience.

Audience ethnographies and other qualitative studies have the potential to fill this gap. Utilizing methods of direct observation, questionnaire, focus groups, and/or interview, such research usually proceeds from the assumption that some resistance to dominant meanings could occur and is interested in discovering how and for whom.

In the last two decades, in a continuing effort to argue that participants in feminine culture are active producers of meaning and not mere dupes of dominant ideology, many feminist media scholars have moved toward empirical yet qualitative audience study. However, with some notable exceptions, such examinations are grounded in an understanding of established generic conventions rather than in close textual analysis. Additionally, few contain more than a perfunctory consideration of production imperatives or practices.

One ground-breaking study of feminine culture to incorporate ethnographic methods with solid assessments of narrative features and institutional aspects is Radway's (1984) *Reading the Romance*. Through questionnaire and focus group encounters, Radway concluded that romance novel reading allows women to make a space for their interests amid otherwise tedious and unfulfilling domestic routines. Moreover, she found that her subjects interpret the genre's heroines as powerful and empowering in their ability to tame roguish heroes. For Radway, such readings and uses are substitutes for and not necessarily evidence of "true" feminist awareness and action (p. 222).

Gender and class are key elements in similar, book-length ethnographic studies of TV. Press (1991) explored relevant imagery and the interpretations of female viewers, adding the element of generation (as opposed to age) in theorizing the reading positions of prefeminist and postfeminist women. Similarly, Heide's exploration of the 1980s' prime-time serial drama *thirtysomething* inspects the larger production environment, general features of the text, key episodes, and data acquired via audience ethnography.

Although Intintoli (1984) examined fan letters in conjunction with his backstage production study of *Guiding Light*, the earliest qualitative studies of soap opera audiences have concentrated on British programs and viewers or on cross-cultural reactions to *Dallas*, the American prime-time serial and international hit. As mentioned earlier, Hobson (1982) and Buckingham (1987) consulted both creative personnel and fans in their analyses of British soaps—*Crossroads* and *EastEnders*, respectively. Age is a factor in each of these studies, with Hobson noting that *Crossroads* provided a much-needed source of entertainment for housebound seniors and Buckingham discovering that adolescent viewers of *EastEnders* seemed more enthralled with the older characters than with the teens. Liebes and Katz's (1990) work on the impact of *Dallas* in non-Western cultures demonstrates that audiences can negotiate the meanings of culturally alien texts according to their own frames of reference. Ang's (1985) textual readings and mail solicitation of *Dallas* viewers in the Netherlands led to theorization of fantasy, pleasure, and the melodramatic imagination (see Brooks, 1976) involved in women's apparent identification with heroines such as Sue Ellen Ewing—the neglected, alcoholic wife of J.R.

Other soap opera scholars maneuver in the direction of audience analysis in the U.S. cultural studies mode, foregoing specific attention to text or production. The Seiter (et. al, 1989) dissection of group interviews with viewers in Oregon reveals that working-class women, among others, appear to reject the subjectivity of the ideal mother, which Modleski (1982) saw inscribed in the soap opera narrative. Brown's (1994) study of Australian viewers of British, American, and Australian soaps found that interaction within fan "friendship networks" (pp. 37-39) facilitates pleasure and resistance through collective acknowledgment of women's lot under patriarchy. Similarly, Blumenthal's (1997) cultural feminist perspective on soap opera viewing sees it as an empowering reaffirmation of women's identities. Harrington and Bielby (1995) drew from questionnaire responses, computer bulletin board postings, fan magazines, and similar data in claiming that soap opera fans are active consumers *and* producers of culture.

The contents of soap opera anthologies by Frentz (1992) and Allen (1995) run the gamut of perspectives, although Frentz's is peppered with articles that are more mainstream than scholarly. *The Feminist, the Housewife, and the Soap Opera* by Brunsdon (2000) is meta-analytical, dissecting the subjectivities of cultural critics who have contributed to the literature on soap opera as illuminated through interviews. *Worlds Without End* (1997), an offering of The Museum of Television and Radio, intersperses the insights of scholars, creators, actors, and the press within its pictorial history of the genre. Nevertheless, other popular treatments that contribute to understanding the genre and its backstage processes include Wakefield's (1976) biography of award-winning soap opera producer/writer Agnes Nixon, Lemay's (1981) account of his tenure as head writer of *Another World*, as well as Poll's (1999) commemorative history of this long-running soap opera, Buckman's (1984) overview entitled *All For Love*, and Rouverol's (1984) insider tutorial on soap opera writing.

The contest over meaning in critical media studies surfaces in assorted ways throughout this literature review. One fundamental point of controversy centers on whether empirical audience studies tend to romanticize their subjects and compromise the critical posture of researchers. Modleski (1986) took Radway's (1984) study of romance novel readers to task for its "collusion between mass culture critic and consumer society (p. xii)." Responding to Modleski, Ang (1996, p. 100) refused to concede that "the project of ethnography is necessarily at odds with a critical stance" and argued that encountering actual readers "helps to keep our critical discourses from becoming closed texts of Truth" (p. 100).

However, Ang recognized that ethnography is a tangled adventure with many perils and faulted Radway's work on other grounds. According to Ang (1996), Radway distanced herself from her subjects, insinuating that the feminist potential of romance readers can only be realized if they cease that activity in favor of becoming appropriately political. Thus, Ang believed that Radway romanticized not her subjects, but her own totalizing viewpoint, and ignored the possibility that the pleasure derived from the activity is authentic and not necessarily inimical to feminism. Although Ang is correct about the dangers of oversimplifying ethnographic results so they can be readily filtered through reductionistic theories, I believe her criticism of Radway's work is somewhat overstated. It is valid to ask whether and how pleasure equals *meaningful* resistance, and this can be managed without dismissing the pleasure as insignificant.

Lewis' (1991) clarification of the encoding/decoding model as enhanced by Hall's (1986) elaboration of the concept of *articulation* ground this work. In Hall's formulation, articulation theory demands that analyses of audience readings acknowledge their embeddedness in particular contexts—that is, at the intersection of specific identities, political subjects, sociocultural urgencies, and textual features bound up in the "historical moment" (p. 53).[2] As Grossberg (1992) elucidated: "Articulation is the continuous struggle to reposition practices within a shifting field of forces, to redefine the possibilities of life by redefining the field of relations–the context–within which a practice is located. (p. 54). With an emphasis on texts and readings related to issues of gender, lifespan, and romance, I seek in this research to isolate and consider particular articulations so that their ideological import may be better appreciated. As the opening narratives illustrate, situations and pressures likely to occur at various life stages can lead to significant conflicts among women's negotiations of the same textual matter. Moreover, according to Moffitt (1993), articulation reconciles the British and U.S. cultural studies traditions by reinvigorating ideological critique of texts and, especially, audiences.

These issues, theories, and approaches are illuminated and debated throughout the investigation to come—an investigation that, through its distinctive properties, is apt to raise as many theoretical and methodological issues as it helps to resolve. The first noteworthy feature is its multiperspectival, three-pronged approach to production, text, and consumption. Few of the previously mentioned studies substantively reference and/or perform analysis at all three levels.

Existing research on institutional practices and the discourses of soap opera creators reflected in these studies, in the press, and on the Internet have provided significant data on which to base the production aspect of the study. Every effort has been made to contextualize analyses of text and audience response in terms of the commercial imperatives and processes reflected in these materials. The dual public relations role of soap opera's behind-the-scenes personnel—to inform those in the industry of their economic goals and successes while communicating to fans that they are all equally welcome—are often in conflict and have resulted in revealing insights. On the one hand, a producer will excitedly announce that his or her show has increased viewership in the female, 12 to 34 demographic groupings and, on the other, deny that this same show privileges young audiences over long-time fans.

This study concentrates on daytime soap operas in the United States—programming that best reflects the genre's original *raison d'etre*, format, and content. My experience as a regular or semiregular viewer of six such programs over the course of more than two decades, for periods ranging from 2 to 25 years per soap, generated many of the illustrations used in the analysis. These shows include *Another World, Days of Our Lives, Guiding Light, Young and the Restless, All My Children,* and *General Hospital.* Precise viewing and/or videotaping, as warranted, of five programs—*Another World, Days of Our Lives, General Hospital,* One *Life to Live,* and *Guiding Light*—occurred expressly for this project during its 5-year duration. In addition, plot summaries and magazine articles yielded information about unobserved soap opera stories serving as corroborative data.

In addition to the multiperspectival approach, a second feature of this study involves the intense scrutiny of a long-term storyline in a *timefactored analysis.* This is the assessment of text, production information, and/or audience response *as the narrative unfolds* rather than purely in hindsight. Existing theory related to soap opera remains suspect in the absence of such attention. If soap opera stories achieve closure despite the genre's pretensions of openness and if, as Mumford (1995) argued, stories that seem to challenge dominant ideology at their midpoints retreat into that ideology on resolving, it is vital that close textual analysis and corresponding ethnography occur in this manner. Most examinations of particular plots (see e.g., Nochimson, 1992; Williams, 1992) fail to note or deem significant whether the critic's readings are based on memory, videotaped records of a completed story, and/or perceptions at various junctures during a story. Qualitative audience studies do not often distinguish between fans' recollections of previous plots and interpretations of ongoing storylines. To adequately address issues of textual polysemy, hegemony, and audience resistance, the inclusion of such a time-factored analysis would seem imperative. Moreover, timefactoring assists in tracking the historical moment critical to pinpointing ideological articulations.

The study's audience investigation utilized two overarching procedures—examination of fan letters in magazines and various participation in fan activities and interactions in cyberspace. The ethnography of cyberfans frequenting relevant, discursive sites on the Internet is clearly a third distinctive characteristic of the research.

Like many audience researchers, I distinguish among *audience members* or *viewers* and *fans.* Fans are a subset of the audience—more knowledgeable about and loyal to the text than typical viewers. This study concentrates on audience members who are avid and active enough to take their interest in or views about soap opera online or to the magazines. Consequently, they are fans. However, for variety's sake, the terms audience members, viewers, and fans are used interchangeably throughout the study to designate fans. When a distinction is significant, it is explicitly stated.

Jenkins (1992) took some account of cyberspace activities in his analyses of science fiction fandom. Baym (1993, 1995, 2000) scrutinized interaction among posters on the soap opera newsgroup on Usenet in her assessments of computer-mediated communication (CMC) and fan culture. Blumenthal (1997) collected online reactions to particular shows for a brief period in the course of her study of soap opera consumption. Harrington and Bielby (1995) included survey data gleaned from the Internet and comments on cyberspace bulletin boards as part of their broad-based investigation of soap fans. Hayward (1997) looked at Usenet postings as part of her analysis of fan reactions to controversial storylines on ABC soaps. However, I conducted a naturalistic virtual ethnography involving comprehensive participant observation of 5 years duration and have done so in conjunction with equally extensive textual analysis and an appraisal of production imperatives and processes. As Seiter (1999) acknowledged, most qualitative cultural studies of the audience are labeled ethnographies, but do not adhere to the anthropological criteria for such a methodology—especially those prescribing long-term immersion into a culture.

This research did involve such long-term immersion. Nevertheless, although insights concerning CMC and virtual community emerged, the primary purpose was to investigate the culture of *cyberfans* in the context of designated texts to assess their uses and interpretations against those of the critic and, ultimately, in terms of theoretical positions of hegemony, resistance, and/or opposition. This study also differs from earlier qualitative assessments of online fans in its performance of a multi-sited virtual ethnography, which, as Hine (2000) pointed out, allows one to explore "connections within and around the Internet" that are "not reliant on any one understanding of it" (p. 61).

Three types of data collection were used in the virtual audience study. The first involved lurking—that is, anonymously observing and/or downloading messages and transcripts without actually contributing to bulletin boards or online chats. The second entailed joining these discussions, with a periodic reminder to other fans that I was also engaged as a researcher. Participation in a small, informal mailing list was the third source of data, with the other e-mailers having expressly consented to be included in the study. None of the online scholars previously mentioned utilized all three methods. This naturalistic approach precluded the imposition of standardized methodological procedures in situations in which they undermined the normal flow and tenor of cultural activities of fans on the Internet. Emergent guidelines for this manner of virtual ethnography were, therefore, identified.

Some of the issues attendant to any ethnographic audience research are still at play here. For instance, the fact that I entered the research context as a fan, much as Brown (1994), Jenkins (1992), and others in the U.S. cultural studies tradition have done, subjects me potentially to the charge that I cannot not help but romanticize popular culture products and their partisans and to share the view that pleasure equals resistance.

LONDON metropolitan university
LIBRARY SERVICES

I attempt to demonstrate, however, through a self-reflexive accounting of my own subjectivity and methodology, that conducting ethnography in this fashion can have advantages as well as drawbacks and need not result in an uncritical celebration of commercial culture or its consumers.

Nonetheless, interacting with subjects in a virtual environment presents its own difficulties. Collecting accurate demographic information is one because cyberfans often use pseudonyms or otherwise avoid revealing their vital statistics. In her treatise on virtual ethnographic method, Hine (2000) argued that participation over time is apt to reflect authentic identity and "tracing statements made on the Internet to their real-world referents is not generally impossible" (p. 119). Indeed, in this instance, the genders and ages of regular participants often became apparent in their discourses. For instance, a typical comment such as "my husband and I disagree about our son's choice of a wife" yields information about gender, marital status, and approximate age without the ethnographer having to ask. Moreover, some bulletin boards and online services have allowed participants to submit profiles of themselves that are accessible to others, and the demographic traits of e-mailers can be solicited outright.

Race and class are less apparent without such solicitation, however, and the resulting marginalization of these aspects of difference in the study might invite criticism. Research confirms that the computer revolution initially accommodated the male, the White, and the well-off preferentially (see Interrogate the Internet, 1996; Jacobsen 1996), and the fact that cyberfans probably do not faithfully represent the larger community of soap opera devotees must be acknowledged. However, research also establishes that soap opera audiences are still predominantly female and draw from lower more than upper income groups (see Liccardo, 1996), and the prevalence of women among the subjects of this study is indisputable. Moreover, although sacrificing face-to-face interaction and more verifiable demographics, virtual ethnography allows for a larger number of subjects from a greater diversity of geographical locations.

Additionally, of approximately 50 regular and over 100 occasional participants whose discourses have been considered in the virtual ethnography, more persons of every class, race, and age group are likely to be represented than has been logistically feasible in face-to-face encounters. The ease of virtual participation also allows for long-term knowledge of and interaction with subjects and may tend to compensate for some of the disadvantages attached to such a methodology.

Again it is my contention that the subjectivity and impact of the participant researcher need only be prohibitive problems if they are not properly acknowledged and accounted for as many ethnographers, including Seiter, et. al (1989) and Ang (1985), have attempted to do. Methodological specifics are included in the appendix to this study, and further consideration of the caveats, benefits, drawbacks, and potential criticisms associated with virtuality and other aspects of the method are incorporated into the concluding chapter so that such a self-reflexive accounting take place.

A fourth noteworthy aspect of this study is its effort to provide a legitimate academic contribution to the estimation of the author's peers while endeavoring to employ language that is accessible to students and laypersons. As Walters (1996) argued:

> If we want to reveal the ideological agendas . . . often inscribed in a cultural text, then to use language and analysis that are deeply inaccessible and severely laden with jargon only further removes that cultural text from the comprehension and control of those consumers for whom the agendas are intended. (pp. 150–151)

Although I attach appropriate theoretical vocabulary to the phenomena under scrutiny, plain-language explanations of the processes and elements involved in these phenomena occur before or as theoretical concepts are applied.

The layout of the study is similarly accessible. Following this introductory chapter is a theorization of desire, fantasy, pleasure, and their dimensions in popular culture, as well as an examination of soap opera production and the commercial imperatives that underpin its privileging of some audiences—and some elements of content—over others. In chapters 2 and 3, the soap opera text, its inscribed subjectivities, and representative examples of audience response and interpretation are assessed, particularly in terms of exigencies of gender, age, and romance. Chapters 4 and 5 relate a detailed case study of production imperatives, content, and consumption of a single, long-term soap opera storyline manifesting issues of power relations significant to the larger investigation. Chapter 6 highlights the readings of participants in an e-mail group devoted to the story and characters featured in this case study, while Chapter 7 examines meta-textual influences such as magazines and the impact of online *netiquette* on the politicization of soap opera fans. The Conclusion self-reflexively dissects the use of virtual ethnography and summarizes the findings of the research and its contributions to theory and method. All of this occurs with the key elements of gender, age, romance, fantasy, and power in mind.

NOTES

1. A colloquy debating these issues appears in *Critical Studies in Mass Communication*, 12, 62-100. The colloquy includes lengthy statements by Garnham and Grossberg (1995) among others, as well as rebuttals.

2. The concept of *relevancy* (Cohen, 1991; Cooper, 1999) has also been proposed as a way to appraise readings shaped by linkages between the identities and circumstances of the reader and the subject matter of the text. However, especially in its application, articulation theory enables broader consideration of prevailing cultural filters of the historical moment at which decoding occurs.

1

Marketing Desire Fantasy, Soap Opera, and the Preferred Audience

*I don't necessarily want in my own life
what I can have an appreciation for in fiction.*

This chapter establishes soap opera as a conduit of shared, public fantasies and reconceptualizes notions of desire, fantasy, and pleasure as they are provoked and satisfied by popular culture. It considers popular culture's ability to reach people on a visceral, *affective* plane as postulated by Grossberg (1992), and introduces the idea of *currency* to theorize a particular dimension of that plane. Next, it explains how and why soap opera's commercial and creative interests conceive of and address the most desirable audience with fantasies deemed most complimentary to that audience. Finally, questions are posed concerning the meanings of pleasure and fantasy vis-à-vis the ability of the audience to resist and actively oppose hegemony.

DESIRE, FANTASY, AND PLEASURE

The *pleasure of resistance* is matter of factly proclaimed in the subtitle of Brown's (1994) study of female soap opera viewers, and she is not alone in suggesting that resisting hegemonic, preferred meanings of a text can be pleasurable or that realizing pleasure from popular culture—even hegemonic popular culture—is, by its nature, resistive. Ang (1996), who theorized the pleasure *Dallas* fans derived from identifying with outwardly unliberated, melodramatic heroines (1990), faulted other researchers for dismissing similar pleasures as vicarious rather than real and profound. Although she was careful not to equate pleasure with defiance of or support for the status quo, she contended that the quest to

1

attain the feeling of romance perpetuated in and by romantic fiction, for instance, "should be taken seriously as a psychical strategy by which women empower themselves in everyday life . . ." (Ang, 1996, p. 107). Coward (1985) concurred that women's identities are "formed in the definitions of desire" provided by the cultural discourses she examined, many of which "sustain male privilege." However, she also thought it is crucial to search for "pleasures which escape" (p. 16) and directly challenge those definitions.

Desire, fantasy, pleasure, and so on—in the relevant literature, these terms often appear interchangeable, lacking in precise definition, or mystified in intricate psychoanalytical jargon. For our purposes, it is important to distinguish between private fantasies, which play out on an individual basis, and shared, public fantasies, which reveal themselves in popular, mass-communicated texts such as soap opera. According to Coward (1985), the latter variety is less likely to sway from the course of gender hegemony. Ang (1996) insisted, however, that they "still involve the occupation of imaginary subject positions which are outside the scope of our everyday social and cultural identities" (p. 93), consequently creating alternative spaces from which patriarchy can be contested.

Moreover, private fantasies can develop out of public ones. Star Trek and X-Files fans, among others, create their own fan fiction out of the private fantasies they extrapolate from the characters, settings, and basic premises of their favorite programs (see Jenkins, 1992; Scodari & Felder, 2000). Once written and publicized on the Internet or in fanzines, fan fiction makes its way back into the public arena by way of fan culture. These fans' desire to poach the given text by imagining their own value-added stories, and then to give these private imaginings public expression, suggests that the sharing element is crucial. The conclusions of Jenkins' study imply that engagement in such rewriting and sharing begins to compensate for the failures of the original text, but others might argue that such labor-intensive practices are simply making do— that they are not sufficient substitutes for having subversive desires play out in living color and on hundreds of channels. Those without the time and/or energy to devote to the reading or writing of fan fiction are left out of the equation in any event.

Whether public, private, or a blend, fantasies can be viewed in the psychoanalytical sense as reflections of and responses to desires, which in some respects are or cannot be achieved in reality. Fantasizing then becomes a reality of everyday existence (see Ang, 1996) and produces pleasure—in the case of public fantasies, partly through the process of interpellation, or the taking up of subjectivities to share the feelings and experiences of fictional characters even if those feelings and experiences might not be sought in real life. Consider the elaboration of the middle-aged, female cyberfan whose quote opened this chapter and for whom a romance on *General Hospital* was apparently reminiscent of an unhealthy relationship from her past: "Now, I don't want to have that unhealthy relationship again regardless of all its highs & that exhilaration, but I definitely enjoy watching it play out on the screen."

It is no wonder that audience ethnographers argue that assessing possible opportunities for reader interpellation through textual analysis alone is not satisfactory. Without ethnographic study, Ang (1996) might have supposed that the gender identification offered by the disempowered character of Sue Ellen in *Dallas* is surefire evidence of popular culture's patriarchal hold over its audience. Instead she discovered that Sue Ellen served as a fantasy—not as a role model—and a way for women to realize that "one can never have everything under control all the time," and to indulge the "weighty pressure of social reality upon one's subjectivity, one's wishes, one's desires" (p. 95). Similarly, the Seiter et al. (1989) ethnographic account of real viewers yielded the judgment that working class women do not easily adopt the subjectivity of the ideal mother figure, which Modleski (1982) considered essential to soap opera's narrative function and often take pleasure instead in the character of the villainess.

Despite these unexpected outcomes, many scholars report that the ability to identify with character and/or story can be facilitative of pleasure, whatever the ideological implications of that pleasure might be (see Brown, 1994; Feuer, 1995; Hobson, 1982; Press, 1991). Before the ideological question is addressed, the occupation of multiple identities and its impact on that ability require appraisal.

IDENTITY AND INTERPELLATION

Clearly, representations of such aspects of identity as gender, class, race, and sexuality are studied precisely because it is not only logical but psychoanalytically valid to claim that, if given the option, real social actors are more inclined to be interpellated by and adopt the positions of protagonists with identities similar to their own. Commercial TV, in fact, operates on this basis when catering to desirable demographics. This is the reason that NBC's hit series of the 1990s, including *Seinfeld*, *Friends*, *ER*, and *Will and Grace*, are populated by White, middle-class, urban, professional characters between the ages of 18 and 49. With such programming, the network has been successful in attracting viewers with these same traits.

However, the relationship between reader and text is more problematic than a simple image of women or role-modeling approach would have us believe. For one thing, the fact that each of us has many identities at once muddies the issue. As Ang (1996) wrote:

> Each individual is the site of a multiplicity of subject positions proposed to her by the discourses with which she is confronted; her identity is the precarious and contradictory result of the specific set of subject positions she inhabits at any moment in history. (p. 93)

The fact that soap operas provide an array of female characters with whom to identify renders other aspects of identity, and the range of female identities in the mix, more consequential.

Age is one marker of identity that has been marginalized in feminist cultural studies of TV. Although soap opera ethnographers often catalogue the ages of the viewers they study, the ways in which these subjects respond to the text based on the existence or lack of age correspondences have not been thoroughly analyzed.[1] Similarly, textual studies often fail to account for age in their assessments of narrative subjectivities. For instance, Modleski's (1986) conceptualization of the ideal mother subjectivity in soap opera presupposed that viewers do not take up the positions of some female characters more than others due to identities other than gender. Consequently, although she criticized ethnographers for ascribing too much resistive power to their research subjects, she implied through her ideal mother theorization that audiences do not easily cooperate with the expressed intent of advertisers and creators to draw in younger or racially diverse viewers by populating and gearing their narratives accordingly. In so doing, she neglected a key means by which society's definition of womanhood and its predominant subjectivities become animated according to the structures, processes, and imperatives of commercial TV. As Ang (1996) affirmed: "It is through the meaning systems circulating in society and culture that subjectivity is constituted and individual identities are formed" (p. 93).

Life stage and other variables of feminine subjectivity are manifested, first and foremost, in the culture's prevailing embodiments of active, productive, desirable subjects. Before exploring this further, some relevant and serviceable concepts warrant introduction.

AFFECT AND CURRENCY

Grossberg's (1992) conceptualization of *affect* as a defining facet of the popular culture experience is intimately related to, although not synonymous with, prevailing notions of desire and fantasy. For Grossberg, affect is the visceral, sensory passion and feeling of life that often accompanies engagement with popular culture and that, when articulated to ideological investments particular to the textual and contextual moment, can be exceedingly powerful. This notion appears to nullify Barthes' (1975) distinction between *jouissance*, or feelings of ecstasy and sensuality, and *plaisir*, feelings of pleasure in the act of textual reading. Even without specific ideological articulation, Grossberg's affect is still potentially empowering in its "construction of possibility . . . the feeling that one is still alive and that this matters," and which "enables one to go on, to continue to struggle to make a difference" (p. 85).

According to Grossberg's definition, affective emotions would seem to relate to the present and future more so than to the past and memory. This is not to say that nostalgic popular culture has no affective component, but rather that limiting available avenues of identification to memory and nostalgia could contain affectivity in meaningful ways. If one's energy and vitality are aroused primarily in and through invocation of the past, a feeling of present and future potential can be sacrificed.

I propose the term *currency* to refer to this element of present and future possibility. Long-lived currency is the feeling that one matters and will continue to matter for some time to come. Power relations of age and gender, therefore, may be associated with an affective sense of long-lived currency, which, as upcoming analyses corroborate, is largely denied the feminine subject in popular culture. Because affect operates at the level of the physical body and its senses, articulation to embodiments of gender and life stage in the range of subjectivities offered real audiences for inhabitation becomes crucial and has ideological implications. For instance, it logically would be difficult for a 60-year-old woman to become energized about the present and future as a result of viewing cultural texts in which the majority of active, competent, and desirable bodies do not resemble her own in most respects. This type of cultural discourse may contribute to what Brennan (1999) referred to as the constructed *social inertia* of the psyche associated with aging. Younger women might glean a sense of the here and now from such representations, but a sense of long-term potential and opportunity is another matter. Although research by Buckingham (1987) showed that young audiences preferred the older characters in the British soap *EastEnders*, and Hobson's (1982) investigation of another British program, *Crossroads*, revealed senior women's investments in younger heroines through the mechanism of nostalgic reminiscence, these effects occurred in the absence of significant story given to characters of their respective generations. As we see, American soaps reverse the equation for their most desired audience by placing younger characters at the center of the action. This forces older audiences to relate nostalgically rather than in terms of their present and future lives.

The significance placed on embodiment is also a culturally gendered matter and has definite implications for feminism. Gergen and Gergen's (1993) study of lifespan as represented in the autobiographies of men and women indicates a deeper connection between women and their skin than exists for men, who consider their lives to be "above bodily concerns" (p. 50). In her article entitled "Theorizing Through the Body," Probyn (1992) cited Gallop's (1988) belief that feminism's twin tasks are to ask not only "who am I?," but also "who is the other woman?" The embodiments of age are markers of the *other* in this quest and are unique in the sense that they may be exploited not only to pit women against one another, but, more insidiously, against their present or future selves. Particularly for women, then, the subjectivity and embodiment of life stage are crucial, and the currency aspect of affective pleasure associated with these factors is inescapably ideological.

Currency is used as a nominal form of the adjective *current* and also as a reference to the economic and political forces that may influence its disbursement. In commercial TV, identities represented with currency tend to be those that are most valuable as commodity audiences sold to advertisers—the viewer demographics with the most buying power. Among other hegemonies, a cultural double standard of aging may be reproduced as a result of these preferences. As this investigation unfolds, manifestations of opposition to and complicity with such a double standard in production imperatives, narrative interpellations, and actual audience identifications are evaluated. Toward that end, the process and commercial goals of soap opera production, particularly in terms of demographic targeting, require explication.

SOAP PRODUCTION: BLUEPRINTING CONSUMPTION

To appreciate the ideological element in the intents of soap opera producers, the processes, imperatives, and constraints under which they operate should be assessed. Additionally, it is important to determine whether fans know, understand, resist, and/or oppose the rules governing the content they receive. Therefore, it is necessary to discover the degree to which individual creators—as opposed to the system—bear the brunt of fan displeasure.

Anonymity Unlimited?

The mechanisms of the soap opera production process have changed little since Allen (1985) reviewed them in his classic work, *Speaking of Soap*

Operas. The executive producer oversees this process and is a primary decision maker in terms of deciding which actors and/or characters are retained, introduced, featured, or dismissed, and regarding overall story trajectory and tone. He or she answers to the network, studio executives, and sponsors. In fact studio executives and sponsors are one in the same in the case of Procter and Gamble (P&G), the only advertiser that still produced its own soaps in the 1990s, including NBC's *Another World* and CBS' *Guiding Light* and *As the World Turns.*

The head writer is responsible for story projections conceived and deliberated months in advance of airing, although changes in plan can be accommodated. Again the wishes of the network, studio executives, sponsors, and executive producer are taken into account. Associate writers then convert the stories into daily scripts.

As the major players in a soap's creation, the executive producer and head writer take the most heat from avid, disgruntled fans. Cyberfandom has altered the condition about which Allen (1985) remarked: "Authorial anonymity is also a requirement of the soap opera production situation. Because creation of the soap opera text is ongoing, its world and characters cannot bear the mark of a particular creator" (p. 56). Online enthusiasts refer to executive producers, head writers, and network executives by name and occasionally by initials or pseudonyms, condemning them when favored stories, characters, and/or actors are, in their view, mishandled. Executive Producer Jill Farren Phelps, veteran of such programs as *Santa Barbara, Guiding Light, Another World, One Life to Live,* and *General Hospital,* has been referenced quite casually as JFP or, in fans' angrier moments, "Jill Fire'em Phelps." This moniker derives from her penchant to eliminate actors from programs when she arrives on board only to substitute performers from programs she has departed. Leah Laiman and Richard Culliton, head writers who made the rounds of several shows, have been referred to as "Lethal Leah" and "Richard Cullitoon" by fans angry about the former's tendency to leave a show worse off than when she arrived and the latter for his supposed proclivity to render formerly complex characters as one-dimensional cartoons. Similarly, head writer Maggie DePriest has been referred to as "Maggie the Beast" and executive producer Charlotte Savitz as "Charlotte Savage." Although the anonymity of backstage personnel is now curtailed when it comes to ardent fans, average viewers are still not fully conscious of the authorship of the programs they watch.

The musical chairs played by studio and network executives in rotating creative personnel in efforts to bring new blood to ailing soaps has not plagued some productions as much as others. Until the late 1990s, top-rated *Young and the Restless* (CBS) had been written and coproduced by one of its creators, Bill Bell. Bell also created *The Bold and the Beautiful* (CBS), which he produced and wrote with his son. NBC's *Days of Our Lives* has been produced almost exclusively by members of the Corday family including, most notably, Ken Corday. It might not be a coincidence, then, that these three soaps were consistently in the top four in the late 1990s, although Corday did not escape the wrath of some fans who referred to him as "Dorkday" and blamed him for allowing the show to be subjected to profound alterations as the millennium loomed.

Such changes have been a gradual outgrowth of demographics strategies conceived in the late 1970s and early 1980s. Moreover, the big three networks have become increasingly determined not to concede their most valuable audience to competitors. A brief history of this evolution is essential to understand how economic imperatives affect representations of gender and lifespan.

Are You Demographically Correct?

By its name, soap opera telegraphs its *raison d'etre*; women's domestic and consumptive roles are both reproduced and exploited by a segmented, repetitive format allowing women to simultaneously engage in their household duties while beholding stories affirming the importance of hearth and home and by ads for soap and other products used to keep home and family tidy (Brown, 1990; Spigel, 1992). Because women hold the *power of the purse* when it comes to foodstuffs, clothing, cleaning products, health and hygiene products, and cosmetics, daytime dramas were designed for radio in the 1930s and are still intended to sell commodity audiences of homemakers to those who advertise such items.

Women spend more on these products when they are first establishing their households, forming brand loyalties, and having and raising children, making those between the ages of 18 and 49 the most lucrative target audience for soaps and their advertisers (Intintoli, 1984; Rouverol, 1984). Because "some advertisers want an even younger group, women between 18 and 34" (Rouverol, 1984, p. 178), it is they who are "the primary object of the current programming and advertising strategy" (Intintoli, 1984, p. 63). This tendency is further complicated by the fact that most fans begin watching soaps in their teens or early 20s and become hooked, allowing producers to eventually take them for granted (up to a point) and continue skewing content and representation in favor of the younger audience they hope to entice and secure for the future (Intintoli, 1984). Younger women, then, are the most "demogenic" (see McAllister, 1996, p. 46) audience in the eyes of soap opera powers that be.

Moreover, as the number of TV sets per household has increased, advertisers have become more interested in assessing numbers of individual viewers according to their demographic characteristics as opposed to enumerating which homes are tuned to particular programs. Ratings *sweeps* periods in the months of February, May, and November become a focus of creators' efforts to reflect and establish demographically desirable viewership. During these periods, secrets are revealed, romances are consummated, and audience numbers form the basis for subsequent advertising rates.

This concern for younger demographics is a manifestation of the double standard of aging that pervades patriarchal culture. Just as patriarchy perpetuates this inequity, valuing women primarily for their youthful appearance and reproductivity, rather than for qualities honed by age and experience (see Stoddard, 1983), the imperatives of commercial TV favor women whose life stage and cultural understandings determine or foster the need or desire for products linked to youthful appearance and reproductivity. These include disposable diapers and tampons as well as, according to the advertisers' own market research, more generous quantities of mascara (Youthful Demographics, 1995). Conveniently, although not coincidentally, capitalism and boardroom politics facilitate patriarchy and bedroom politics and vice versa.

In the early 1980s, soap opera writer Rouverol (1984) endeavored to justify this preference:

> Those faithful soap-watching women over fifty don't make as many household purchases as their younger counterparts. They're no longer raising children. . . . And (an even more depressing thought), they have fewer years of viewing ahead of them. So, although the reasons are economic rather than aesthetic, Daytime's targeting of the younger audience seems to reflect the attitude of society at large today: young is beautiful. (p. 178)

Give Us Your Daughters 'Til They Are Sixteen. . . .

. . . and they will be ours forever? Soap opera's privileging of the 18 to 49 age demographic does not preclude a focus on even younger teenage fans in the hope that they will form a lasting allegiance. Teens have become an ongoing concern for many soaps, but traditionally summer recess from school has been the time when "events involving the sons and daughters of the show's principals will suddenly move to the foreground, and young love, licit and otherwise, will crowd its more mature counterpart off the screen" (Rouverol, 1984, p. 32). The summer storyline also ushers in a flurry of ads peddling back-to-school supplies and acne medications.

According to *Soap Opera Digest* (Bonderoff, 1995a), the tactic can be traced all the way back to the summer of 1958, when "virginal Penny

Hughes eloped with Richie Rich kid Jeff Baker on *As the World Turns*" (p. 30). However, this is not the only type of summertime plot. In the mid-1980s, *General Hospital* devised summer adventure storylines involving regular characters, and this tended to keep the teen crowd placated (Rouverol, 1984). Recently, however, this soap and many others have devoted little of their summertime script to characters much beyond 30 years of age.

Even when older characters are incorporated into a summer plot, there is an effort to flatter younger viewers by making their fictional contemporaries smarter and more proactive than the grownups. In the summer of 1997, for instance, *Another World* featured a story in which Toni, a tough African-American rookie cop, was raped after being knocked unconscious by her assailant. Wealthy, White, college-aged Nick Hudson was accused based on a plethora of circumstantial evidence. Nick's middle-aged lawyer, Cass, had some good courtroom scenes defending his (obviously) innocent client, and Nick's father and Toni's mother dutifully stood behind their children. These three were restricted to primarily reactive roles, whereas a quartet of Generation Xers including Nick's loyal sweetheart, Cass's law partner, a newlywed and pregnant police detective, and her gumshoe husband uncovered clues implicating the true culprit. Soon the rapist was subdued by the victim, and the older generation was not only impressed, but also outdone by the cleverness and efficiency of its progeny.

Before summer storylines can be crafted, however, teens and young adults must be woven into the canvas. Occasionally a character will simply be born or brought in as a child and grow up normally, entering the adult world as appropriate. Kimberly McCullough, *General Hospital*'s Robin Scorpio, was an impressive child performer and retained into adulthood.

More often than not, however, young adults emerge by one of two alternative routes. The first occurs when the relative (usually a child) of an existing older character leaves the canvas and then reappears with a new face, having aged beyond real-time calculations. This often happens incrementally before the young adult emerges so that viewers are eventually presented with a 17-year-old who they may remember to have been born years after their own preteen children. The multifarious implications of this phenomenon, dubbed the "soap opera rapid aging syndrome" by Internet fans, are detailed more thoroughly in the next chapter. One of many examples is the character of Michelle Bauer on *Guiding Light*. The actress who portrayed her for many years was not yet old enough for a love story in the mid-1990s, and so her character was abruptly dismissed. When Michelle reemerged some months later, she was depicted by an older actress as a nubile high school senior and was later the focus of a 1997 summer romance with Jesse, a newly introduced young hunk.

Such introductions provide the second means by which soaps are populated at the lower end of the adult age spectrum. Frequently these characters are already connected or are soon discovered to be connected to an older character on the canvas, as linkage to a core family allows viewers to more readily accept an unfamiliar player. Occasionally the need to create a young character permits an older one to return or be inaugurated. In fact virtually the only time middle-aged or senior characters are introduced or reclaimed is when they can be linked to a new or established younger face. In 1997, *Another World* rehired an older actor whose character, Lucas, had been killed off years earlier, but cast him in a new role so he could be joined by a teenage daughter—a plan that never came to fruition due to a change in writers. The late 1990s' resurrection of *Guiding Light*'s fortyish Reva might have stood up on its own, but the show soon invented a twenty-something, long-lost sister for the popular diva.

Instant paternity is a popular mechanism for associating established characters with young newcomers. *Another World*'s Michael Hudson was reintroduced in 1995 along with Nick—the teenage son he never knew he had. Sudden maternity is a more complicated task for the writers and usually involves the mother having relinquished the child for adoption or believing him or her to be deceased. In the early 1990s, a backstory was devised for *All My Children*'s Erica Kane concerning her rape as a teenager and the child she consequently conceived and surrendered. Naturally, this soon led to her reunion with Kendall—the daughter in question. However they emerge, young soap hunks and babes, as fans refer to them, are inevitably infused into a summer potboiler and become part of the soap's larger effort to capture succeeding generations of consumers.

Baby Boom or Bust/The "X" Factor

The summertime push for demographics is still only a fragment of the larger effort to attract younger viewers. Historically, it was the influx of Baby Boom consumers in the 1960s and early 1970s that first inspired the tactics that have since evolved into a seemingly unimpeachable conventional wisdom. Allen (1985) traced the origins of this paradigm shift to the late 1970s, when producer Gloria Monty was hired to save ABC's *General Hospital* from extinction. She promptly replaced older cast members with younger ones in an effort to appeal to the Baby Boom market and then centered her storytelling strategy around confused teenager Laura Webber Baldwin and her tangled romance with older bad boy

Luke Spencer. This successful duo inspired the term *supercouple* and became the model for dozens of soap opera love stories to follow.

Monty's success became soap opera legend. As a producer for CBS' *Guiding Light* confessed to Intintoli (1984) in the mid-1980s:

> Now ABC made a concerted effort over the last 15 years to go for a younger audience . . . and that audience is in the middle of the baby boom. That baby boom grew up and went home to have kids and they are sitting number one, a lot for that reason. . . . What we have to do is get some younger viewers into the pipeline so that the person sitting at this desk ten years from now doesn't commit hari-kari. (p. 70)

Still some in the soap opera business resisted the strategy. Harding Lemay (1981) insisted in the memoir of his tenure as *Another World*'s head writer in the 1970s that the show's top-notch ratings began to decline when sponsors began pressuring him to feature younger characters. With the Baby Boom audience in place as an ongoing meal ticket for the soaps, some researchers of the early 1980s speculated that, "as the younger audience ages, soap opera content will again shift to reflect the interests of the older audience" (Cantor & Cantor, 1983, p. 220).

A decade after the anxious *Guiding Light* producer envisioned a possible suicide scenario for one of her or his successors and as Baby Boomers began to creep past that "magic 49," the soaps continued their attempts to lure viewers at increasingly younger ages. A late 1990s addition to the list of daytime dramas, Aaron Spelling's *Sunset Beach* (NBC), was expressly created to feature largely unrelated Generation Xers, eschewing the traditional soap opera focus on multigenerational families (Baldwin, 1997; "NBC Wants", 1996).

Soap creators have honed what were early on awkward attempts to write for teenaged characters (see Intintoli, 1984) and now regularly inject finely tuned maneuvers that lavish the younger generations with cajolery. In fact the Baby Boom generation is now positioned at the dubious end of a divide-and-flatter marketing approach designed to seduce their younger counterparts, as illustrated by a Pepsi commercial in which hip teenyboppers relish their soda and glare disbelievingly at self-indulgent, balding, pot-bellied mid-lifers frolicking at the Woodstock site in commemoration of the music festival's 25th anniversary (see Bowen, 1994). Once thought to be comparatively ad-proof, Xers are now viewed by Madison Avenue as a cohesive, predictable, well-behaved consumer market (see Hornblower, 1997). The younger Baby Boomlets, born between 1977 and 1993 and nearly as numerous as their parents, have already been probed by demographers anticipating a 21st-century windfall (see Mitchell, 1995). It is this generation, also referred to as

Echo Boomers or Generation Y, who may have become the true targets of the soaps' millennial *youthification* trend because a focus on slightly older Xers is likely to have aspirational appeal.

It is not as if Baby Boomer audiences have faded silently. After being the center of consumer culture for so long, it may be twice as intolerable to suddenly be belittled or ignored. As a later chapter demonstrates, protestations of soap opera's youthification trend occur and can emanate from younger as well as older viewers. However, the interesting thing is that these objections seem to materialize only after older actors are axed or otherwise forced out. Younger fans, especially, seem not to mind the backburnering of older characters. It is enough that these veterans supportively circle around their children as reminders of the soap opera's history. When a fortysomething couple, Sean and Tiffany, were eliminated from the *General Hospital* community in the early 1990s, online fans objected vehemently. However, the fact that the duo lacked a storyline for a couple of years previously did not provoke the same outrage, and the fans had found more than enough to enjoy in the screen time given to the remaining, mostly younger players.

Despite the general lack of a critical stance in soap opera magazines, which after all rely on the soaps for storyline spoilers, access to actors, and other content (see Fiske, 1987), they also have been known to register editorial exception to youthification strategies. For instance, *Soap Opera Now!* touted research revealing that aging Baby Boomers could be a more lucrative market in the eyes of some daytime advertisers and suggested that the soaps should take heed (Is the Youth, 1997). Yet is simply reversing the age bias or substituting a class bias for an age bias really the answer?

This overview of producer goals and strategies grounds upcoming explorations of particular soaps, stories, characters, creative decisions, and audience readings pertaining primarily to age and gender representations and their connection to the range of fantasies—especially, romantic fantasies—offered to and/or stimulated in female fans. As the study considers whether engaging in and receiving pleasure from such fantasies is a vicarious waste of potentially resistive energy, a prerequisite for political action in the private and/or public spheres, or something in between, the apparent motivation for producers to limit the character and breadth of public fantasies in terms of their economic goals accumulates relevance.

NOTES

1. Moreover, quantitative studies of audiences often depend on the younger college community for subjects and may assume that the responses of such women are indicative of women of all ages.

2 IMAGINED SUBJECTS AND THE GENDERED TEXT

. . . the guy in the leather jacket . . . who storms in on a cloud of grit and testosterone that obscures his heart of gold. . . .

The initial task of this chapter is to probe the soap opera text and its purported openness, and to consider whether and in what ways the attainment and/or delay of narrative closure might have gendered, ideological implications. Accordingly, formulaic textual articulations of gender, lifespan, fantasy, and romance are explored, and a tendency to reinstate hegemonic generic preferences at the point of storyline closure is detected. A map of typical stories and characters is also laid out—not merely as a matter of description, but to show how such traits flow from hegemonic production imperatives related to age and gender. This in turn sets a context for examining viewer interpretation.

In their 1994 study of soap opera, Liebes and Livingstone demonstrated that textual ethnography of the relationships represented within formulaic genres can be a tool for assessing power hierarchies of gender, age, and other identities. Although this chapter does not render its results diagrammatically as the authors did, it draws conclusions and presents examples based on long-term, detailed observation of such formulae.

As we proceed in this chapter and thereafter, a number of daytime dramas are regularly mentioned. Just as soap opera magazines and fans on the Internet employ acronyms to reference the titles of particular programs, so do we here (see Fig. 2.1). As each soap opera first appears in this and succeeding chapters, its full title and acronym are given. Thereafter, only the acronym is used.

SOAP OPERA TITLE	ACRONYM
All My Children	AMC
Another World	AW
As the World Turns	ATWT
Bold and the Beautiful	B&B
Days of Our Lives	DOOL
General Hospital	GH
Guiding Light	GL
One Life to Live	OLTL
Young and the Restless	Y&R

Fig. 2.1. Soap Opera Titles and Acronyms

SOAP TEXT: PREFABRICATED CONSTRUCTION

A Flexibly Feminine Format?

Feminist and/or cultural scholars of soap opera are virtually univocal in appreciating the genre's privileging of feminine subjectivity and its similarly gendered defiance of narrative closure (see Allen, 1985; Brown, 1994; Fiske, 1987; Modleski, 1982). As the cover notes of Nochimson's (1992) book on the genre assert: "In breaking the linearity and closure of traditional narrative, daytime serials decenter patriarchal power strategies and articulate instead a feminine politics of inclusion." Some researchers (Allen, 1985; Flitterman-Lewis, 1992; Geraghty, 1991) have also recognized the existence of miniclosures resolving particular narrative questions. Thus it is appropriate to wonder about what happens when narrative questions and their resolutions are fraught with ideology—ideology that might mitigate against the supposed feminine subjectivity of the soap opera form.

Mumford (1995) issued a serious challenge to the celebratory posture greeting soap opera's textual openness by proposing that the genre features an excess of definitive closures at the level of the individual storyline and that closure occurs when a story's key narrative enigma—the issue around which the story revolves—is settled. She contended that the "specific *content* of the moments of closure, the way that individual story resolutions insist on the correctness of the patriarchal status quo and women's position within it," performs soap opera's "most important ideological work," functioning to "endow all that preceded it with a retrospective meaning," which can then be assumed as inevitable by the reader (pp. 90–91). This occurs even as soap opera's production and reception over time increase the likelihood that a particular closure was not anticipated by the authors or audience at the story's inception or midlife. Whereas scholars have viewed the idea of narrative closure as a conservative, masculine trait and its refusal as feminine (see Deming, 1990; Fiske, 1987; Nochimson, 1992), Mumford contended that the mere fact of closure is not always patriarchal, but "could easily be turned to oppositional ends and stories could be resolved in ways that demonstrate, say, a wide range of romantic and sexual alternatives . . . " (p. 92). In contrast to the views of White (1994), who claimed that viewers' apparent tendency to accept the reversibility of a soap opera story through "selective memory loss and willful amnesia" (p. 339) can be seen to challenge the strictures of patriarchal power, Mumford maintained that the ideological content of the story and its reversal are the crucial factors.

This author (Scodari, 1995) theorized the culturally gendered demeanors toward both the happy endings punctuating romantic comedy films of the 1930s and 1940s and the evasion of monogamous commitment characterizing the derivative love stories of prime-time TV series such as *Cheers*. Here, too, is evidence that the tidy resolution might provide more opportunity for women, in particular, to read egalitarian struggle into the unseen futures of the films' monogamous lovers than is permitted by the deferment of commitment in the TV derivations. Still the insistence that closure is a patently and necessarily masculine feature regardless of content persists in the literature.

Mumford's definition of soap opera closure as the resolution of a narrative enigma characterizing a story is logical, but I propose that any issue of power relations manifested in the story embodies one or more corresponding ideological enigmas also demanding settlement. To illustrate the need for analysis in these terms, I resurrect and reexamine aspects of two case studies Nochimson (1992) offered to support her claim that soap opera romances embrace defiantly feminine fantasies.

The Case of the Well-Married Heroine

Nochimson (1992), a former soap opera writer, textually explored the courtship between Kayla and Steve on *Days of Our Lives* (*DOOL*) in the 1980s—a period during which the show was fine tuning the *supercouple* paradigm initiated by *General Hospital's* (*GH's*) Luke and Laura. She described how Steve, an eyepatched voyeur known as Patch who first stalked nurse Kayla at the behest of Salem's resident crime boss, was redeemed in the course of a blossoming romance with his mark. His criminal past was a persistent barrier, however, and when his respectable brother Jack surfaced, fell for Kayla, and developed a serious illness, Steve bowed out in what he believed was the better interest of two people he loved. Kayla married Jack, but her continuing attraction to Steve led to marital rape. Several crises later, Kayla bounced back with Steve's help and the two eventually found happiness.

Nochimson's psychoanalytical analysis, especially her argument that Kayla's choice of Steve rather than Jack can be interpreted as a renunciation of traditional, masculine narrative convention, stalled at this point. In applying Mumford's theory of soap opera closure to this story and the standard plot it exemplifies, the key narrative question might be whether the couple surmounted the obstacles and wed successfully—which they did. The ideological enigmas, as Nochimson implicitly framed them, would involve whether Kayla's quest for liberation as reflected in her preference for rebel Steve over safe, well-heeled Jack amounts to a counter-hegemonic departure from patriarchal expectations. This is akin to what emerges in studies by Radway (1984) and others who have investigated romance novels and/or their readers, in that spirited heroines who tame "heroes with dark and dangerous pasts" are, to varying degrees, consequently viewed as empowered and empowering (Barlow & Krentz, 1992, p. 17).

However, romance novels are not serialized, and the ability to envision adventure and challenge as continuing features of their heroines' lives may actually be facilitated, rather than hampered, by a closure that leaves the future progress of the romance up to the reader's imagination. Indeed DuPlessis (1985) identified a tendency in female writers of the 20th century to fashion their endings for the benefit of readers inclined to read beyond them. Soap opera seriality could, consequently, frustrate such an option. If we frame the enigma in Steve and Kayla's storyline in terms of their ongoing relationship and its ideological component, we would find that the newly respectable Steve and his blushing bride eventually became bastions of the establishment—their marriage troubled only by interlopers of the character Steve initially embodied. As a supercouple romance, Kayla and Steve's union was subject to being regarded by creators and fans as an inalterable and unimpeachable symbol of a patriarchal order from which any truly rebellious and adventurous heroine might seek deliverance.

The Case of the Retroactively Redeemed Rapist

In detailing the prototypical supercouple, *GH's* Luke and Laura, Nochimson (1992) proclaimed, once again, the genre's privileging of feminine desire. She admitted that "marriage, which conventionally operates as a form of closure (p. 77)," must be disrupted to create this subversive aura. However, she identified Laura's first marriage to Scotty as *the* patriarchal albatross without acknowledging that any subsequent nuptials between Luke and Laura could have served to reinstate the predicament she decries.

More important, her analysis of this story raises the key issue of what can happen when a critic idealizes her own interpretation over that which might be gleaned from actual audience readings. Paradoxically, although such audience study is often chided for being too celebratory of popular pleasures (see Walters, 1996), Nochimson's conviction that soap operas are emancipatory is buttressed by her failure to reach beyond the text. This potential shortcoming is most evident when she considers an ideologically potent element of this saga—the fact that the romance took off after Luke raped Laura.

Before returning to this point, it should be noted that the redemption of rapists on soap operas has repeatedly led to controversy among creators, critics, and fans, and that the Luke and Laura incident is only the most prominent in a long list of such cases (see Logan, 1995; Martin, 1995a). After raping Kayla on *DOOL*, Jack sought and received salvation as half of another supercouple. On *Another World* (*AW*), Jake's rape of ex-wife Marley was gradually erased from the backstory so that he could heroically couple with Marley's twin while, at one point, Marley enviously pined. More notably, on *One Life to Live* (*OLTL*), the rape of college student Marty at the hands of a gang led by Todd (Roger Howarth) did not dissuade creators from capitalizing on Howarth's charisma by reforming Todd and linking him with other heroines. Hayward (1997), in fact, concentrated on this divisive redemption in her analysis of ABC soaps and audience readings. Howarth departed the show in protest of his character's redemption, having endured screams of "rape me, Todd" from fans (Waggett, 1997), and later agreed to return only if Todd did some backsliding (Logan, 1996b). Although similar situations have occurred with Roger and Holly on *Guiding Light* (*GL*) and Bill and Laura on *DOOL*, Luke and Laura's is still the most memorable case in which a rapist was subsequently portrayed as the worthy paramour of his victim.

Or is it? Using video clips of the rape scene and TV interviews with actors and creators, the documentary video *The Power of Suggestion* (Segal, 1987) illustrates what appear to be backstage efforts to retroactively rewrite the story. Soap opera magazines have either skirted this question (Martin, 1995a) or stated outright that, "when the chemistry between [the two actors] became apparent, the encounter was explained as a seduction and Luke and Laura fell in love" (*General Hospital*, 1996, p. 54).

This debate crystallizes Mumford's assertion that a story's resolution, regardless of whether it is anticipated, can reinvigorate patriarchal understandings even when they are initially contested. Only a time-factored textual and audience analysis—that is, one performed as the story unfolded beginning in 1979—would be able to determine how it could be and was interpreted over its course. However, in 1995, the recollection of a long-time fan offered a clue:

> She screamed "No!" for God's sake. And when a woman says "no" several times the way Laura did and a man violates her anyway, that's rape. . . . But as time went on, it was cleverly termed a seduction, and the audience went along with it, myself included. (Martin, 1995a, p. 14)

Similarly, in commenting on the Todd Manning redemption on *OLTL*, some fans used the Luke and Laura case to argue against whitewashing such a heinous act as rape (Hayward, 1997).

At the same time, former head writer Pat Falken Smith insisted that she conceived the story as a seduction from the beginning:

> When Laura screamed "No!" it was a cry to herself for succumbing to his advances. Afterward, when she realized what she'd done, she had to cry rape because she was married. That's what I wrote, and that's what was filmed. . . . I'm a woman; do you think I'd write a story where a woman falls in love with her rapist? (Martin, 1995a, p. 14)

Her rhetorical question begs another. Would she, as a woman, write a script that deliberately muddies the issue of whether no means no? As the fan's sentiments indicate, such a muddying was foreseeable. Although this fan was cognizant of the possible manipulation involved, confusion could have been the likely outcome for many viewers.

Still Nochimson (1992) viewed the event precisely as Smith claimed to have intended it, but did not reveal whether her reading was informed by the soap insiders she consulted and/or based on recollection or videotape viewing only after the story's completion. She dismissed the possibility that the tale might have begun as anything other than what it seemed to her after the fact, ignoring the actual (or possible) interpretations of real viewers. Her ultimate assertion was that the ambiguity of the seduction was merely a way to show Laura coming to grips with "her fear of shedding conventional limits" (pp. 81–82).

Early in 1998, in an effort to create a rift between Luke and his teenage son by Laura, *GH* decided to resurrect the incident between the couple (Fig. 2.2 and 2.3) and weave it into the ongoing story. A related interview with actor Anthony Geary (Luke) resolved the issue of how the story was originally envisioned: "It was played as a rape, desperate and dirty, and then there was a quick rush to rewrite it as a seduction" (Logan, 1998b, p. 46). Eventually, in a confrontation with Luke, Laura admitted that it was a rape and that she had been in a state of denial since. Those who might have absorbed the backpedaling some 15 years earlier and at a formative stage of life might not have been rescued soon

Fig. 2.2   Luke and Laura's saga continues on *General Hospital*.

Fig. 2.3   1998's resurrection of Luke's "rape" of Laura serves as a distancing mechanism.

enough by the turnabout, however. Moreover, they would now have to face the dissonance of having supported and, perhaps, continuing to support this supercouple despite its questionable genesis.

Clearly, the saga of Luke's "seduction" of Laura exposes the need for time-factored consideration of both text and audience, as well as the applicability of Mumford's (1995) theory of storyline closure and the conceptualization of both narrative and ideological enigmas to gauge such closure. Moreover, it can be argued that Laura evolved into yet another well-married, conventional heroine for whom ongoing rebellion would be anathema.

What's Behind Door #3?

The apparent optimism of many soap opera researchers requires further comment at this juncture. There is no doubt that soap opera's validation of the feminine—the private sphere, its dramas, and its heroines—distinguishes it from the dominant culture in positive terms. Still it is pertinent to wonder what feminine fantasies are not publicly sanctioned in soap opera—fantasies whose masculine corollaries *are* authorized in soaps and the larger culture. The case study outlined in subsequent chapters illustrates how fantasies inscribing long-lived currency reside, for women at least, beyond a forbidden door.

Similarly, the denial of shared feminine fantasies is revealed by briefly exploring race, gender, and romance on the soaps. Several instances of love between an African-American woman and a White man have been seen in American daytime drama. For instance, *GH* had the blue-blooded brothers Jason and A.J. Quartermaine battle over African-American Keesha and a second White man/African-American woman combination in the marriage of Doctors Simone and Tom Hardy. However, a taboo has persisted against the reverse configuration, although romances between Latina women and African-American men, such as Julia and Noah of *All My Children* (AMC), have been dramatized. The motivation behind the African-American man/White woman taboo is evidently the backstage sensitivity to vestiges of White racism in the viewing audience.

A couple of examples deserve note. After Kayla's happiness was dashed because of Steve's demise, a new love interest was sought for the widowed heroine. Fans of *DOOL* recall that Steve's African-American friend, Marcus, seemed positioned for that role, and the chemistry between the two performers was promising. However, the former true love of Kayla's sister Kimberly was available, and the tide turned in an effort to join the halves of two supercouples. A decade later, cyberfans continued to complain that this romance was forced and lacking in both propriety and passion, and that the Marcus/Kayla coupling would have been preferable. One online viewer also remembered letters written to the magazines in favor of the pairing and her anger on discerning the show's reason for balking—that such a story would be too controversial.

Years later, when *TV Guide* publicized *AW*'s plan to unite the middle-aged, White Felicia with an African-American newcomer (see Logan, 1994), there was apparently sufficient negative fallout to bring the story to a screeching halt. Even after the hype, the show felt no obligation to explain the change of heart. Yet the male actor involved, Randy Brooks, had given them away in a magazine interview (DeLosh, 1994), stating: "I have heard that we have been getting some flak about this story, and therefore have been cooling it a little . . . . I would like to see it happen the way it was initially spelled out to me" (p. 2). Barely a hint of this flak appeared on the bulletin boards or in fan letters to the magazines. However, one African-American male cyberfan did indicate that he was drawn to the program in anticipation of the romance, but was disappointed to discover that it would involve a menopausal White woman instead of her comely daughter—thus appearing to validate the suspicions of some African-American women that White women are sought as mere trophies by too many successful African-American men (see Norment, 1994). The heroine's age might have mitigated against this particular objection while increasing the likelihood that some of her fans—fans of her generation and older—might protest on other racial grounds. The show clearly feared such impulses and backed off without apology.

In 1998, *Young and the Restless* (*Y&R*) embarked on a romance between White Victoria, pregnant with her former husband's child, and African-American Neil, whose estranged wife was expected to show up momentarily (Fig. 2.4). In this instance, nonracial landmines stood to provide an easy out for writers if the racial backlash became prohibitive. Judging from mail received by *Soap Opera Digest* (*Y&R*'s Interracial, 1998), such a backlash began brewing early.

Somewhat later, *AW* finally violated the taboo with a romance between White Marley and African-American Tyrone, but interestingly Marley could not be considered a protagonist at the time. Rather, she was in the process of conniving against her twin sister Vicky—a much-beloved heroine on the show. Had Vicky been paired with Tyrone, it would have been far riskier for the show and, consequently, far more ground breaking.

This is only one nontraditional romantic fantasy that daytime drama traditionally denies a large segment of its female viewers. Again it is evident that the defiantly feminine delights associated with soaps have their limits and that such limits may be vital to the genre's ideo-

Fig. 2.4 *Young and the Restless* ignites a fan backlash
when it attempts to romantically pair African-
American Neil with White Victoria.

logical function. Many fans were exhilarated by these potential
romances and baffled by their refusal. On one level, their objections
could indicate a healthy resistance. On another level, the stories had to
be at least hinted at for such protests to surface. Otherwise their
absence does not seem to be an issue. Most significant, the quashing of
desire associated with their blatant revocation may be more disheartening
to fans than their blanket absence. In any case, collective commiseration
is little compensation for the loss of potentially subversive public
fantasies because it pales in comparison to the empowerment felt
through shared celebration of their endurance. Such fantasies are rare,
emerging as exceptions to the rules of "least objectionable programming,"
which appear to condition and characterize the soap opera
genre and, thereby, to reaffirm their own correctness.

SOAP TEXT: PARCELLED PASSION

This section explores the archetypal characters, couples, and stories that
populate soap opera's preferred universe, the gendered subject in the
soap opera text, and the genre's manipulation of age and time. It examines
the formulae of standard storylines such as the supercouple and
romantic triangle and subtle but consequential differences among soaps
in this regard. The stars in soap opera's prevailing familial and romantic

constellations are logged so that ideological implications of gender and lifespan representations, and the economic imperatives that motivate them, can be better appreciated.

Hunks, Babes, Divas, Vixens, and Harridans

The mechanisms by which young adults typically debut as characters on soaps have already been detailed. These appealing young *hunks* and *babes*, as they are referred to by fans and creators alike, are carefully selected and molded to be magnets for the most sought-after audience—young females. The interpellative pull of characters and text is crafted so that young female viewers identify with the nubile young woman in desiring and, especially, in being desired by the virile young male. Shirtless hunks gratuitously adorn soapland while maintaining some element of subjectivity. In the 1990s, however, fans and pundits complained that these players were being drawn from the ranks of modeling and that the caliber of acting began to suffer as a result. Still it can be said that there is no double standard of gender and beauty among these neophytes. If anything they reflect a higher expectation of masculine pulchritude, with many of the young heroines sufficing to be cute, spunky, approachable and, therefore, somewhat less intimidating to young girls in the audience whose body image may be a source of insecurity in a beauty-dominated culture.

In the tradition of the romance novel, these spirited ingénues are often destined to tame bad boy hunks who are, despite their cynicism and rough edges, goodhearted. One fan described the archetype as "the guy in the leather jacket and motorcycle who storms in on a cloud of grit and testosterone that obscures his heart of gold." As this characterization indicates, a rebel veneer is established from the beginning and often reproduced in ads and promotions in which angst-ridden pouts, scowls, and smirks prevail over toothy grins (Fig. 2.5). *AW's* Nick hitched a ride into Bay City with two women in a classic convertible, replicating the scene in which filmdom's notorious *Thelma and Louise* (1991) first encountered J.D., the seductive outlaw portrayed by Brad Pitt. *DOOL's* Lucas bedded a Madonna wannabe pop star on his way into Salem. On *GL*, the James Deanish delinquent Jesse literally crashed onto the Springfield scene by nearly colliding with wide-eyed heroine Michelle on his motorcycle. Not only did Michelle detect Jesse's good heart through his rough-and-tumble facade, but the heart in question turned out to be transplanted from her dearly departed mother.

When a teen heroine is not enamored of a bad boy, it is usually a somewhat older, professional male who inspires her devotion. This

Fig. 2.5 Scowls and smirks are trademarks of the angst-ridden soap opera "hunk."

trend became entrenched in the early 1980s when Douglas Marland, then head writer for *GL*, consulted his own 15-year-old niece about her romantic fantasies to develop story ideas that would attract the younger generation (Waggett, 1997). When she stated that she would be flattered if a college guy was interested in her, Marland proceeded to link 17-year-old Morgan with medical student Kelly and to have them consummate the relationship while Morgan was still a minor. Having the older man prefer the innocent teen over a less-deserving and sexually sophisticated woman older than she was also added to the formula in the person of a troublemaking rival—Nola.

Not all younger soap babes are heroines. Like Nola, Sami on *DOOL*, or Annie on *GL*, they set their sites on an unavailable male and scheme to keep him from happiness with his true love. Occasionally, however, such *vixens* become exceptionally popular and undergo some measure of redemption before evolving into heroines. *AW's* aforementioned Vicky, an evil twin whose teenage manipulations wreaked havoc in the life of her outwardly identical but saintly sister Marley, began to soften with age and acquired more of a following than her counterpart. Her guts and spunk remained, however, until the third actor to play the roles, Jensen Buchanan, decided she could no longer pull double duty. Marley was sent away, and Vicky procured much of her timid demeanor in the process. Later the first actor to play the twins, Ellen Wheeler, was lured back to portray Marley only and was positioned as a vixen ready to square off against her sister, who had become the more established heroine.

Babes who become exceedingly popular and survive a show's weeding process into middle age can develop into *divas*—a term used in reference to both the characters and their portrayers. *AMC's* Erica Kane (Susan Lucci), *DOOL's* Marlena Evans (Deidre Hall), *Young and the Restless'* (*Y&R's*) Nikki Reed (Melody Thomas Scott), and *GL's* Reva Shayne (Kim Zimmer) have been among the most celebrated divas, although all soaps feature one or, at most, two examples of this archetype. The daytime diva retains some measure of protection against the fates that often befall other older females, in that she remains somewhat complex and central to the storyline. Divas with notorious pasts such as Reva and Erica may show vestiges of their former selves, but the shows risk viewer backlash if they allow such heroines to regress too far. When *AMC* promised in 1997 to reinstate Erica as the woman fans "love to hate," and had her kidnap a baby she believed was fathered by her wayward husband, fans revolted and the story was cut short (Henderson, 1997; Logan, 1998a).

Female characters introduced in middle age or who remain on the canvas without attaining the status of diva might not escape being represented as the desperate, cartoonish *harridan*. When comely young Carly began competing for the attention of Vivian Alamain's nephew Lawrence on DOOL, fiftyish Vivian retaliated by having Carly buried prematurely. In an effort to alienate the other object of her affection, Victor Kiriakis, from his true love, Kate, Vivian purloined their embryo from a fertility clinic and used her own uterus as an incubator. Less conspicuous in her methods was *OLTL's* Dorian who, nevertheless, could always be counted on to vex resident diva Viki Lord. Because there is a greater number and range of characterizations for babes and vixens than there are for older divas and harridans, a limiting, good mother/bad mother dichotomy often develops for mature female characters. In contrast, a more diverse array of older male characters continues in evidence.

Satellites, Supervillains, and Supercouples

When not a harridan or diva, a middle-aged or older soap female is likely to be underutilized and serve as a *listening post* or *satellite* character whose primary function is to evoke the soap's history and revolve around and/or facilitate the stories of younger characters—especially her children. This contradicts, in part, the conclusions of Liebes and Livingstone (1994), who argued that mothers in mothering roles are not plentiful in American soaps. Although it is true that younger mothers rarely defer to their children's needs in lieu of pursuing a free-wheeling romantic adventure, many mothers of grown children are relegated to little more than parenting duties. In fact grandma is often conveniently available as a babysitter—the reason a younger mother is able to be away from her children. Judging from American soap operas, grown children are more of a hindrance to parents seeking to live their own lives than small children are. This reversal, of course, facilitates the demographic imperatives of producers.

Aging male characters become satellites, too, but usually at a later stage in life. The middle-aged male is often coupled with a younger heroine and thereby maintains his centrality. In the mid-1990s, five of *GL's* forty- and fifty-something males—Roger, Alan, Ross, Buzz, and Ed—were each involved with at least one woman 10 or more years younger. This occurred because three out of five of *GL's* middle-aged women—Nadine, Alexandra, and Lillian—had no front-burner romance or storyline of any kind. By early 1998, *AW* had reduced its number of older male characters to three and only one of these was paired with a comparably aged woman. Soon that popular role was eliminated, leaving all four middle-aged women with no apparent romantic prospects.

Despite that retired persons are a ready-made audience for soap opera, senior characters are virtually always restricted to satellite status and in some cases, as with *AW* in the mid-1990s, are stricken from the canvas entirely. *Loving's* Nada Rowand (Martin, 1995b) lamented: "I've certainly had less story as my character has aged, and I'm not going to lie and tell you it doesn't bother me, because it does." Wizened and/or crusty matriarchs and patriarchs such as Tom and Alice Horton of *DOOL* and Edward and Lila Quartermaine of *GH* are or have been fixtures, but outside of intervening on behalf of the family business and/or rendering approval or disapproval of the life choices of their progeny exist more to evoke history than to make it. They may have enduring romantic relationships, but such uninterrupted contentment is often the side effect of having no story. Occasionally female characters such as Katherine Chandler of *Y&R*, remain harridans into their dotage.

When not center stage escorting a younger heroine, the older soap male may achieve notoriety (and job security) as a *supervillain*. From

DOOL's supernatural miscreant Stefano DiMera, who has devoted each of his several lives to ghoulish mischief among Salem's denizens, to the comparatively earthbound degeneracy of *AW's* Grant Harrison, with his endless machinations to wrest custody of his son away from ex-wife and long-suffering heroine Vicky Hudson, the supervillain delights soap fans through his utter, unwavering evil. Most accept and even embrace his cartoonish or, at least, tenacious wickedness, but occasionally a righteous heroine will succeed in redeeming him without prohibitive fan backlash. The virtuous matron Rachel Cory tamed and wed the infamous Carl Hutchins on *AW* and made way for Grant Harrison to emerge as their arch-nemesis and new resident supervillain. Backsliding is always a possibility, however. *GL's* sinister Roger Thorpe seesawed back and forth from salvation owing to the intermittent good graces of true love Holly.

Soap opera couples such as Carl/Rachel and Roger/Holly have been the focus of fan attention and discussion. A majority of Internet posts register an opinion of an existing couple, a former couple, or a prospective couple. Fans often refer to themselves in terms of their allegiance to a love story, and e-mail groups form accordingly. A number of fan Web sites are devoted to a particular soap opera romance, and these may endure despite the dissolution of the relationship. *GL* fans have been known to allude to romantic storylines by fusing the first names of the characters involved. Mattessa indicates the Matt/Vanessa love story, Bloss is shorthand for Blake/Ross, and supercouple Josh/Reva are rendered as Jeva. Even romances that are not fan favorites are subject to this treatment; fans of Roger/Holly or Rolly were quick to express their disapproval of Holly's new romance with Fletcher by labeling them Folly. Cyberfans of all soaps often display their devotion to an actor, character or especially, couple in their choice of an Internet screen name or handle. The focus on couples is so primary that a mail solicitation for renewal of a subscription to one of the soap opera magazine beckoned: "Help keep a nice couple together."

Rarely, a couple is created by accident. Platonic interactions or brief affairs can result in an outright pairing when the couple's chemistry is obvious to creators and/or fans. If a promising match can be accommodated without inordinate changes in story projections, and if the couple is not too controversial and/or commercially counterproductive, soaps sometimes pursue the unplanned love story. The enduring romance of Mac and Rachel on *AW* began in this manner (Lemay, 1981), as did the duos of Holden and Lily on *As the World Turns* (*ATWT* Waggett, 1997) and Buzz and Jenna on *GL* (Why *GL's* Vanessa, 1994).

Regardless of whether a love story is envisioned from the outset, when creators are fully behind it they will employ various tactics to get the audience behind it too. Budget permitting, one or several couples will be sent on location to secluded, romantic spots during sweeps periods. If location shooting is not financially feasible, exotic sets will be invented within studio confines for this purpose. Favored couples might also be given their own signature music or song. Of course, the addition of an evil third party is further evidence of a soap's commitment to a romantic storyline. These mechanisms are enhanced when producers detect viewer resistance to a couple deemed demographically lucrative and withheld when this dynamic is reversed and a breakup is planned.

As previously indicated, the early 1980s saw the emergence of what soon came to be called the *supercouple*. Luke and Laura of *GH* were the archetype for this brand of romantic duo, and soon inspired emulation in *DOOL's* Bo and Hope, Cruz and Eden from the now-defunct *Santa Barbara*, and numerous others. Reep (1992) defined a supercouple as "a man and a woman who have found perfect love for each other, so perfect that they are incapable of having romantic feelings for anyone else under any circumstances" (p. 96). As with any soap opera love affair, obstacles delay consummation and marriage. Yet, for a supercouple, such obstacles can never be "personal flaws or idiosyncracies that could interfere with their perfect love" (p. 96). Neither are they likely to be real-world obstacles related to identities of class, age, race, appearance, or physical ability. Instead it is that external force—a devious schemer, supernatural power, and/or criminal element—that keeps the couple at bay. The notion of forbidden love, then, is associated with some outrageous and unlikely roadblock causing problems for otherwise gorgeous, healthy, well-off, homogeneous, and age-appropriate lovers. Especially once they wed, these pairs can transform into rigid and static characters who restrict the evolutionary structure of the narrative.

Viewers are so intensely loyal to these romances that they will not accept a breakup under any circumstances. If an actor involved in a supercouple story wishes to resign, it is more likely that she or he will die or vanish as a result of foul play than be written off on account of relational deterioration. In the case of Justin and Adrienne on *DOOL*, Reep (1992) pointed out that the remaining member of the couple was dismissed so that the pair could ride off into the sunset together.

If a death occurs, it is sometimes merely presumed. This allows for the actor's return to the role at some later time. If bodily remains are fully present and identifiable, however, it is a sign that the creators have had their fill with the story and want to head in a totally new direction. When Vicky's fiancé and true love Ryan was shot to death on *AW*, not only was Vicky shown crying over his body, but the audience was subsequently told that his corneas had been harvested for transplant. Because the writers hoped to capitalize on Vicky's popularity by inserting her into another supercouple romance, they did not want fans to resist investment in the new story because they believed Ryan might be resurrected. That did not keep a few fans from hoping, long after Vicky's period of mourning and her involvement with other men, that he would be.

Along with the "destructive slide toward closure" represented by the supercouple (Reep, 1992, p. 96), the traditional notion of one true love invoked by their depiction and confirmed by their reception appears to fly in the face of the rebellious feminine subjectivity celebrated by Nochimson (1992). The vehement hunger for stories featuring previously established lovers who are meant to be together is widespread among fans and a possible impediment to efforts to portray growth throughout the life cycles of the characters. Attachment to such couples constrains romantic possibilities for older female characters because many of those who survive into middle age will have had a long-term love at some point. If that true love is still on or returns to the canvas, there will be significant numbers of fans who vehemently protest the idea of the woman moving on to another relationship at her stage in life.

Younger heroines with a string of romances are another matter. Despite that serial monogamy is the standard pattern for soap opera relationships, efforts by the writers to recontextualize prior relationships can work to reinforce faith in fated and forever love. Although *AW* capitalized on Vicky and Ryan's popular romance by orchestrating an otherworldly rendezvous during Vicky's brief sojourn to the afterlife, only a year later they were writing Vicky's stormy romance with Jake as if the relationship with Ryan had never occurred. Dialogue and story asserted that Jake and Vicky had always been "soulmates." When it suits creators' goals and, especially, when it involves a younger heroine, viewers are encouraged to believe that the current true love coupling is (and always has been) it. Because many fans approach soaps with corresponding hopes and expectations, such encouragement is rarely wasted.

Tethering Time

The real-time authenticity of soap opera heralded by Brown (1994) and others has its exceptions. While residents of soapland do celebrate holidays—including each new year—along with viewers, and they may be born, grow old, and die as the decades unfold, certain conventions may render life-event connections with the audience rather tenuous.

One such convention is referred to as *SORAS* (soap opera rapid aging syndrome) by fans. It is the rare child who grows up in real time on a soap, and investment in any child born to the soap community pays off only when she or he reaches an age sufficient to attract romantically minded adolescent viewers. As previously illustrated through the character of Michelle on *GL*, accelerated aging accomplishes this feat at a time—often in the months preceding summer—when producers can mold these characters and use them to greatest advantage. So a viewer who remembers that her son was born about the same time as Rachel Cory's son Matt came into the world of *AW* may have forfeited that connection when Matt was SORASSED into a teenager overnight.

A by-product of SORAS is the spate of young, unusually attractive grandmothers. By the time a female soap character is 40, it is rare if she does not have a child who is in her or his late teens or older. The only noteworthy exception has been *AMC's* Erica, whose children have been depicted as younger and for longer periods in an apparent effort to make Erica seem younger and, therefore, more acceptable to a wider range of viewers. When adult offspring are not the result of instant child stories of the kind previously discussed, they are usually the work of SORAS and, in either case, grandmotherhood typically follows in short order. This effect creates young grandfathers too. However, because the men are generally somewhat older than their female counterparts when children are born, it is not as pronounced. An extreme case of the former is Reva of *GL*, who in 1999 was being written as the fortyish grandmother of a 12-year-old. Again for the many viewers who have reached 40 and are still caring for pre-teen or even younger children, the sense of shared experience may be lessened.

Indeed the ages of characters who are parents of grown children may be distorted because of SORAS or similar conventions because an actor may not be old enough to have reasonably borne the child (and/or the actor playing her or him) in reality. Anna Stuart (Donna on *AW*) is a mere 15 years older than Jensen Buchanan, the third actor to play Donna's twins. In some cases the improbability of parenthood is inescapable. *GL's* Holly appears to be only about 8 or 10 years older than daughter Blake, and the same meager disparity exists between *GL's* Buzz and son Frank. Ironically, however, viewers who were too young and/or not watching when SORAS occurred in a given soap family sometimes perceive the parent as older than both the actor and her or his character as traditionally depicted, as in the case of the viewer who questioned how Donna could still be in her 40s given the ages of her children. This questioning occurs despite these older characters' exceedingly youthful appearance. Because female characters find themselves in this bind more so than male characters, a perception on the part of both producers and viewers that the woman is too old to be coupled with a character portrayed by a male actor her own age can result.

Although the acronym is only used occasionally by fans, *SOADS* (soap opera age deletion syndrome) also operates in the soap opera universe. Age deletion most often occurs when a role is recast with a younger actor. This can be a matter of design or happenstance. In either case, however, it serves to extend the romantic viability of the character, and this is especially desirable when he or she is a fan favorite. Additionally, SOADS can point a character who was previously SORASSED toward real-time alignment. When the sister or brother roles of Matt and Amanda Cory were recast on *AW* in 1996/1997, a few of the approximately 10 years each had acquired through SORAS were instantaneously expunged.

Age deletion can also be accomplished by fudging a long-term character's history. On *AMC*, when the daughter Erica supposedly bore as a young teen was written into the program and played as and by a spritely teenager, fans protested in magazines and on the Net. Those who had matured along with Erica and were in their 40s wondered how their contemporary could suddenly be some 10 years their junior. The show's scribes recognized their error and began to write the daughter as a 23-year-old, but this still fixed Erica on the shy side of 40.

The tendency of soap operas to kill characters off only to miraculously resurrect them also breaches life cycle associations. On most soaps, resurrections are given some plausible, if not likely, explanation. Often deaths occur when departing actors are too closely identified with their characters to be immediately replaced. As mentioned earlier, if the character is half of a supercouple, a breakup would violate fans' sacred memories, and so an untimely demise is deemed preferable. Yet if a fan favorite wishes to return, he or she is often accommodated in an effort to boost both story options and ratings. So, it is *de rigueur* for deaths to yield no recognizable remains except when creators wish to discourage fans from hanging on the hope of the character's return, as was the case with *AW's* Ryan. When Kathleen McKinnon reappeared on *AW* in the early 1990s, a tale about her involvement in a witness protection program was used to explain her apparent death in a plane crash several years earlier. In the case of *DOOL*, however, resurrections had become so habitual by the 1990s that explanations ceased to be offered. As we see, such plot holes are in keeping with the program's flourishing fantasy orientation and camp sensibility.

Despite these violations of the timeline, the soap opera format is still more closely meshed with the life cycles of viewers than that of any other popular genre. Fans appreciate any evocation of their soap's history, whether it be the rekindling of an old flame, the eruption of an old feud, or the mere mention of a long-gone incident or character.

However, this hankering for history tends to contradict another unique by-product of soap opera seriality—the ability to portray character evolution with an iota of verisimilitude. Nostalgic longing for characters to revisit their old selves could conceivably create a canvas populated with static, one-dimensional caricatures and make a soap opera indistinguishable from a sitcom.

Still core families and characters carry much weight in evoking a soap opera's history. When new characters are introduced, they are often linked with the core in some manner so that viewers accept them more readily. Supercouple hopefuls Jake and Paulina of *AW* were broken up temporarily so that a new Australian hunk, Ian Rain, could be tied to the core through Paulina. The more of a *tentpole* a core character is, the more likely that she or he will have satellite characters circling about. This is not purely a function of fan favor, however, but of the demographically motivated tactics of creators because a front-burner storyline can stimulate fan support for most any character. However, it is the younger core characters who are most prized and protected by creators, often despite multiple recasts, because it is these characters who can be exploited in efforts to attract the most desirable audience.

Triangulation Station

The core character with his or her satellites is just one constellation endemic to soap opera. Another configuration—and one that is a staple of the genre—is the triangle. When a supercouple is involved, it is almost always a scheming interloper who completes the triumvirate and persistently endeavors to spoil the true lovers' chances for happiness.

DOOL has come to specialize in this type, moving from the supercouple formula established in the 1980s to an era of *supertriangles* in the 1990s and beyond. For much of the 1990s, under the direction of flamboyant head writer James Reilly, the show focused on four such trios: Marlena/John/Kristen, Billie/Bo/Hope, Carrie/Austin/Sami, and Jack/Jennifer/Peter. Despite peripheral suitors, these triangles dominated. The fact that all but the Jack/Jennifer/Peter threesome feature two women vying for one man is noteworthy.

Only the second, Billie/Bo/Hope, can be said to have featured some even-handedness. Bo and Hope were the premiere *DOOL* supercouple of the 1980s and were eventually written off with their son as a happy, intact family. Their re-emergence as a major force in the 1990s was preceded by Hope's apparent death and a recast of the character of Bo. Bo resurfaced after Hope's demise to be coupled with two other women—each of whom, in her own way, was played as a true love. The second of these matches, Billie, was extremely popular in that role—especially in the view of younger fans who admired the new, age-deleted Bo. However, with the appearance of a woman of uncertain identity who resembled Hope, a battle commenced between fans of the celebrated supercouple and those too young to have witnessed their heyday. The return of the original actor to the role of Bo, the exit and eventual recast of Billie, and the revelation that the mystery woman was, indeed, Bo's beloved wife eventually gave the edge to the long-time fans. Only then did the program dare insult either faction by making one of the women—Billie—into a vixen.

It is significant that the first successful coupling fans witness first-hand is generally the one they favor. Many who had expressed pleasure with the Bo/Billie duo were quick to shift their allegiance on Hope's return, with some vociferously denying that they ever accepted Bo with anyone but his one true love. This does not appear to be conscious hypocrisy on the part of these fans, but rather evidence of their facility for negotiating and adapting their own readings to the tenor of the moment. This displays both a potential to resist *and* to be molded according to wishes of the powers that be. However, a show rarely establishes a somewhat even-handed triangle. The Jax/Brenda/Sonny and Brooke/Ridge/Taylor supertriangles on *GH* and *The Bold and the Beautiful* (*B&B*), respectively, cultivated vocal adherents and fan investment on all sides.

A snapshot of daytime's triangles during the fall of 1997 speaks to the genre's prevailing stance toward age, gender, and romantic viability. Of 29 clear-cut triangles, 18 featured a man at the center. Eight of these men were over 40, whereas only 1 of the 11 women desired by two men had reached midlife. Also the triangles featuring a woman at their core were more likely to be depicted in even-handed fashion and less likely to portray either of her suitors as desperate and pathetic. The increasing use of the evil vixen or harridan as a menacing third party colors viewer perceptions of forbidden love because it is this female rival, and not hegemonic power relations of gender, race, age, or class, that stands as the impediment to happiness.

Front Burner, Back Burner, and Ye Olde Chopping Block

Decisions about which characters should be featured or on the front burner, which should be back burnered or serve as satellites, and which should be axed and removed from the canvas entirely, can depend, in part, on factors coincidental with age such as seniority. The specifications of the actors' contracts are relevant. Generally, a newly contracted actor receives an agreement of 3 years duration with a 13-week option for the first year and a 26-week option thereafter (Allen, 1985). This means that at the appropriate intervals, the show can decide not to pick up the option and the actor can be dismissed. However, the actor usually has no privilege to release him or herself until the contract term is up. Additionally, a pay rate is set on a per diem basis. The number of days per week for which an actor is to be paid is referred to as her or his "guarantee"—in other words, the actor is guaranteed pay for that number of appearances whether or not he or she is called to duty. The actor can be required to work more than the guarantee provides, but must be compensated for the additional time (Rouverol, 1984). If an actor becomes (or is) exceptionally popular and possesses greater leverage than the typical performer, he or she can negotiate a contract of shorter duration, interim release options for him or herself, longer release option intervals for the show, a limit to the number of required appearances, and, of course, a larger per diem rate.

Regardless of whether an actor rates such privileges, seniority generally brings with it an increase in overall income. Therefore, when a show's budget gets tight and demographic pressures loom, the first actors jettisoned or moved to the back burner tend to be older actors with seniority. During *AW's* Baby Boomer purge of 1996 to 1998, four middle-aged actors portraying characters with relatively long histories were dropped from the cast. Another was rumored to have resigned when the show failed to offer him the minimum guarantee and/or salary he previously commanded (Logan, 1998d). Yet another was reported to have accepted a reduction in pay to remain employed. Whether due to soap opera youthification trends, economic constraints, or both, the dearth of older characters and the meagerness of their storylines have become all too evident.

The *DOOL*ification of Soap Opera

Many of the conventions described in this chapter and previous assessments of the genre began to be challenged in the 1990s and reformulated by the trajectory of one particular soap—*DOOL* (see Logan, 1996a). Although a decade earlier, *Santa Barbara* (NBC) attempted to lace traditional generic elements with an outrageous campy feel, the soap audience was not quite ready, and the show was canceled after 8 years. However, during the 4-year tenure of writer James Reilly in the mid-1990s, the innovative tone, texture, and text of *DOOL* were responsible for attracting large numbers of young viewers and propelling it into second place in household ratings and first place in terms of the key demographic groups. Its ascendance made it a trendsetter in daytime as other soaps attempted, with varying degrees of success, to emulate it.

Since the early 1980s, *DOOL* had been an especially fantasy-oriented show, incorporating gothic costume dramas into its romantic narratives and fiddling with the lives, deaths, and identities of characters with greater than usual fluency. When the actor playing Marlena's husband, Roman, quit the show, a new actor was eventually brought in to replace him, and Roman's altered appearance was written into his story. An archvillain had treated him to brainwashing and plastic surgery, forcing him to become the enigmatic John Black. Eventually Black's true identity was revealed, and the Roman/Marlena romance flourished. When the original actor was available to return, however, the show banked on two popular stars and devised a way to retract the previous story and return the second Roman to his enigmatic identity—a mystery to be saved for later resolution. The first Roman's reappearance was shortlived, and when the actor was not available to reprise his role a few years later, the solution was to cast someone who had previously portrayed a totally different character. Fans seem to adjust to these character, actor, and identity gymnastics with relative ease, as the program's postmodern sensibility has become more and more accommodating and as they have been youthified to the point of widespread unfamiliarity with the show's history.

Ironically, although it had been the first serial to venture into supernatural territory with Luke and Laura's *ice princess* story in the early 1980s, *GH* gradually evolved toward an ambience of comparatively hard-hitting realism in the 1990s, offering critically acclaimed stories about breast cancer, sexual harassment, organ transplantation, and a ground-breaking one in which teen Robin Scorpio, who had literally grown up on the program, contracted the AIDS virus by engaging in unprotected sex with her boyfriend, who later died of the disease. These stories did not, however, stimulate the viewership of newer, younger audiences nearly as much as *DOOL's* increasingly far-fetched leaps into fantasy. Strangely, a large number of *DOOL* fans appeared to also watch *GH*, perhaps owing to the number of *DOOL* alumni on the ABC show. Exasperated *DOOL* viewers often pointed to *GH* as the superior soap, but the opposite sentiment was also evident when fans stated their preference for *DOOL's* escapist, postmodern fare over *GH's* reality-based, but comparatively cheerless, plots. To posters bemoaning *DOOL's* lack of realism, another fan responded emphatically:

> AIDS, drug/alcohol addictions . . . handicapped kids. . . . Uh, *hello!* That kind of realism is *depressing!!*. . . . *DOOL* has carved out its own little niche. . . . Yes, *DOOL* is escape; yes, it's fantasy; yes, it's campy; yes, it's *unrealistic!!!* *DOOL* is what it is and plenty of people *like it that way!!!!*

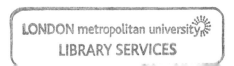
LONDON metropolitan university
LIBRARY SERVICES

The unyielding aspiration of many viewers to dodge real-world issues, be they in the public or private domain, becomes pivotal as the investigation continues.

Reilly's escapist vision spawned storylines involving premature burial, embryo theft, demon possession, execution by guillotine, and never-ending supertriangles pitting true lovers against vicious, persistent schemers who literally talked themselves into believing that their love would someday be returned in kind. Plots revolved around four or five demographically staggered but mostly youthful romantic heroines, with all other characters engaged in facilitating or sabotaging their happiness. For much of the 1990s, forty-something Marlena, thirtyish Hope, late twenty-something Jennifer, and twentyish Carrie anchored the show. Happiness for women, in particular, was defined in terms of romantic, as opposed to financial or professional, success.

Additionally, the one-dimensionality of characters was enhanced and logic was defied on a daily basis. When Sami's baby was kidnapped and taken to France, the French government refused to return the child unless Sami married its father. Carrie's beloved, Austin, was consequently hijacked into a marriage of convenience with the scheming Sami. Even-handed triangles, when they did occur, were shortlived; in no time, any ambiguity was erased and the identity of the *persona non grata* became fairy tale clear. Rather than rooting for favored couples, who were generally portrayed as foolishly vulnerable to their victimizers, many fans tuned in day after day to see a manipulator get his or her comeuppance. Lessons did not stick, however. The rule of the new *DOOL* was that, although most male villains began as such and did not change, female evildoers were typically and, as of this writing, irreversibly created when good women, such as Kristen and Billie, turned bad on account of desperate, pathetic, and unrequited love. Lovelessness led, inevitably, to lunacy.

Character consistency was virtually nonexistent because the program was story-driven, as opposed to character-driven, in its execution. Triangles dragged on, but mini-cliffhangers kept viewers intrigued. Marlena's possession by the devil was good for a plethora of these. As ridiculous as many fans found the story, they could not resist making return visits as she levitated, morphed into a feline, and paraded *au naturel* before family and friends.

DOOL's increasingly postmodern tenor allowed younger audiences, among others, to appreciate older characters who seemed most likely to be involved in the wooliest tales. However, the incompatibility of their pleasures with those of older, female viewers seeking engagement and identification with characters like themselves is problematic. *DOOL's* new formula made many long-time fans unhappy, as have the

*DOOL*ification efforts of other shows—such as *GL's* attempt to literally clone the character of Reva.

The ideological impact of demographic preferences can be seen in these prevailing and, especially, evolutionary soap opera tendencies. Although women are the intended audience, a large portion of this audience is routinely marginalized and constrained in terms of romantic viability and the number and array of subject positions offered for inhabitation. Yet, could cyberspace provide a rallying space for consumer resistance to demographically based content? If so can such resistance begin to compensate for the denial of collective fantasies coveted by marginal audiences? Empirical examination of viewers can begin to address these issues.

3 ACTIVE INTERPRETERS AND THE SOCIAL AUDIENCE

I'm not trying to have a war on the Internet,
but hear me out. I think Morgan Winthrop is gay.

This chapter assesses the ideological posture of fans' interpretations of soap opera stories by highlighting readings associated with articulations of gender, age, sexuality, and/or romantic fantasy. In addition, it explores cyberspace in terms of how it may facilitate and/or hinder fan negotiation, pleasure, and opposition. The insights it produces begin to answer the key question of whether counter-hegemonic readings, to the extent they exist, signal meaningful resistance.

SOAP AUDIENCE: UNAVOIDABLE DISRUPTION

Collective Bargaining

Hall's (1980) encoding/decoding model, with its three-pronged desig-nation of preferred/dominant, negotiated, and oppositional meanings (or readings), has been employed in myriad efforts to assess textual reading positions and/or actual decodings. Lewis (1991) elucidated this model by considering definitional ambiguities and inconsistencies in its application. The idea of a preferred/dominant reading, or one that is expected and/or desired on the part of the encoder(s), is most tricky because it assumes that the intentions of the source can be accurately gauged. This study has begun to argue, however, that through an accounting of soap opera's institutional practices and imperatives and the proclivities of the genre and/or text, such intentions are, with general regard to issues of age and gender, determinable. Lewis also contended

41

that "the basis for investigating the preferred meaning" is that it is presumed to be the "exercise of [ideological] power within a set of shared cultural assumptions" (p. 64). That is, it is assumed to be consistent with hegemony. The negotiated reading is a subtler concept and not to be confused with the term *negotiation* when applied to any encounter of reader with text. It is used to identify readings that depart in some minor aspect from what is intended, but not in terms of their overall, hegemonic crux. Lewis defined an oppositional reading as one that recognizes the preferred reading as such and then explicitly opposes it.

However, Lewis also cites Condit's (1989) essay, which illustrated these concepts by employing a text in which the preferred meaning is one favorable to a pro-choice position on abortion and provokes an oppositional reading from a pro-life viewer who acknowledges the story's intent but disagrees with it. Here pro-choice is established as the preferred reading—in this instance, the intended reading—because both this pro-life advocate and an abortion rights supporter concur about the program's ideological bent. Yet the preferred meaning is not consistent with the dominant ideology of patriarchy in the first place. Therefore, the pro-life viewer's opposition cannot be seen as resistive to hegemony—that is, to many of the shared assumptions of a larger culture, which continues to value women, first and foremost, for their reproductive role. Yet Condit's evolutionary usage of the term oppositional reading is consistent with that of other scholars attempting to identify self-conscious disagreements with the preferred reading regardless of whether that reading is hegemonic.

To fill some of these gaps, a fourth designation—the *resistive* reading—has evolved. According to Lewis (1991), resistive readers question the idea of preferred reading and work in concert with the text by "exploiting the message's ambiguity s they see fit "(p. 69).

Condit's (1989) distinction between *polysemous* and *polyvalent* texts is complicating but relevant in this regard. According to Condit, what is frequently mistaken for contradictory interpretation arising from textual openness may actually be contradictory evaluation of a common reading. Many studies touting resistance among audience members attribute this judgment to textual polysemy, but may instead be confronting polyvalence.

Even with these clarifications and designations in mind, there is a need to indicate when a reading, true to the spirit of Hall's (1980) original idea, subverts hegemonic structures of power, whether it is labeled as preferred, negotiated, oppositional, or resistive. I propose adding the qualifier *hegemonic* or *counter-hegemonic* to perform this function. In other words, when the pro-life viewer in Condit's (1989) study agrees that the text in question supports a pro-choice view, but takes issue with that view, this would be a hegemonic oppositional reading. The concept of articulation (Grossberg, 1992; Hall, 1986; Moffitt, 1993) thereby enters into the equation because the question of whether a given text may be said to evoke a hegemonic response largely depends on what is expected from the text by particular groups of readers at particular textual and historical junctures.

Armed with these concepts, we can briefly inspect the results of existing investigations of the soap opera audience. Soap opera scholars in the U.S. cultural studies tradition (Brown, 1994; Harrington & Bielby, 1995) eschew specific attention to text or production in favor of audience ethnography and have observed counter-hegemonic postures in marginal subjects. Brown's (1994) study is especially noteworthy in this regard because it focused on interaction within fan "friendship networks" (pp. 37–39) as an opportunity for collective negotiation and resistance. Such collectivization is stressed by Condit (1989) in arguing that private pleasures are fleeting and largely inconsequential in their potential for social impact. One would expect that with a multiplicity of sites for fan interaction in cyberspace, the likelihood of interpretive play would be enhanced. Although there are striking instances of such an effect in the data uncovered throughout this project, a conclusion of meaningful opposition is more problematic. After all, the larger a collective is the more diverse and prone it is to reflect hegemonic as well as counter-hegemonic aspects. The mere fact of polysemy and/or polyvalence, for instance, does not necessarily indicate opposition to the preferred reading, which may anticipate and, in fact, favor contentious reactions in the first place.

Tabloid Talk/Tabloid Soap

The *DOOL*ification of soap opera and the general trajectory of daytime TV in the 1990s reveal an impetus to stimulate confrontation on the part of audiences, whether it be in the TV studio, at home, or online. The tabloid talk genre, which expropriated a staple of soap opera—the catfight—and took it to new levels became the most visible example of confrontational, feminine TV during this era. The success of these comparatively inexpensive productions, in turn, forced soap operas to compete in terms of tone and content. Hit films targeted to female audiences, such as 1997's *My Best Friend's Wedding* starring Julia Roberts and Cameron Diaz, borrow from both daytime genres. Roberts' character resorts to scheming in an attempt to lure her ex-boyfriend away from his bride to be (Diaz) and, eventually, confronts her in a public restroom as onlookers cheer and hiss their mutual recriminations. Unlike what was occurring on contemporaneous soaps and talk shows, however, Roberts admits defeat and embraces her rival, eliciting applause from the same group of women.

After 1994's premature burial story resulted in a ratings hike for *Days of Our Lives* (*DOOL*), other soaps began to feel the pressure to create plots that would lend themselves to female versus female conflict. Claimed one P&G executive (cited in Hinsey, 1995): "Never mind that our shows have never been about that. The message we got was 'Do catfights. Have the women pull each other's hair.'" *DOOL* took the standard catfight and made it obligatory and indicative of larger confrontational themes in the text and viewers' reception of it. If creators expect contradictory interpretations, the only remaining issues could be whether and which audience views are at odds with hegemonic structures of power.

The middle-aged love triangle of Felicia, John, and Sharlene on *Another World* (*AW*) serves as a case in point. In the mid-1990s, the program and its new executive producer, Jill Farren Phelps, were handed a mandate to improve demographics by becoming more compatible with *DOOL*. Phelps promptly fired all the actors over 55 and attempted to focus the attention of older fans on a single story involving middle-aged characters. She abruptly separated the stable, happily married couple, Dr. John Hudson and Sharlene Frame, and steered them into adulterous territory courtesy of romance novelist Felicia Gallant.

This turn of events seemed implausible to many fans because the couple had only recently renewed their marriage vows and Felicia had spent the last several months lecturing her daughter about her affair with a married man. Although negative reaction was immediate, many in Felicia's legions of fans loved her relationship with the handsome doctor, thereby adopting a preferred, hegemonic reading.

Flame wars soon erupted on several cyberspace bulletin boards. Although Baym (1993) was upbeat in her appraisal of soap opera fan interactions in cyberspace, she warned that the "voicing of multiple interpretations" can lead to flame wars—that is, hotly contested debates featuring belligerent posts. Celebrating the John/Felicia romance was tantamount to gender heresy to fans who saw the doctor as a "self-absorbed asshole" and his recent behavior as cold, arrogant, insensitive, and sexist. Their reactions were oppositional and counter-hegemonic, asserting that John was but a weak, unfaithful cad unworthy of the two women's rivalry.

However, a third group of fans took Sharlene's side and were quick to lay the primary blame on Felicia, creating uncomplimentary nicknames or aptonyms (Baym, 1993) for her, including Floozia, Fellatia, Fallopia, Fleaslut, and Fauxlicia. Although these viewers were pitted against Felicia fans, it is also appropriate to label their responses as preferred and hegemonic because the text appeared to anticipate a clash between the two groups. Catfights between the two characters were a frequent occurrence, and soon the normally reserved Sharlene was being referred to by Felicia fans as Shrewlene or Shoutlene. The tabloid style was all too apparent, as anyone channel surfing between Sharlene and Felicia's high-decibel slapfests and *Ricki Lake* could plainly see.

Not surprisingly, fans' online deliberations soon mimicked this tabloid style, complete with name-calling and personal attack. Accusations of a double standard emerged from the anti-John contingent, one of whom complained that he was getting off scot free while the battle raged on between the women: "At the risk of harping on this . . . why, oh why does this play out again in the absence of John, who is the most culpable of persons who began this debacle?" These fans also lamented that John had not inspired any negative aptonyms. Eventually, Dr. Hudscum, John Juan, and Teflon John were submitted.

Privately, those who chose to place the primary blame on John could revel in that view, whereas on the newsgroup they seemed appalled to discover that others' readings did not coincide, and that many Felicia enthusiasts hastened to forgive him anything by virtue of the fact that he was a handsome guy deigning to lay his blessings on the beloved but lonely diva. Felicia's fans on America Online (AOL) bulletin boards, showing their negotiative (and hegemonically resistive) sleight of hand, angered other fans by reinventing the backstory to justify the affair. They argued that John and Sharlene had been in trouble for years, even before the new management took over, because of Sharlene's problems with a psychological disorder that required John to sacrifice his own needs. Sharlene's fans defended her by saying that John had lovingly and appropriately rendered his support and that character assassination by the new creative team was the culprit.

Although those criticizing John, bemoaning the double standard, and, thus, embracing the counter-hegemonic position could find allies, their collective acknowledgment of sexism in the representation of the love triangle was more than offset by the readings of those who adopted Felicia's gaze in opposition to Sharlene or Sharlene's in opposition to Felicia. As other cases show, the net effect of exposure to such disputes can be to diminish, rather than enhance, marginal pleasures associated with soap opera. The show's focus on Felicia as home wrecker and Sharlene as bitter harridan, rather than on John as philanderer, as well as its multiple dramatizations of disputes between the two women, indicate that the encoders of this tale bargained for polyvalence and, potentially, tabloid catfighting among viewers. Confrontation among women interpellated by female characters competing for a prize—the love of a man—was a preferred, hegemonic response not opposed as such by the majority of online participants.

"Why Would a Campy Gay Man Keep a Lady in a Cage?"

An unsuspecting viewer switched on *DOOL* for the first time as Gothic supervillain Stefano DiMera held diva Marlena captive in his lair, and her initial impression of gay *camp* may have been on target. As McRobbie (1994) observed in her overview of Sontag's (1967) essay on the topic, camp is an edgy, theatrical sensibility that "pronounces good taste in bad taste" and exhibits "self-conscious artificiality (pp. 85-87)." In *DOOL*ified soap opera, camp reveals itself in, among other things, exaggerated, cartoonish manifestations of good and evil, scenery chewing by actors, paranormal elements, and periodically outrageous scenarios, settings, and costumes.

Although no definitive data exist, participation in soap opera fan activities reveals a definite gay male presence. Feuer (1995) chronicled gay activations resulting from the camp sensibility in the prime-time soap opera *Dynasty* and centering on Alexis, the extravagant *bitch* portrayed by Joan Collins. Daytime, too, caricatures many of its middle-aged characters. Griffin's (cited in Feuer, 1997) interviews with gay male cyberfans confirm that they often "see things through the eyes of 'camp'" and defend Alexis-like characters such as *All My Children's* (*AMC's*) Erica Kane. However, it is not only gay fans, but youthful ones, who seem to relish seeing veteran players awash in a camp aesthetic, although their delight is in booing and hissing these characters online and, implicitly, as they watch. One effect of preferring older characters in this mode may be to further marginalize articulations in which older fans seek verisimilitude in characters/subjects by which they might be interpellated. If camp concocts, as McRobbie (1994) contended, "a simultaneous feeling of immediacy and disengagement" that can "never be confused with realism or with the search for authenticity" (p. 86), fans whose love of the genre developed over time through attachment and investment, and who are less accustomed to a postmodern sensibility than their younger counterparts, are apt to feel increasingly shut out.

Nonetheless, soap opera's portrayals of gay characters and the negotiations of gay male viewers are more relevant to explore at this juncture as evidence of marginal fans' ability to negotiate in ways that augment their pleasure. The interpretive fluency exhibited by such fans in reading gayness into what appears to be intended as standard, heteronormative fare is nothing new. D'Acci (1994) recalled CBS' ambiguity reduction efforts meant to thwart similar readings of the relationship between female cops—the title characters of the 1980s program *Cagney and Lacey*. On the Internet, readings of gay fans can acknowledge the hegemonic intentions of creators and still dwell between the lines—that is, be oppositional and resistive simultaneously. One fan's interpretation of a character on *AW* is exemplary:

> I am not trying to start a war on the Internet, but hear me out. I think Morgan Winthrop is gay. I think his relationship with Brett was doomed from the beginning. I think he has told Lorna his true feelings and Lorna is very understanding. Next, I think Morgan left medicine to sort through his sexual identity. However, I don't think *AW* will attack this storyline but this type of story needs to be told.

The poster gathered story details that did occur—Morgan's breakup with his girlfriend, his career confusion, his friendship with a female confidante—and supplemented them with what he felt was a logical (and desirable) explanation: Morgan is gay. He "exploits the text's ambiguity," but follows with a qualification suggesting that he knows the given text is not likely to fulfill his wishes, situating this counter-hegemonic reading on the bridge between oppositional and resistive modes.

This was not an isolated case. Several months later, another gay fan scrutinized *AW's* new cop, Gary Sinclair:

> Most of you know that I think *AW* should have a gay character. Here is my idea. Hopefully it will work out but probably not. Gary is an alcoholic. We know this. He could use his drinking as a way to cope with his homosexual tendencies. . . . Maybe that is why he is afraid to open up at AA. He also mentioned his last post because of officers harassing him. Josie may be the person he confides in and they develop a strong friendship. . . .

This reading is remarkably similar to the first, right down to the career issues, the female confidante, and the realization that such a story evolution was doubtful. After all, Josie was to become more than just friends with the dazed—but not sexually confused—Gary.

Gay fans recognize their own enhanced facility to read against the grain. When *AW* reintroduced a popular middle-aged character and made it clear that he returned with a secret, a female fan wondered online: "Does anyone feel that they are leading up to Michael coming out of the closet?" She was promptly chastised by another female poster for her insinuation: "Bite your tongue! If that gorgeous hunk turns out to be anything but fuel for my fantasies, I'll die." At this point, a gay male fan chimed in to declare his interpretive dexterity: "Hello, if he turns out to be straight, *I'll* find a way to use him as fuel for *my* fantasies." As it happened, Michael's secret was Nick, the illegitimate son he discovered while in absentia. Another self-conscious effort to read oppositionally is seen in the comment of a gay poster who viewed *Guiding Light's* older woman/younger man duo of Matt and Vanessa as a "metaphor of gayness" because they kept their taboo romance a secret and were seen engaging in phone sex while hiding in their respective closets. Also, perhaps recognizing a subtext of forbidden love in such an intergenerational romance, a fan identifying himself as a "26-year-old GWM" had this to say about *AW's* Donna and Matt: "Matt was a mature young man not finding what he needed in a woman his own age . . . ."

Yet another reading, submitted by a poster of uncertain sexuality, proved to be something else entirely. Of a recently added, thirtyish character on *All My Children* (*AMC*), a fan observed:

> Anyone else think Michael is gay? It seems to me that the writers are working so hard to show that he's a man's man (no pun intended) that they have something up their sleeve. . . . Think about it, why else would they bring up his military service and catalog the sports he likes in one scene if not to set . . . us up for such a revelation.

Indeed this was a preferred reading of a potentially counter-hegemonic message because the program *was* building up to this very revelation over a period of several months. Their strategy, it seemed, was to get the audience to warm up to the character apart from his sexuality before breaking the news.

This was not the first serious attempt to portray gayness on a soap (see Caploe, 1995; Is America Ready, 1995). In the late 1980s, *As the World Turns* (*ATWT*) featured Hank Eliot, a gay fashion designer. In the early 1990s, *One Life to Live* (*OLTL*) told the story of a gay teen, Billy Douglas, focusing on the inability of Billy's father to accept his gayness. The reactions of other members of the community, including those of a sympathetic minister, were also highlighted. As Fuqua (1995) reported in her analysis of the storyline, the effort was watered down from its original conception, which was to have Joey Buchanan, the teenage son of Llanview's primary core family, come out as gay. Shifting the role to a peripheral character was, in the institutional mindset, more acceptable. Although short term and an example of the "sexuality-as-a-problem paradigm" (Fuqua, 1995, p. 209), the story was popular and ground breaking.

So when Michael's story unfolded on *AMC*, those loyal to ABC's soap lineup might have been well-cushioned. Although Michael was a member of one of *AMC's* core families, he was a new character rather than one already ensconced as a heterosexual hunk. Having an established male character suddenly emerge as gay would probably be deemed too risky by the powers that be, who would worry about disappointing female fans accustomed to being interpellated by the targets of his affection. The *AMC* story did not break out of the sexuality-as-a-problem mold either because its main focus became Michael's dismissal from his high school teaching position on account of his sexuality and the court case that ensued.

Negative and positive mail reacting to Michael's tale was highlighted in an issue of *Soap Opera Digest* (Love It/Hate It, 1996) and reflect hegemonic and counter-hegemonic positions of every variety. Those on the hate it side of the issue included the male fan who wrote:

> I'm not too pleased with *All My Children*'s gay storyline but not because it's dealing with homosexuality. . . . My problem is that the story is about Michael being gay and how everyone feels about it. . . . I'd like to see Michael treated like any other character—give him a love life, scandalous secrets from his past, stuff like that. (p. 63)

This counter-hegemonic, negotiated reading approves of the show's desire to deal with gayness, but prefers that Michael's sexuality be treated matter of factly and not as a *problem*. However, a fan on the love it roster argued that the story should be about family and support issues (p. 62). Although it rejects the larger culture's homophobia, this preferred reading nonetheless is consistent with the program's hegemonic containment of the story.

Hegemonic, oppositional readings also appeared in this feature, although they were comparatively infrequent in cyberspace. "I am tired of having homosexuality crammed down my throat," an angry consumer complained. "I watch soap operas as an escape, not as a news magazine" (p. 63). The view that soaps are only political when they overtly challenge the status quo, and that they should not be political at all, is commonplace. The bridge between soap opera readings and broader political contexts may be a difficult one to traverse.

Michael's story on *AMC* halted when the actor playing him opted against re-signing his contract. Although a love interest had been introduced, their story existed primarily as background, and Michael eventually exited Pine Valley. *AMC* followed Michael's departure with a gay teen story in which the conflict, once again, centered on the homophobic attitudes of family and friends.

Other than half-hearted, short-lived attempts on *AMC*, *DOOL*, and *Young and the Restless* (*Y&R*), soaps had mostly veered away from representing lesbian characters until such time as *AMC* planned to reveal, late in 2000, that Erica Kane's daughter, Bianca, harbored such a secret (see Logan, 2000). Their hesitancy might have been due to the fact that lesbian soap fans do not appear as open about their sexuality or as

vocal as gay male fans. The only time this researcher observed such
self-disclosure was when actor/comedian Ellen DeGeneres announced
her gayness and her romance with film actor Anne Heche. Because
Heche had been the second popular performer to portray *AW's* infamous twins Marley and Vicky, many fans of the program commented
on this news. A handful of the many who praised Heche and
DeGeneres for their courage identified themselves as lesbians. Most of
these had not been regular posters. Whether the *AMC* story would significantly diverge from the sexuality-as-a-problem paradigm remained
to be seen at this writing.

Overall, soap opera's overt treatment of gayness has been limited,
although the closures of these stories do allow viewers to envision a positive future for gay characters. Interjecting a camp aesthetic seems to be
the more nebulous, commonplace, and acceptable way to collect this
audience in the process of courting younger viewers. Yet counter-hegemonic readings of straight characters by gay fans exist as evidence of the
interpretive playfulness of some marginal readers. That such playfulness
is fully compensatory for the dearth of explicitly gay characters and storylines in soap opera seems doubtful, however. Additionally, the fact
that most of the conspicuously camp characters so pleasing to gay viewers are over 40 presents a conundrum. Their representation may alienate
another marginal group—older women—whose quest to locate engaging, authentic characters like themselves can be left unfulfilled.

SOAP AUDIENCE:
NEGOTIATING CURRENCY

Research on the interactions of soap opera viewers, both on and offline,
applauds the feminine subculture created out of the primary text.
However, there is little attention paid to what vested interests connected
to soap opera consider to be the most crucial marker of identity in addition to gender—age. If women may find solace as women within a community of soap opera enthusiasts, it should not be assumed that these
women are not at cross-purposes, both within and beyond this subculture, in terms of age and other aspects of identity. Again it is the particular articulation that is key.

Age, gender, class, and race are considered separately in analyses of
representation on the Net. Nonetheless, although the prevalence of
women in soap opera discussion groups might mitigate against their
underrepresentation elsewhere in cyberspace and in the larger culture,
this is not likely to be the case with respect to class, race, or age. The
cyberspace generation gap observed by Baym (1993) may persist within
soap opera discussion groups. Baym's (p. 171) further concern about the

eruption of flame wars—disagreements reflecting polysemic and poly-valent interpretations—is pertinent. When flame wars break out, the panacea of collective pleasure and empowerment may be confounded.

Moreover, it is not the mere fact that negotiations in such groups often float behind the text to the motivations of the powers that be (TPTB) or, in more indignant critiques, "the idiots" (TIIC) or "mother fuckers" in charge (TMFIC), which signals resistance to hegemony, but whether the consensus remains one of resignation to and acceptance of these motives and/or the content they generate as natural and immutable.

In her article entitled "Who Says Older Women Can't/Shouldn't Dance?," Wade-Gayles (2000) lamented: "Age and gender biases are invisible particles in the air we breathe; they get into our bloodstream and change the chemistry of our attitudes toward other people and, if we are women, toward ourselves" (p. 9). Similarly, Russo (1999) pointed out that when older women do things considered to be beyond their purview, such as wearing trendy fashions or becoming pregnant, it is regarded as scandalously anachronistic and more contemptible than parallel behavior on the part of men. Films in which monstrous older women turn on their philandering husbands highlight the "'unnatural' conjunction between middle-aged female flesh and still youthful desire" (Sobchack, 1999, pp. 202–203). No matter how empowered a woman dares to feel in the face of age and gender discriminatory culture, Gullette (1999) argued that "putting discourse on the defensive cannot be accomplished as long as only a few people do it" (p. 51).

On the surface, at least, there is much commentary by fans on the Internet and in letters to the editors of soap opera magazines that evi-dences their awareness of and concern about age and gender representa-tions. Yet, whether this signals meaningful resistance is still at issue. In an effort to explore this question, it is useful to enact an appraisal of fan negotiations online and elsewhere as they pertain to the currency of male and female characters at various life stages and, consequently, the subject positions offered to viewers with corresponding identities.

As it repeatedly faced extinction during the research period, the long-running soap opera *AW* provides a focal point for investigation. Cyberfans rallied after discovering, late in 1995, that NBC was threaten-ing cancellation if the program did not boost demographics by emulat-ing *DOOL* (see Logan, 1996a). *DOOL* was immediately ridiculed by *AW* fans for preferring models to actors, victimizing women, and for its out-landish plots. However, the fact that *DOOL* also tended to relegate its older cast to its most bizarre stories and/or pigeonhole them as over-the-top villains or sanitized, storyless listening posts was not discussed in this context. In an oppositional moment, one *DOOL* viewer discerned the real reasons she did not appreciate the program's older characters: "I don't like watching Alice, Maggie, or Caroline either. It's not because of their age, but because they are never given anything interesting to say or do. They just show up at weddings, funerals, or if somebody needs a babysitter." However, most fans of the program described these characters as dull, as if this quality were somehow intrinsic to their age group.

Although soap opera collectives generally provide a sanctuary from the criticism of nonfans who belittle the genre, some online forums encourage what could be interpreted as elitist condemnation of one soap by the fans of another. A Usenet fan unhappy with the trajectory of *AW* directed her ire at *DOOL* fans and their postings, saying that she felt "insulted and ashamed" to weed through subject headings such as "Sami is a big fat whore. . . ." Although a good many watched both and NBC would have liked nothing better than for all who watched either to watch both, a considerable number of *AW* devotees prided themselves in not watching *DOOL*, which they often referred to disparagingly as *DROOL*. Posts unfavorably contrasting *DOOL* with *AW* were common at this juncture, and the characteristics described earlier were used as justifications. In these cases, instead of directing blame to the powers that be, the onus was placed on the tastes of other fans.

However, as the intention to *DOOLify AW* became known, some fans encouraged others to write the powers that be, especially the controversial new executive producer Jill Farren Phelps (JFP), and warn them that the current trend would not sit well with loyal, long-time viewers. Yet months later and with the changes wrought by the new mandate coming to fruition, one fan saw her soap becoming a haven for female characters who were "stupid, thoughtless, man-hungry floozies" causing problems for all the "saintly men." Another fan concurred:

> All the women have changed into idiots. No one has a job any more, everyone is obsessed with their man. When . . . all the women on the show get "screwed" . . . while the men are forgiven, getting laid, and enjoying themselves, we know that TPTB are either aging men not getting any at home or brain-damaged women.

Yet another fan playfully reported visiting the JFP Clinic, where one would be "forced to watch the 'new *AW*'" and would then be given the "'shock' treatment of watching the 'old' *AW* where the women were smart, independent, and basically ran the show" in marked contrast to *DOOL*—"the preceding program." In a clever posting, a fan bemoaned the back burnering of one of her favorite characters, thirty-something Frankie Frame, by hypothesizing an announcement from the powers that be:

> Until we can find a plot line where she can desperately degrade her-self over a man, Ms. Frame will only be seen hanging up her family's clothes and providing expository one-liners for others. The part has been recast. After a long search we have chosen a 15-year-old model with no previous acting experience. . . . We know you will enjoy the next Frankie Frame storyline, in which the young lass . . . thinks of this really cute guy she likes, but he doesn't like her, so she cries a little and goes shopping.

The poster later offered a new translation for the acronym TPTB: "the penises that bite." He or she was to be further outraged when the show opted to have Frankie brutally murdered by a serial killer in an apparent effort to liberate a mid-level actor's salary for more demographically gainful uses. These fans' readings do, however, represent counter-hege-monic opposition, in that they recognize the hegemonic intent of pro-ducers and take it to task.

The youthification efforts of creators were designed to attract newer, younger clientele in the hopes that they would soon compensate for any erosion of the established fan base. Indeed there was, in the course of this researcher's observation of *AW* cyberfandom, a turnover in online participation, which, despite the uncertainty of cyberspace identity, appears to reflect a shift from an older to a younger population. This could be detected in the cyberfan reactions to a story on *AW* in February 1998 in which two characters met their untimely ends in a vehicular col-lision. Shane, a relative short-termer, was portrayed by a thirty-some-thing actor popular with primarily younger fans who considered him a hunk of unimpeachable credentials. His resignation from the show was reason enough for many of them to declare: "I'm outta here." The sec-ond victim, Michael, was a long-term character—the father of the soap's premiere young heroine—whose demise was occasioned by the actor's dismissal as the latest in a spate of firings of veteran performers. On one Web site bulletin board, there were no less than five subject headings and 25 posts bemoaning the death of the younger hero, whereas only two subject headings and 6 posts expressed regret over the exit of the veteran. These latter posts were exceedingly intense, but their "whistling in the wind" quality was palatable. "They just don't care about us," a "32-year viewer" observed. The paucity of like-minded responses indi-cates that they included the younger generation of fans who by omis-sion, if not by outright antagonism, appeared to devalue the pleasures of their older counterparts.

Antagonism is a more conspicuous manifestation of age-related biases transferred from the balance sheets of the networks and advertis-ers into cyberspace. With the demise of the older hero in the spring of 1998, *AW* effectively reduced its number of Baby Boom characters to three, and only one middle-aged woman remained as part of an ongoing romance. This fifty-something duo, Carl and Rachel, had its share of enthusiasts—one of whom had been attracted to the show for what she described as the "passionate love between two people in my age group." Others took exception, however. "Personally it disgusts me to watch them," stated one of several outspoken dissenters. "Carl reminds me of the dirty old man down the street," another agreed. "Nauseous is the word that comes to mind," echoed a third. The wishes of these naysayers were soon granted when the actor who portrayed Carl was fired, leaving the program potentially bereft of any love stories featuring older women.

Age-discriminatory sentiments have not been limited to this couple or to *AW*. "I have absolutely no interest in watching John or Marlena get passionate," remarked a poster about what was the sole midlife romance on *DOOL*. "[It] reminds me too much of my parents." Of diva Erica Kane (Fig. 3.1) on *AMC*, one fan bristled: "She makes me want to puke, she has to be almost 50." Another chimed in: "I'm sick of all the stories and men revolving around her dried up behind." Middle-aged mavens Stephanie and Sally from *The Bold and the Beautiful* (*B&B*) fared even worse, being dismissed by one discriminating viewer as "flaccid, shriveled monsters."

Additional signs of this generational divide can be seen in responses to the Matt and Vanessa love story on *GL*. In contrast to most others, this older woman/younger man relationship was taken seriously by

Fig. 3.1. *All My Children's* Erica Kane. . . . Well preserved, or all "dried up?"

creators and had endured into marriage, perhaps owing to the vigilance of its mostly older fans. Still there were persistent protests from viewers who found the idea of such a marriage ridiculous and from younger fans who hoped that Vanessa's scheming daughter, Dinah, would steal the heart of her stepfather. When Vanessa underwent a near-death experience after the birth of her child, one detractor began a bulletin board subject heading entitled, "Vanessa, go toward the light." Added a like-minded fan: "I agree, send Vanessa into the light. Then let Dinah and Matt raise the baby." These remarks were in direct conflict with the delighted reactions of Matt/Vanessa followers happy to see some atten- tion paid their favorite couple after a long dry spell. Their marginal pleasures were, in this instance and at this juncture, consecrated by cre- ators, but not by the derisive judgments of other fans. In smaller, face- to-face fan groups such as those studied by Brown (1994), affirmation of these pleasures might be possible. Amid the larger, more diverse collec- tive inhabiting cyberspace, however, cohesion and validation are con- stantly threatened in a sea of polyvalence. The counter-hegemonic opposition of many posters slowly erodes as the preferred audience asserts its privilege, demonstrating that not everything women do together acknowledges their aggregate, marginal position in society or seeks to remedy it.

If the gradual silencing of marginalized audiences can foster the goals of the powers that be, so too can the interventions of those powers. Obviously official network Web sites constitute one type of forum for these interests, but their visibility elsewhere has escalated. *Soap Opera Digest*, for instance, instituted its own forum on AOL, which included message boards that soon exceeded the unsponsored AOL boards in traffic and gradually led to an integrated Internet Web site. The forum and Web site also provided interviews, polls, and tidbits linked with its current issue, the cover of which is prominently displayed.

Accordingly, the agenda of the magazine helps set that of the mes- sage boards. As Fiske (1987) observed, the magazines are not indepen- dent of the larger soap opera enterprise because they "rely on studio press releases and cooperation for their material and access to their play- ers for interviews" (p. 118). The networks' sites on the Web and else- where also house soap opera bulletin boards subject to the same spillover. Thus, the soaps' desire to promote younger stars and their sto- ries registers on these sites and filters into the content of the message boards.

One article in *Soap Opera Digest* fueled a scant, short-lived, but angry outcry on the magazine's AOL site and illustrates how soap opera publications can embrace the imperatives of the industry on which they depend. In a critique of *One Life to Live* (*OLTL*) (Thumbs Up, 1997), the magazine argued that the program was "wasting" too much story on its aging cast members when the younger audience would not be enticed:

> What were they thinking by showcasing so many graphic scenes of, shall we say, "mature" people having sex? . . . fans are "treated" to Carlotta's fantasies of Hank, which has us thinking 9 1/2 Eeks. . . . As for Dorian, it's nice that post-menopausal women can still rip up the sheets with the best of them. (pp. 74–75)

If the previously recounted slights against older women and couples on the soaps are any indication, the sentiments of this piece concur with the preferences of the favored audience and may contribute to the marginalization of older viewers and their identifications.

Additionally, media-sponsored forums provide an expanded means by which diverse groups of viewers can, however fleetingly, experience an illusion of empowerment when any actual audience influence proceeds primarily from market research keyed to the producers' demographic goals. As Intintoli (1984) concluded from the comments of an insider in his exhaustive, backstage analysis of *GL*: "[W]hereas the degree to which the story could be changed by mail was limited, suppliers liked the audience to *feel* it can affect the show" (p. 183). Despite the privileging of youthful stories, characters, and outlooks, soap opera cyberfan sites still offer equal access and participants may overestimate their impact accordingly.

Yet, what about industry encroachment on the presumably independent Usenet soap opera newsgroups? The evolutionary structure of these newsgroups is relevant. When a single soap opera newsgroup became too unwieldy, the solution was to divide it into three separate newsgroups according to network. So like many of the commercial bulletin boards, these newsgroups now reproduce and assist the networks' efforts to create a flow that carries the same audience from one of their soaps to another. It is necessary for someone who watches soaps on two or more networks to subscribe to and manage more than one newsgroup—a disincentive to channel surfing.

Other examples of indirect influences emerged when *AW* was under the axe in 1995/1996. Those who protested content changes linked to the push for demographics were consistently chastised by other fans and accused of endangering the soap's status. Fans who had endeavored to keep the show on the air through letter-writing campaigns had taken a leadership role and determined that such negative commentary was counter-productive to the goal of keeping the show afloat at all costs, even if it was becoming *AW* in name only. Although well intended, these leaders were instructing fans to do exactly what the powers that be hoped—that is, to continue watching even if the new *AW* did not suit them, and thereby allow themselves to be taken for granted while other audience segments were courted. Tom Freeman, an avid fan of the program, established an *AW* Fan Brigade on behalf of which he waged an online war to keep fan morale up and dissuade viewers from jumping ship for several years as the massive and mostly unwelcome changes were occurring. By the spring of 1998, however, he disbanded the group and admitted to *Soap Opera Weekly* (DeLosh, 1998) that he might have continued his efforts if those in charge had given any indication that the Brigade's efforts were: "a) appreciated; b) important; and c) served some purpose beyond . . . trying to keep fans off their back" (p. 9). In his estimation, the program had exploited his unpaid labor to keep long-time viewers watching even though their interests were not being served.

Those in the industry have also exerted some influence through their participation in discussion groups. During *AW*'s 1995 cancellation hubbub on Usenet, an insider began providing insightful information on decision-making behind the scenes. Although he did not reveal his official position, his input was highly valued, with much of it eventually confirmed in magazine articles and interviews. Quick to toe the party line, he defended Phelps, the controversial executive producer who had improved the show's demographics, and scolded fans who did not appreciate the changes that preceded this: "Why the sniping at *AW*? If bottom line-motivated NBC sees reason to give the show a chance and continued support based on the numbers, why can't the people here?" Amazingly, nobody (except this researcher) contested the notion that NBC's profit-motivated criteria should also be their own. The act of (politely) challenging this insider's recommendation seemed to border on heresy and was dismissed by some as a violation of network etiquette.

Despite some wrangling over demographics, fans do seem to accept the system that determines what they will see. For instance, they argue that the advertisers are incorrect in their preference for teens and twenty-somethings when Baby Boomers possess equal or greater numbers and disposable income. Declared one 45-year-old: "I have two children, ages 16 and 7, and I buy plenty of laundry detergent and every other thing that 'younger' women who have school-age children buy." Younger viewers question the assumption that they are only intrigued by youthful characters and storylines. The issue of whether gender, age, race, or class should make an audience a more valuable commodity in the first place is, however, seldom raised. The mechanisms by which commercial TV operates are a given. Readings that protest youthification and the "dumbing down" of female characters may be viewed as counter-hegemonic in isolation, but they are not predominant. Neither do they quarrel with the commercial logic of targeting a lucrative audience and, therefore, cannot be said to demonstrate significant resistance. In essence, these viewers may simply "cry a little" about the loss of empowering public fantasies and then "go shopping'" for products they believe should make them a worthy target audience.

After feminist scholars initiated a justifiable defense of female audiences who had been summarily dismissed for their devotion to soap opera and other feminine texts (see Brunsdon, 1995), many of them neglected to adequately deliberate the limits of the pleasure and resistance they chronicled. This researcher acknowledges that many soap opera fans are able to intuit the reasons their enjoyment is belittled by the larger culture. Consider this letter to a magazine addressing the issue of why soaps get no respect (Why Soaps, 1997):

> . . . the answer is simple: because it's a woman thing. . . . Powerful women in leading roles don't appeal to most men. . . . I will not buy a . . . soap magazine if a man is behind me in the checkout . . . as quite a few times men have made comments like, "Do you really read that garbage?" I shrug, "No, I just look at the pictures. I read Playboy for the really informative stuff." (p. 37)

Although a haven from such external disapproval, discussion groups on the Net appear to provide new spaces for the disparagement of marginal women's pleasures as much or more so than for the collectivized celebration of such pleasures. When posters insensitively slight older female characters in romantic contexts, the fact that the ages of participants are not apparent in virtual reality may be little consolation to older cyberfans who are well aware of their age and marginality in the larger culture and who, consequently, seek respite and validation online. As Interrogate the Internet (1995) contended, "the structure of the technology and the content" are intimately entwined with the "broader cultural context" (p. 127) and commercial imperatives of media filter into these groups and privilege the pleasures of the producers' preferred segment of the audience.

This occurs when the more marginal segments—especially, older female viewers—are compelled to incessantly defend their interests amid the diminishing options and returns offered by soap opera creators or else fall silent. As Condit, (1989) argued, there is a "greater work load imposed on oppositionally situated audience groups" (p. 109) and the effect of such burdensome labor may be to muffle their voices.

My purpose here is not to advocate a reductionistic, political-economic view of these processes, but to caution against oversimplification on the other side of the equation. Just because many soap opera fans are savvy, critical consumers of the genre and, in certain instances, the economic imperatives behind it does not mean that their views are typical or part of some large-scale, resistive impulse. Just because the Internet has been touted as a place where marginal voices can be heard does not mean that existing cultural and economic arrangements have no bearing on the disposition of these voices and perspectives. Additional study must continue to focus on the push–pull of hegemony versus resistance on the Internet as elsewhere.

As this chapter's analyses indicate, however, the advertisers' strategy of divide and flatter subjects the feminine subculture of soap opera fandom to rupture along other lines of identity. Older characters, viewers, and themes are slighted and cultural hegemonies—such as the double standard of aging—persist and even flourish.

Such dissonance demands that soap opera stories and their readings be analyzed according to particular articulations of age, gender, romance, and fantasy. As the inquiry proceeds, a case study manifesting these articulations is detailed, the parameters of soap opera fan resistance are further established, and the likelihood of empowering public fantasies and overt political action arising from cyberfandom is ascertained in light of the commercial imperatives of the genre, network etiquette, and other pertinent variables.

NOTES

1. Fan Eddie Drueding, whose Another World Home Page (http://www.igs.net/~awhp/awhp.html) became an extensive repository of the program's history detailing everything from first kisses to shootings to exit lines, departed from his typically objective posture to issue an "Eddietorial" lambasting the Felicia/John/Sharlene triangle.

4 HE'S MAY, SHE'S SEPTEMBER, BUT ARE THEY BOTH FROM ANOTHER WORLD?

I don't find the concept unreal at all.
Matt is a very smart man—
sees past age and bustline.

. . . this fundamental inequity—that women are considered "over the hill" at forty when . . . they are just coming into their own, sexually and intellectually, while men of that age are "in their prime"— is . . . one of the most profound injustices of our egomaniacal society. (Haskell, 1987, p. 14)

So wrote Molly Haskell in her germinal book on women in film, *From Reverence to Rape*. Nothing in the culture or the reality it constructs demonstrates this more than the gender/age double standard in romantic relationships. "Time and time again," observed Haskell (1987), "women are paired with men twenty years their senior and nobody thinks twice about it; yet a man paired with a woman a mere five years older is . . . often a joke or a perversion" (p. 14). This chapter unearths some of the historical/cultural roots of the older woman/younger man taboo and begins a critical examination of the power dynamics among source, text, and audience regarding a specific representation of such a story in a TV soap opera. Because the story's content addresses hegemonic intersections of age and gender, and because it is appealing to female viewers seeking a sense of long-lived currency via romantic fantasy, it was appropriately scrutinized by establishing a time-factored approach examining data as the story unfolded. This allowed assessment and reassessment of an evolving context of multiple, relevant, and variously articulated elements.

SAUCE FOR THE GANDER

Certainly, Hollywood has helped perpetuate the cultural norms contributing to the older woman/younger man taboo, but the disparity of options and power they engender are more deeply ingrained. Banner's (1992) definitive work, *In Full Flower: Aging Women, Power, and Sexuality*, includes a reading of the film *Sunset Boulevard* (1950), but wanders back into history to trace the evolution of the values resonant in that film. Banner and others (see Derenski and Landsburg, 1981; Huston, 1987; Sunila, 1980) acknowledged that the double standard has, at its core, two cultural myths responsible for much gender bias: First, a woman's value to society is in her reproductive role; and second, a woman's sexuality and attractiveness are, likewise, tied to her fertility.

Couple these two myths with physiological realities made more significant by a culture that equates sex with intercourse and a crucial basis for the double standard can be appreciated. Consider the song "Younger Men" recorded by country music star K.T. Oslin, in which the fortyish female protagonist shamelessly questions the conventional wisdom of relationships with age-appropriate males when, sexually speaking, it is older women and younger men who are apt to peak simultaneously.

Not surprisingly, a culture fostered by older men has sought to conceal the sexual compatibility of older women and younger men. Banner (1992) noted that early Europeans were aware of the effects of aging on male sexual function and that this is a subtext in many literary classics—as the reason behind "Othello's overreaction to charges of his [younger] wife's infidelity" (p. 199), for example. However, she also indicated that the cultural upshot has been to minimize the impact of age on male sexuality, deny the sexuality of older women and/or regard it as perversion, and simultaneously contain the sexuality of young men who occupied a "privileged gender position" (p. 199) because their strength was needed to fight wars, which kept older men in power. Accordingly, young men were "rendered in terms of a sexual passivity considered inappropriate in adult males" (pp. 200–208) or characterized as hot blooded and lacking in property and/or status. Because women were denied property in their own right, the selection of a mate on this basis *seemed* natural. Haskell (1987) put some of these cultural dynamics into a nutshell: "One doesn't have to be inclined to the conspiracy theory to feel an unconscious drive working to keep women in their place, a taboo that has arisen out of a fear, or awe, of women's greater survival and sexual powers" (pp. 14–15).

Modern celluloid culture further demonstrates how the attributes of older men—authority, power, wealth—are framed as sexually appealing, whereas women over 40 simply do not appear as romantic leads in the majority of Hollywood films (Haskell, 1987). Wade-Gayles (2000) commented on these biases:

> In the media, they are the stark and seductive images that turn on the projector, amplify the sound, color the scenes, and write scripts that give leading lines to women who are young and only a nod to women who are older. To men, however, they give the enviable ability to be more attractive, more sexy, more suave, more everything desired precisely because they are older. (p. 9)

Curiously, young men are a key target audience for, but not the main protagonists in, blockbuster movies. The action/adventure hero is often well over 40 and made sexually attractive by virtue of his authority, his smooth approach, and the very fact that he is there to drive the narrative—to make things happen. Young women flock to him, his vitality is unquestioned, and there are no little blue Viagra pills in evidence. In this fashion, an affective sense of long-lived currency is affirmed for male audiences of all ages.

However, when older woman/younger man relationships are represented in film, stereotypes emerge of "barracudas who feed on young flesh or misfits who can't attract a 'real' man" (Lovenheim, 1990, p. 48). A common rendering is of a pathetic older woman who seduces and/or keeps a confused or ambivalent young man who will never love her, as in *The Graduate* (1967) and *Sunset Boulevard* (1950). Another cliché involves the older woman facilitating the sexual education of the younger man who will inevitably move on to occupy the male's proper position of greater experience, as in *Tea and Sympathy* (1956) and *Summer of '42* (1971; Haskell, 1987). A clear implication of this cliché is that young men necessarily lack sexual *savoir faire*. A few older woman/younger man films depart significantly from these stereotypes. Haskell (1987) and Stoddard (1983) regarded *All That Heaven Allows* (1950) as one such departure. *White Palace* (1990) and *How Stella Got Her Groove Back* (1998) might also qualify.

TV series targeted to Baby Boom generation women such as *Sisters*, *thirtysomething*, *Murphy Brown*, and *Designing Women* have fared somewhat better with the older woman/younger man scenario, although the disposition of some of these romances has been less than encouraging. Andersen (1995), highlighting 35-year-old Melissa's relationship with a younger man on *thirtysomething*, argued that a fulfilling sex life was depicted as "a ratings draw," but that the story's closure suggested that "such an arrangement simply will not work" (p. 131). Similarly, a promising older woman/younger man romance abruptly ended on the

NBC series *Sisters* so that the sister in question could reunite with her middle-aged ex-husband in the program's final episode.

Nonetheless, because it is seen to embrace female subjectivity, one might expect the daytime serial to be in the vanguard with potentially subversive representations of older woman/younger man relationships that articulate to women's affective desire for long-lived currency. In what follows, this assumption is examined and the case study unfolds.

MRS. ROBINSON IN SOAPLAND

As Chapter 2 demonstrates, although Modleski's (1982) conception of the ideal mother figure is still present in the guise of soap opera's satellite characters, the aging of Baby Boomers forced some changes in the representation of middle-aged women. In 1994, *Soap Opera Weekly* editor Mimi Torchin observed that over-40 soap heroines had stories involving their own "dynamic careers and active sex lives, more and more often with younger, hunky men" (p. 4). Yet an erosion of this trend was evident in the 1990s, in that romantic and other story opportunities for older women increasingly left much to be desired. This is also true of those linking older women with younger lovers.

Outside of brief, illicit affairs, gigolo situations, and/or matches made primarily for comic relief, the most common older woman/younger man cliché in soap opera frames the older woman as interloper between a younger couple who are destined, by the text's manipulations, to be together. This appears to be a blatant, formulaic strategy to flatter younger female viewers interpellated by the soap babe, as if having an older (and, therefore, comparatively unworthy) woman as a rival makes winning and/or retaining the young man's devotion all the more sweet. Such stories tend to foster intergenerational competition among women and could serve to construct an audience of female fans whose sense of lifespan opportunities and long-lived currency is narrowed.

Mother/daughter triangles involving a younger male were not uncommon in the 1990s. On top-rated *Young and the Restless* (*Y&R*), gorgeous socialite Nikki, in her late 30s, vied with her 18-year-old daughter for the affection of Cole, in his late 20s. The text clearly directed viewers to favor the young(er) heroine, and her success sent Nikki into an alcoholic tailspin.

Similarly, on *Days of Our Lives* (*DOOL*), mid-40s Laura happened into an affair with a younger man who, unbeknownst to them both, was her daughter's wayward ex-husband. Fans were outraged, because they had long hoped for the young couple's reconciliation despite the daughter's engagement to another man. Predictably, Laura continued to pine for her former son-in-law even after their true identities became known, whereas *he* only had eyes for her daughter.

In the early 1970s, a somewhat more sensitive but still stereotypical treatment was given to the story of Addie and Doug on *DOOL*. Doug's age split the difference between Addie and her nubile daughter, Julie. Doug married Addie, producing a child, Hope, but a mutual attraction between Doug and Julie deepened (perhaps owing to the actors' off-screen romance). The writers soon eliminated Addie by having her suffer the fatal blow of an oncoming vehicle after rolling Hope's carriage to safety. While viewers were assured that Doug sincerely loved Addie, he was now free to romance fair, young Julie. Ironically, this soap's eventual youth-orientation would make such a story practically unthinkable today, and Addie would likely be depicted as Laura—a desperate, lonely matron trespassing on a young woman's rightful territory. At least, in this case, she might not require euthanasia.

In many older woman/younger man stories, there are indications of overkill in the writers' efforts to stack the text from the outset so there is little negotiating room. On *One Life to Live* (*OLTL*) in the mid-1990s, 47-ish Dorian entered into an affair with the virginal, 19-year-old son of her archenemy, Viki, and an apparent motive of revenge. The young man, Joey, had recently undergone SORAS, so viewers still remembered him as a child, and cyberfan commentary reflected the preferred response of disapproval. Through these mechanisms, the powers that be saw to it that the audience would be dissuaded from rooting for this romance. They wanted nothing to spoil their plan to introduce a young woman for Joey in time for the summer teenfest.

Despite these tendencies, during the late 1970s and 1980s, several counter-hegemonic examples of older woman/younger man married couples appeared on soaps. ABC's *All My Children* (*AMC*) featured Mark and Ellen, whose 10-year (or so) age difference was less of an obstacle than Mark's drug addiction. They were eventually written off as an intact couple. CBS' *As the World Turns* (*ATWT*) showcased Casey and Lyla, whose love remained unblemished despite an even larger age gap and Casey's untimely demise. In the 1990s, a 15-year breach separated *ATWT*'s Susan and Larry who had a child and survived into their third year of marriage before a breakup was necessitated by cast downsizing. Matt and Vanessa of CBS' *Guiding Light* (*GL*) were the premiere (and only) legitimate older woman/younger man married couple in daytime in the late 1990s and, ironically, might have been inspired by the romance that is the focus of this case study.

THE "CHEMISTRY YOU DON'T OFTEN SEE"

On NBC's *Another World* (*AW*), petite, 42-ish Donna Love Hudson and ponytailed, 23-ish Matthew Cory began interacting in the fall of 1992. Actor Anna Stuart (Donna) was told by the head writer that young Matt, played by Matt Crane, would befriend her character (Bonderoff, 1995). At this point, little more was sanctioned in the blueprints of NBC and Procter and Gamble (P&G) Productions—the latter entity also responsible for *ATWT* and *GL*.

Set in fictional Bay City, Illinois, *AW* premiered in 1964. It saw its heyday in the 1970s, but thereafter experienced a gradual decline in ratings and, as earlier chapters have discussed, repeatedly faced the threat of cancellation (see e.g., Susman, 1993). Although a low-rated soap will sometimes take risks it might not otherwise take (Cantor & Cantor, 1983), *AW's* quest for demographics would be the key factor in decision-making respective to this age-related story.

At the beginning of their interaction, Donna and Matt were already well-established characters on the canvas from two core families woven into the soap's history. Both had been raised in the upper crust, but Matt was adopted into it and, therefore, had tried to make it on his own outside of his family's publishing empire. Despite several relationships, he had never been married. Donna had been married four times—three times to the same man. At this juncture, she was portrayed as an idealized version of a forty-something woman, but the audience was constantly reminded that she was a grandmother and that her twin daughters were older than Matt.

It began, as one magazine later put it, as a "chemistry experiment in the writer's lab over at *Another World*" (Who's Getting, 1994, p. 16) and became an example of "the chemistry you don't often see," as a caller on E! network's now defunct *Pure Soap* program described it (1994, Sept. 8). Matt and Donna were brought together as owners of the local TV station, KBAY, after Matt accidentally discovered the pampered socialite, his nephew's grandmother, working as a party hostess because her accountant had bilked her out of her fortune. Afterward Matt helped Donna recoup her wealth through a counter-scam, and Donna bought into KBAY as Matt's not-so-silent partner.

This placed Donna in the thick of the action rather than strictly relegating her to the satellite role of mother hen to twin daughters Marley and Vicky. Donna was ecstatic about her new opportunity, having confided to Matt that she was eager to prove to herself, Bay City, and her patronizing ex-husband, Michael, that she could be competent and self-reliant. Except for a brief visit at the time of Vicky's wedding in February 1993, just as the grifter accountant was being foiled, Michael had last been seen 3 years earlier exiting Bay City with a young woman after having divorced Donna for the third time. Michael and Donna's relevant backstory is related piecemeal as the case study proceeds, but the latest divorce resulted from Donna's clandestine but sensitively rendered affair with a younger man—Marley's rebounding ex-husband, Jake. Michael, a businessman who moonlighted as a spy, had feigned love for another woman to protect Donna, and this led to her short-lived, validating fling. After Michael explained himself, Donna neglected to reveal her indiscretion. When the truth later surfaced, Michael was unforgiving. Donna pined for him as he romanced other women and then left town. So, with Donna's new career, the theme of a divorced woman acquiring independence and a sense of growth and renewal in midlife was clearly established. This is the key enigma initiated by the first phase of the story. In keeping with Mumford's (1995) theory of closure and ideological reification, it is crucial to note whether or not subsequent textual developments appear to maintain or neutralize this counter-hegemonic element.

Little would happen between Matt and Donna for several months; the writers were careful to have Matt and a young woman, Brett, engage in a flirtation during the summer when age-sensitive teen viewers are generally courted. Almost like clockwork, this flirtation began to fizzle in the autumn, just as a new wrinkle in Matt's relationship with Donna appeared.

As we recount this story in the literary present from this point on, Donna Hudson, intrepid reporter, is determined to investigate a prostitution ring fronted by the party hostessing business by which she was employed when she was destitute. After she receives a death threat, Matt cautions her to back off. Donna ignores him and prepares to go undercover to investigate a state political party chairman who is dallying with prostitutes while preaching family values to the citizenry. On Halloween night, Matt becomes wise to Donna's intentions and catches her in a seductive outfit with a miniature microphone tucked into her cleavage. Extracting it, he explains that he is concerned for her safety. "You're driving me crazy. I care about you," he declares—punctuating his declaration with a passionate kiss. The kiss is immediately dismissed as "just one of those things," but the fantasizing of both parties suggests otherwise.

The classic screwball romantic comedy style that characterized the pair's earlier antics is honed during the next month as they jointly pursue their journalistic prey. Matt's over-protectiveness leads to miscues, however, and the duo ends up hiding under the bed as the politico is entertained by the prostitution ring's madam. Several close calls later, Matt and Donna find themselves snowbound in the TV van and nature, predictably, takes its course (Fig. 4.1). It is December 1993, a full year after their initial interaction. This is the point at which the as-it-happened, time-factored analysis of production, text, and audience in the case study commenced.

Donna insists that their tryst remain a secret and vows that it will never happen again. Matt, however, cleverly plays to her continued attraction by flirting with the station's new weather person, Misty. This foreshadows the New Year's Eve arrival of Josie, Matt's high school sweetheart, who has just returned to town after several years' absence. Josie is clearly interested in reigniting the old flame, and viewers are immediately presented with the prospect of yet another inconsequential affair of an older woman and younger man. The only question seemed to be whether they intended to play Donna as the stereotypical wedge between young lovers, and Donna's palpable jealousy as Josie and Matt share a New Year's kiss is telling despite her subsequent efforts to push a reluctant Matt in the direction of his first love.

Even with a breakup, it seemed probable that Donna would retain her career and sense of independence, and that a warm and mutually respectful friendship and partnership with Matt would endure. It is important, however, to ascertain how viewers were negotiating the message at this juncture and whether their readings and interpretations might have influenced the plans of creators.

Fig. 4.1.   Nature takes its course for *Another World's* Matt and Donna.

GEESE UNITE! "NO STATUS QUO"

Mind Your Own Genre

By examining fan publications and cyberfan reactions along with text, it is possible to ascertain that the Matt and Donna romance was supposed to be short term and the audience was responsible for coaxing the network, sponsors, and creators into switching gears from their original, formulaic plan. Magazine articles eventually confirmed that actor Amy Carlson (Josie) was slated to play Matt's girlfriend (Sloane, 1994), noted that the plan changed because "Matt is too popular with Donna" (On the Set, 1994, p. 41), and identified the exact point in the story at which Carlson was told she would not be paired with Matt, but positioned for a romance with another "soap hunk" (Cukor, 1994b, p. 45). Lynn Leahey, editor-in-chief of *Soap Opera Digest*, also stated that audience sentiment was responsible for making Matt and Donna a long-term story while answering a fan's inquiry on CNN's *Soap Update* (1994, May 9).

Matt and Donna's romance was to have been a transitional, back-burner story giving then underused actors something to do while the pivotal role of Josie was recast. Donna was to end the affair in what she deemed to be their better interest, and Matt was slated to rekindle his relationship with the young heroine for a front-burner story targeting the much-desired Generation X audience. It is logical to assume that the liaison with Donna was also intended to show that Matt had grown up since he was last in a love story, as the character had been marketed to the teen crowd in the past. This invokes the film stereotype of the older woman initiating the young man into mature sexuality and, because Josie's secret on her return was that she had been involved in the same call-girl ring that Matt and Donna were investigating, this reconfiguration of Matt's character was apropos.

The story was designed to make Matt and Donna's light-hearted pranks pale in comparison with the damsel in distress scenario that was developing for Matt and Josie. Although Matt's undercover (and under the bed) rescue of Donna from the clutches of the party chairman was played for laughs, we soon discover that Josie had been this customer's favorite, and that he and the unscrupulous madam were coercing her back into the fold. Matt, of course, was to be a real champion and lover for Josie.

Because there was a generation's age difference between Matt and Donna, and because the storytellers kept it light by adopting the romantic comedy mode, the creators likely believed that few in the audience would take the relationship seriously and that viewers would effortlessly fall in line behind the idealized and conventional Matt and Josie pairing.

They were mistaken. As Allen (1985) noted, when soap opera melo-drama is hybridized with another genre, the narrative is further opened to conflicting interpretations. Many in the audience had learned to read more into that screwball comedy interplay by seeing it unfold in other soap opera romances, movies, and prime-time TV shows such as *Cheers*, *Moonlighting*, and *Northern Exposure*. Inevitably, in these romances, real feelings lay beneath the surface of comic barbs and antagonism (see Scodari, 1995). In cyberspace, comparisons were made between Matt and Donna and married private eyes Nick and Nora of the *Thin Man* film series. Fans also recognized and lauded Matt and Donna's cat-and-mouse game of pursuit as well as their sexy and humorous repartee—both common conventions of screwball comedy.

Although the couple's fans constantly worried that the story would end, it is clear that they hoped it would not. Cyberfans on a soap opera bulletin board exulted. "Donna deserves a life," stated one. "[T]his woman is fantastic," another concurred. "I don't find the concept unreal at all. Matt is a very smart man–sees past age and bustline." According to Lewis' (1991) distinctions, such readings can be labeled as resistive rather than oppositional, because these fans do not explicitly acknowl-edge the hegemonic preferences of the text and oppose them, but rather "exploit the text's ambiguity as they see fit" (pp. 68–69). At this point, the textual polysemy giving rise to such resistive negotiation appeared to be unintentional.

At the same time, there was little indication that people were enthu-siastic about a Matt and Josie coupling. Scenes between the two fell flat as sparks continued to fly between Matt and Donna. At one point the writers might have been trying to fuel interest in Josie and Matt by set-ting them up according to a love/hate, screwball-inspired formula. Yet, it quickly became obvious that this actor's flair for romantic comedy fluctuated with the experience of his leading lady. Later *Soap Opera Digest* concurred that Matt Crane (Matt) did his best work opposite vet-eran Anna Stuart (Donna; Ten Things, 1994).

However, this was not enough for the powers that be to veer from their original course. Early in the story, a letter published in *Soap Opera Weekly* asserted: "*AW*'s newest couple, Matt and Donna, is disgustingly unappealing! Watching them is like watching my mother in an intimate relationship with my 20-year-old son's best friend; not a pretty sight" (Perry, 1993, p. 42). For several weeks this was the hottest topic in *Soap Opera Weekly's* mailbag, with fans expressing their displeasure with the letter and giving a thumbs up to Matt and Donna (Mail Call, 1994). Yet the letter that the magazine chose to feature in answer to the diatribe was decidedly political:

> This reader painted Donna as some old biddy engaged in an unnat-
> ural alliance with someone young enough to be her grandson. Let
> me point out that Donna is a sexy, vital woman in her 40s, not a
> withered relic. Moreover, where is this reader's ire at the even more
> unequal older man/younger woman matches rampant on the soaps?
> (Stolley, 1993, p. 41)

The letter goes on to recount several examples of this double standard in soapland and ends by congratulating *AW* for forging past the "objections of the know-nothing, demographic-dependent NBC network, considering that NBC would never have blinked if [the age difference] were reversed" (p. 41).

When confronted with an exchange such as this, the application and significance of concepts such as preferred, negotiated, resistive, and oppositional meanings (or readings) become slippery even in the light of previous clarifications. As posited in earlier chapters, it is because few audience ethnographers consider the specific production imperatives behind the characters and situations their subjects interpret that significant implications of these readings can be overlooked. In the case of Matt and Donna's early storyline, it has been established that the creators wanted to present a light-hearted story that could be easily dismissed with the inauguration of the more conventional romance. Although the writers probably had no desire to disgust viewers at this juncture, they were certainly aware that the shared assumption of soap opera fans and the larger culture is that relationships such as Matt and Donna's fall short of the ideals of youth, beauty, and everlasting love.

Because the authors of these contentious letters apparently believed that the romance was intended to be taken seriously at this time, we might conclude that the preferred reading is counter-hegemonic—meant to significantly challenge the gender/age double standard—when it is not. Actually it is more reasonable and productive to label the first reading criticizing the couple as preferred and the second defending the couple as oppositional and resistive. The viewer who found Matt and Donna distasteful had been successfully seduced by soaps and the larger culture into interpreting such a relationship as unnatural and untenable, and this stance was consistent with the writers' long-term goals. The fan who applauded the show was exploiting the story's ambiguity (e.g., the romantic comedy element) in his or her presumption that it had legs, but was also acknowledging and actively opposing the gender/age double standard—a cultural assumption that is unjust and generally rampant on soaps. This viewer was not alone, as similar sentiments appeared elsewhere in magazines and cyberspace (see e.g., Age-Old, 1994; Norris,

1994; Your Turn, 1994). It soon became apparent that the creators had underestimated many fans' willingness and ability to invest in this uncommon romance.

Curiously, the negative letter and scattered, online denunciations of Matt and Donna were eye openers to many of the couple's supporters. Despite the rarity of older woman/younger man romances on the soaps (and elsewhere), these fans denied awareness of any reasons such a story might be offensive to others or resisted by soap opera creators. Consequently, these fans' initial exposure to age- and gender-related criticism of the story was jolting. However, more often than not, the implications, pervasiveness, and political character of the double standard never became fully comprehensible to most of them in the same way that they were, for example, respective to the African-American man/White woman taboo. Paradoxically, many of those criticizing the couple were similarly stunned that anyone could accept the pair as legitimate.

Reducing Ambiguity

Despite the excitement generated by the story, *AW* still banked on its carefully laid scheme. Shortly, a feature article on Matt and Donna appeared in *Soap Opera Update* and included interviews with the two actors and the show's head writer, Peggy Sloane (Cukor, 1994a). In it Sloane confessed that their mail was overwhelmingly positive, but stated, as a foregone conclusion, that the "love affair ultimately resolves" (p. 69). She also talked up Josie's reintroduction and admitted that her concern, and the concern of P&G, was that teenage girls would be turned off if their hunk was paired with an older woman long term. Both actors conceded that the story would be short term, and Stuart (Donna) discussed her approach, arguing that Donna would not be able to continue the affair because she is middle aged and knows that the young man will "walk on by her" (p. 68).

It is interesting that *AW* would choose this story to give the audience a dose of reality, culturally crafted as it is, when at the time Matt's mother was being courted by a man who once tried to murder her and his adoptive sister was renewing her romance with Jake, the man who had the affair with Donna and later raped his ex-wife—one of Donna's twins. As discussed earlier, these "realities" occur with some regularity on soaps and are often defended with the argument that soap opera is, after all, about fantasy and not about reality. Yet when the goal became to discredit Matt and Donna's romance, the reality yardstick was unabashedly and repeatedly summoned by the text, fans, and creators. This irony was not lost on one focus group participant who was incensed that the text was going out of its way to equate the three controversial romances. Even a poll conducted by a magazine took this tack, beckoning readers who disliked Matt and Donna's romance to vote in favor of the following proposition: "Matt and Donna are amusing to watch, but they should get back to reality and find mates their own age" (Networks, 1994a, p. 29).

In any case, the *Soap Opera Update* article was probably meant to give the story and its fans their due, but also to warn them not to get too attached. It also suggests that the source of the primary, backstage opposition to such a story is the potential loss of very young female viewers who might be turned off and, consequently, turn the show off. The deference given to such viewers and to all those who don't like a story, as opposed to those who do, is obvious. Commercial TV's doctrine of least objectionable programming lingers in this way.

The article also insinuated that those behind the scenes had become well aware of the ambiguity in the storyline and were intentionally trying to reduce it through the magazine meta-text. As Lewis (1991) noted, the "existence of the preferred meaning is dependent upon the suppression of ambiguity" (p. 66), and one might have expected that this suppression would also proceed in the primary text.

With February sweeps fast approaching and a dramatic shift to the Josie/Matt romance apparently in the blueprints, there was no time to waste. Suddenly, in mid-January, Matt and Donna's relationship turns dark. The romantic comedy subsides, as Donna is riddled with motherly guilt for having been out of town on a secret rendezvous with Matt at a time when her daughter was threatened by an accused rapist. Donna and Matt's tryst occurs off camera, and only Donna's seamy, muted flashbacks are revealed to viewers. As Donna tells Matt that what they are doing "is wrong," one cannot help but feel that she is also trying to convince the audience. The conspicuous invocation of motherhood might have been even more persuasive except that Donna's twins were closer to 30 than to 20. Curiously, the fact that Donna's children were older than Matt was also reiterated, but in this instance seemingly intended to magnify the couple's age difference and not to insinuate that the twins were fully capable of fending for themselves.

Additionally, Donna has gotten a new look. Unnecessarily heavy makeup and big hair have added years to her appearance and framed her as one whose beauty is not natural (Fig. 4.2). Matt's protestation that Donna deserves a life is more than countered by the shared cultural assumptions conjured up by Donna's arguments and the accentuated age disparity.

Donna breaks up with Matt, but eventually agrees to resume the affair to forestall Matt's threat to reveal it. These developments can be construed as efforts to manipulate the audience into losing favor with the story—to call on the shared assumptions of the larger culture to

Fig. 4.2   Ambiguity is reduced as Donna suddenly
           appears more matronly.

make the romance seem unpalatable and unrealistic to a greater number
of viewers.

Judging by cyberfan feedback, the strategy backfired. One devotee
"felt cheated" that Matt and Donna's secret rendezvous was not featured—that they were "tossing their illicit evening in as an after-
thought." She was also bothered by Donna "trading her body for Matt's
silence." A letter appearing somewhat later in *Soap Opera Digest* encap-
sulated the feelings of Matt and Donna fans at this juncture: "We found
the romance between Matt and Donna touching and beautiful. . . . We
are angry that in a recent episode, *AW* seemed to be breaking them up
for good. We hope that *AW* is not succumbing to those who would support the status quo" (No Status, 1994, pp. 141–142). These readings are
clearly oppositional, reflecting an awareness of the preferred, hegemonic
meaning, but still hoping that the romance would take a positive turn.

A few weeks later, during the February sweeps period, the "Winter
Masquerade" event offered a clear scenario to switch gears from Matt
and Donna to Matt and Josie. In the light of Matt's promise to reveal
their relationship to his mother, Donna again ends the affair because, as
she puts it, "we have to face reality . . . there isn't going to be a future for
us." She maintains that their attraction is mostly about lust and encourages her young lover to seek a future with Josie. Matt is crestfallen, but
searches for Josie who is busy fending off the salacious party chairman.
Instead of rescuing her, which logically was the original plan, Matt only
confronts her after the fact.

The following day, Donna and Matt clash over a talk show topic. Matt, still stewing over the breakup, argues in favor of the topic for its real-life relevance. "The audience doesn't want reality," Donna responds, consulting the station's research reports. "They want glamor and romance." This is self-reflexive dialogue because the writers had been given the green light to continue Matt and Donna's love story.

Also reflected in this dialogue is the writers' apparent bewilderment at discovering that fans who have come to desire and expect an element of fantasy in other soap opera romances might also embrace and savor this love story regardless of whether or not they deemed it realistic. Again the selective invocation of the reality criterion by fans and creators alike is significant.

At about this time, the aforementioned, nonscientific telephone survey sponsored by a magazine showed that 80% wanted the pair to become "even more serious," indicating the intensity, if not the quantity, of fan interest (Networks, 1994b, p. 29). Still certain parameters might have been in force, judging from head writer Peggy Sloane's statement that they were going to have a "fun time" with the "big age difference"—an approach that would undoubtedly be rejected if that big age gap went the other way (Summer Preview, 1994, p. 12). This is curiously reminiscent of Fuqua's (1995) assessment of soap opera's rules for dealing with gayness: "Gay characters can certainly be represented, but only in terms of the sexuality-as-a-problem paradigm" (p. 209).

In the case of Matt and Donna, it seemed that a go ahead had been given for gently exploring some of the issues attendant to older woman/younger man relationships, but not necessarily for framing them as symptomatic of a sexist double standard or for having the cou-

Fig. 4.3   Donna and Matt demonstrate the "push- pull" of their screwball-inspired romance.

ple surmount them all. However, it is important to note that even in the
previously discussed gay teen storyline on *OLTL*, homophobia was
explicitly rendered as an unfair and irrational cultural bias and the gay
character's transcendence was implicit if not explicit. In part this is
because closure could be achieved by making the gay character and his
storyline short term—a strategy that, despite its conservative motivations, actually opens the text to counter-hegemonic readings and imaginings. As Mumford (1995) claimed, narrative closure is not necessarily
and always patriarchal and hegemonic. It can "easily be turned to oppositional ends and stories could be resolved in ways that demonstrate,
say, a wide range of romantic and sexual alternatives . . ." (p. 92).
However, the fact that both Matt and Donna were core characters and
assumed to be continuing on the canvas could have made any explicit
argument against this double standard seem like a tacit promise to follow through with the romance beyond a certain point.

Nonetheless, a few episodes later, Donna appears with a new, hip
hairstyle and mini-skirt (see Fig. 4.3). She is elated because a pregnancy
scare has proved to be a false alarm. Matt reveals his love for her and
gently coaxes her into admitting the same. Earlier, just at the tale's turning, a brief exchange between the two had piqued this investigator's
interest. "You're getting a little pink," Matt teases. "Well," replies
Donna, "it's hot in here."

"We Can Dream, Can't We?"

This loose thread is not woven into the fabric for several months, and
the narrative proceeds along the same lines as it began. There is a series
of double-edged seductions—traditional seduction and dealmaking—in
which Matt uses all means at his disposal to get Donna to take the relationship to the next level. Again this is done in the style of screwball
comedy, with verbal interplay used as a metaphor for sexual foreplay
(see Scodari, 1995). The scene in which Matt and Donna declare their
mutual affection follows the formula down to the minutest detail, incorporating the screwball hero's use of an endearment—in this case,
"grown-up girl"—to which the heroine feigns insult and his pithy, pre-
smooch speech, to wit: "I love you, you love me, nobody's dying and
we've got plenty of money." As illustrated in Fig. 4.3, even the blocking
of the scene evokes the push–pull of the screwball formula. Now as
before, the seduction occurs with most of the hurdles they encounter—
giving into their sexual attraction, admitting to real feelings, going public with their affair, living together, and becoming engaged.

Matt also sacrifices his ponytail to convince Donna of his ardor and
then faces off with the president of Donna's condominium association
who first assumes he is a gigolo and then forbids their cohabitation.

However, much to Matt's delight, it is Donna who puts the woman in her place by threatening a lawsuit and admonishing her to deal with her sexual frustrations and let them be. Still, after most of Matt's seductions, Donna believes she has struck a brilliant compromise. However, we are assured that Matt has won when he grins like "the cat who ate the canary."

Matt and Donna's love scenes are less explicit, but more adult than typical soap love scenes, often employing veiled sexual references consistent with the verbal quality of the screwball. For example:

> Matt: I don't care if you're older than I am.
> Donna: That's easy for you to say. You're the tender
>   jailbait and I'm the nasty cradle snatcher.
> Matt: I'm not jailbait . . . and I like it when you're
>   you're nasty.

Fan interest in this aspect of Matt and Donna's story was particularly evident and might have been easily exploited. Their sex is not "a religious ritual," commented one cyberfan. "The couple who really has me gasping for air is Matt and Donna," another confessed (Jewell, 1994, p. 41). Others vented frustration with their own partner(s):

> My friends and I can identify with Donna. We too find Matt's sweet-
> ness, sensitivity, and "love conquers all" attitude irresistible. Many
> of the men in our age group (mid-40s) have turned into unadventur-
> ous "couch potatoes." We are still ready for fun and romance. It is
> unlikely a Matt will walk into our lives, but we can dream, can't we?
> (Who's Getting, 1994, p. 16)

These responses reveal a desire to engage fantasies not addressed by age-appropriate soap opera love stories as idealized and marvelous as they might be. Evidently, the story tapped a unique and specific sense of confinement in the lives of these viewers, perhaps meeting their need for a sense of long-lived currency.

Age was certainly an ingredient in the appeal. The traditional screwball dynamic was based on class and gender difference (see Scodari, 1995), but here it is based on generational difference—because it is not configured so much as female versus male, but as Matt and Donna versus the patriarchal taboo. The text interpellates women in the audience to identify with Donna in all her resistance, carrying with them, as she does, the constraints of social convention. However, although many viewers were apt to perceive that Donna wanted precisely what Matt wanted, the text still allowed others to invest in the logic of her protestations and resist acceptance of and involvement in the romance.

For those inclined to root for Matt, his victory meant defying the double standard—a defiance that they desired. After a seduction, Donna often faces society as represented by high society—the ultimate social arbiters. When she finally consents to marriage, but insists on a long engagement, Matt acquiesces provided that she announce the betrothal on the society page of the newspaper.

The text permits and even encourages the audience to trust in Matt's sincerity; he is depicted as a practically perfect human being, perched high atop Maslow's pyramid, who regularly debunks cultural values concerning older women. He plainly states that wrinkles are to be loved and a sedate blue suit is sexier than a red spandex dress, although Donna looks smashing in either. When Donna worries whether he will one day leave her for a younger woman, Matt is steadfast. When Donna first refuses his marriage proposal, predicting that he will one day meet a woman closer to his age who will give him everything he deserves, Matt insists that she is his soulmate. Loath to continue a relationship that is "going nowhere," Matt spurns Donna and feigns interest in Josie after his proposal is rejected. However, when the life of his mother's fiancé is threatened, Matt's poignant entreaty—"I had everything 'til you walked away"—is not rebuffed, and the two reunite.

The turnabout as fair play issues evoked by the story were not lost on the mostly female writing staff. At one point Donna relates a tale about running into her ex-husband while on a business trip and tells Matt that she felt empowered knowing she had him available to her.

Along the way, the tale is conscious of the prevailing stereotypes, at times lampooning them very pointedly. "Who better than a woman of experience to tutor a neophyte?" Matt spontaneously quips on a live talk show produced by their TV station, attempting to take Donna to the edge so she will commit to him. Additionally, the relationship is not a fling. Their sexual compatibility is strongly suggested, and he requires no coaching in that department. She is not pathetic, and he is probably the least confused person in Bay City. Finally, there is no mistaking the fact that *Matt* is the seducer. Of course fans with an awareness of the gender/age double standard and its corresponding clichés might have been the only ones likely to read such references and conditions as overt challenges to the status quo.

At the point of Matt and Donna's engagement in June 1994, one cyberfan conducted a poll to see whether other fans believed they would ever make it to the altar. Most respondents hoped they would. Recognizing soap opera's tendency to delay and defer marital union, others expressed doubts. One suggested that the only thing that might prevent the wedding would be a return of Donna's ex-husband,

Michael. Another demonstrated that the head writer's fear of turning off young women was not unfounded by conveying her loathing of Donna and her unequivocal wish that the couple be split up immediately.

Most fans were not aware that the plan for the story had been altered, and some might have been inspired to send congratulatory bouquets to the network and P&G for this forward-thinking, unexpected pleasure. However, because soap opera couples must overcome obstacles on their way to bliss, it is at such a point that dangling threads reappear and must be tied.

"REAL MEN" DON'T MIND MENOPAUSE

Cyberfans had not blinked at Matt's offhand comment that Donna looked "a little pink," nor did they react when Donna's blushing and rosy cheeks were mentioned in subsequent episodes. The pregnancy scare was the only plot point to elicit the word menopause from a few bulletin board fans, but the suggestion was soon forgotten as the story moved on in an affirmative direction. However, this analyst could not help but speculate that a condition of continuing the story was to develop a contingency plan for ending it. Having Donna become menopausal might do this in a most predictable way—over the issue of children. In so doing, however, the show would trade off numerous cultural stereotypes and taboos by even broaching the subject.

If the culture wanted to, it could regard menopause as no more than a blip on the radar of a woman's life. If the culture wanted to, it could regard menopause as the pinnacle of existence, the height of wisdom and desirability. On the contrary, however, the weight of Western culture suggests that the end of a woman's fertility is also the end of her appeal and her very worth. Consider the best-selling book *Everything You Always Wanted to Know About Sex*, in which Dr. David Reuben wrote that after menopause a woman is "just marking time until she follows her glands into oblivion" (cited in Women's Health, 1992, p. 525). In the politics of meaning, nothing affects older women's perceptions more than the mythology and misogyny of the discourse on menopause. Regardless of whether a woman likes her life the way it is, she is told, by the very naming of the thing, that her life will change.

Moreover, historically, liaisons between menopausal women and young men were often viewed as pathological, and any increased sex drive observed in such women was seen as perversion (Banner, 1992). By explicitly introducing the specter of menopause for the first time in a soap opera, and by choosing an older woman/younger man story in which to do it, *AW* might have known it was inviting controversy.

In any event, the subtle hints resume in the heat of the summer as Donna casually mentions her flushed face and the celebratory love scenes surrounding the pair's engagement are unusually steamy. Donna is in overdrive.

At this juncture, Bridget, the elderly Scottish nanny for Donna's grandsons, returns from a trip to the old country. She accuses Donna of trying to recapture her lost youth by agreeing to marry Matt and notices her fanning herself with a magazine. "The change," Bridget laughs. Donna is mortified, countering, "I'll change when I'm good and ready to change!" In denial, she seeks information from a doctor, claiming to be researching a talk show topic. He tells her that some menopausal women "complain of a lowered sex drive, which has been associated with lowered estrogen levels." Based on this, Donna concludes that she is not menopausal, although her hot flashes persist, because it is an unsuspecting Matt who fans himself down after each heated encounter with his fiancée. At first the story twist is played for laughs.

The myth that women become disinterested in sex at the time of menopause is not entirely debunked in contemporary self-help discourse. Books commenting on the subject acknowledge that many women experience precisely the opposite effect, but also report that diminution of sex drive is not an uncommon complaint (see Reitz, 1977; Wells & Wells, 1990; Women's Health, 1992). Moreover, there is little effort to demonstrate the extent to which such disinterest, when it occurs, is actually a psychosomatic result of the culture's insinuation that one is no longer desirable and/or a reaction to the attitudes and behaviors of one's partner(s).

Donna's story targets this issue. It is only when Bridget consults a book and informs her that for many menopausal women sex gets better that Donna resigns herself to the change. She rebuffs Matt once, and a full-fledged midlife crisis erupts. "I've lost my sex drive," she tells Bridget, who reminds her that only yesterday she and Matt were having "hanky panky in the shower." Yet Donna just frets about her (barely perceptible) wrinkles and sags. "Why couldn't this have happened to some woman married to an old coot?" she bristles. Vexed by her behavior, Matt asks her if there is someone else. Donna responds fervently that she would "never do that." However, believing that Matt would only stay with her out of pity, she abruptly leaves town to be with her daughter. Matt immediately wonders whether Donna has gone to rendezvous with her ex-husband. Neither is seen for 2 weeks.

This investigator (and one insightful focus group participant) interpreted this as a feedback period, allowing *AW* time to assess audience response and make repairs if necessary. She and another group member of menopausal age were irked at *AW's* handling of the issue. One resented the humorous tone. Another wished the writers would have had Donna handle herself better so as to avoid the raging hormones myth. Here she discusses her own experience: "It's not that bad . . . I've never felt more sexual and sensual . . . my life didn't change."

Some cyberfans concurred that Donna should get a grip on her situation. Remarked one: "Come on, Donna, this is the '90s, women don't have the 'vapors' simply because they might be starting the change. . . ." Others did not appreciate the stereotypical implications: "One of the things I liked . . . was that while Donna was embarrassed about their age difference, it wasn't all about an older woman trying to hang on to her youth. . . . But it seems to be heading that way. . . ." Still others defended Donna's behavior. Argued a male cyberfan: " . . . if anything you could accuse Donna of being a bit vain. . . . And with Bridget trying her best to make her feel guilty about Matt . . . well, I think her behaviour is not that far off. . . ." Another online participant agreed: "It's completely in character for her to take menopause as the worst thing that could have happened and it will be interesting to see if Matt's love and support would make her realize that there is nothing wrong with the natural process. . . ." One hard-core Matt and Donna cyberfan was unnerved by the fact that this story was not being told about one of the three women characters on *AW* who were of a more typical age for menopause to occur. However, although a few fans acknowledged that this turn of events might "spell curtains" for Matt and Donna, and although those who considered the couple distasteful from the outset were conspicuously silent, there was no apparent sentiment that this *should* mean the end. This appears to be a preferred and counter-hegemonic meaning of this subplot. Yet the writers had to suspect that Donna's menopause might increase the "ick factor" among those very young fans who already wanted their hunk with a fertile, wrinkle-free woman.

When next we see them, we discover that Matt followed Donna but could not track her down. Still worried that she was seeking to rekindle something with her ex, Matt challenges her to come clean. When she does, he is chagrined: "Menopause? This is the big secret?" He is relieved that she is not planning to break the engagement. She accuses him of being insensitive, adding: "The best years of life are ahead of you if you can share them with someone who's an equal. I'm not an equal any more." "That's ridiculous," Matt snaps back. He apologizes for seeming insensitive, but chides her for wallowing in self-pity. "It's not attractive," he asserts, "and it's not you."

Later, as a solitary, melancholy Donna tidies the studio sound stage, Matt dims the lights from his perch in the production booth and entreats her as if a disembodied voice. He goes on to remind her that he has always known her age. He confesses that he has sometimes wished she were younger, but only because things would be easier for her that way and because then he would not have to face losing her before he was prepared. Finally, he promises that she will always be the "most infuriating, most passionate woman" he knows, and that he will love her through her changes if she will only let him.

These scenes appeared to quiet the fan flak. Anticipating her need for spousal empathy at the time of menopause, one cyberfan observed:

> Matt Cory has grown up to be a "real man" and I wonder why they only appear on soaps. . . . If I was telling my husband about going through menopause he'd probably think it was a wonderful thing. . . . And I don't think I have the only man who needs his consciousness raised.

Nevertheless, an essential debate remained. Some fans saw Donna as Donna, a character whose history makes an old-fashioned response to menopause believable. Other fans wished Donna would follow her own lead when, after defending her relationship with Matt, she claimed to be "the standard bearer" for her generation. In other words, they wanted her to be a role model. For it was, to them, not so much a question of whether real men mind menopause, but whether real women do.[1]

The next time the pair appear, they are frolicking by the pool and she is looking fabulous in a very revealing swimsuit. "Doesn't it make you sick?" a woman joked online. It was as if to say: Okay all you baby boom, soon-to-be-menopausal women out there—here's your new role model! Donna's story also led to a menopause thread on the Usenet soap opera newsgroup when fans, many of whom did not watch *AW*, were inspired to reflect on their own experiences.

Yet, Donna must leave town again to be with her other daughter. Could this be another feedback period? When she returns, Matt has arranged for her to see a doctor, and it seems as if Donna's psychosomatic symptoms might be explicitly labeled as such so the important point is not lost. But the doctor has been called away, and she only receives a blood test. After listening to the results on the phone, Donna passes out, creating a cliffhanger. Predictably, fans speculated—and hoped—that she was pregnant. Alas, we find that her hot flashes were due to a "slight hormonal imbalance" and that she is not menopausal. "Not that there's anything wrong with that," she and Matt declare in unison, aping a popular episode of *Seinfeld* dealing with gayness. Donna goes on to explain that she's "very susceptible to the power of suggestion" and that she started exhibiting symptoms when Bridget kept bringing them up. They celebrate, and a tipsy Donna is elated that she has time before menopause is upon her. Matt assures her that whenever it occurs, it will be "no sweat." We are clearly shown that Donna's libido is quite healthy as she beams and announces: "I'm delirious with relief that my body hasn't betrayed me."

This questionable characterization of menopause as the "betrayal of the body" contradicts the implicit message about psychosomatic effects. No matter, viewers on the Net did not react to either point. Instead, they were dissatisfied with the anticlimax: "It doesn't make sense . . . maybe she fainted before Morgan [the doctor] could finish. . . . Anyway, I hope she ends up pregnant or I'm going to be bummed. . . ." The abrupt change in a story that had obviously been planned for months and the inadequate explanation for Donna's symptoms (hormonal imbalance would have to be attributed to some specific condition) suggest that someone high in the chain of command determined that the story was "too hot to handle" and instructed the writers to duck out of it any way they could. Indeed, actress Stuart later reported in an interview that there had been a sudden change of heart about Donna's change of life (Bonderoff, 1995b).

The network and P&G might have assumed that the soap audience did not want to hear about menopause; this study reveals that it was not a menopause story *per se* that turned viewers off, but its handling and interjection into this romance. After all the quest for a pregnancy would be a plot eventuality the writers would not want to preclude if marriage were truly in the picture.[2]

It is doubtful that the subplot was meant to end the relationship in the short term. However, the ratings for the program remained low, and with the O.J. Simpson hearings and trial threatening further attrition, it became apparent that backstage pink slips and shake-ups might be more of a threat to Matt and Donna's story than onscreen rosy cheeks and hot flashes.

IT'S A WONDERFUL MIDLIFE

Cyberfans had long been aware that actor Matt Crane (Matt), an accomplished sculptor, eventually intended to leave acting for his other art. There had been indications that this would happen when his contract expired in the summer of 1994. Although he did re-sign, there could have been a contingency plan to write the character out of the show. Indeed this was the point at which Matt and Donna had (temporarily) broken up over her refusal to marry. Noticing that Matt was to be in the line of fire at his mother's wedding to a former gangland kingpin (Donna's *other* ex-husband), cyberfans speculated that he might get shot.

Whether this was ever actually contemplated, Matt's demise would have been a way to end Matt and Donna's romance while fully preserving its positive message—a fitting closure to a sweet, neat, Capra-esque fable. Matt helped Donna face midlife with optimism, it is Matt who assumes the role of the angel in this retelling of the holiday classic. The scene in which he reassures Donna as a disembodied voice from on high takes on additional meaning in this context. He is a very *carnal* angel, but that is precisely what the wonderful life is about in this tale. As the angel, he would have to leave his earthly existence and earn his wings, perhaps having transformed Donna into Madonna—hardly an immaculate conception, but a miracle of its own kind. In this way, the Matt and Donna story might live on intact, in memory, and in a brand-new character. The story also appeared to borrow from the 1955 film *All That Heaven Allows*, in which the middle-aged widow ultimately rises above the disapproval of friends and grown children to reunite with her injured younger lover—a free spirit who has inspired her to live life for herself and to the fullest. Still a soap would not be likely to sacrifice a younger core character to preserve a romance to which they were never fully committed in the first place.

Late in the summer of 1994, head writer Peggy Sloane hinted that Matt and Donna would be staying together, but not without complications involving one or two young women with designs on Matt (Fall Preview, 1994). Many fans suspected that one of them would be Angela, a deceitful, gold-digging teenager they referred to disparagingly as "Puff-face" or "Moonbaby" and mocked as being no match for Donna—a "real woman."

Hence, at what might be considered the story's midlife, we are presented with what soap opera theorists have characterized as the "indefinitely extended middle" (Porter, 1977, p. 783)—the open-ended narrative in which polysemy and interpretive playfulness reign. Yet because we have incorporated Mumford's (1995) assertion that soap storylines are not indefinite and do reach closure, and have indicated that the final answers to ideological enigmas are paramount, it is important to assess the key questions driving the story at this interim point and how they could be and were negotiated in the text and by viewers.

It has already been stipulated that whether this middle-aged woman could begin anew with a career and an autonomous outlook *in the context of her connection to this young man* was a key issue in this story even before the decision to continue the romance was made. Including a committed romantic relationship with Matt as an added element in that revitalization does not necessarily nullify it. At this juncture, there had been numerous situations showing that Donna felt able to forge ahead on her own. Yet if heterosexual monogamy—and indeed the institution of marriage—had been configured according to this pattern, the traditional power relations associated with the institution might have tilted toward balance. Therefore, a preferred meaning of Donna's renewal and independence endured at the story's midlife, and there were no contradictory interpretations evident in viewer response.

Additional key issues arising from story developments are threefold: (a) Was Matt an unusually mature young man and, therefore, wise enough to appreciate, love, and commit to an older woman? (b) Was Donna sincerely in love with and able to commit to Matt? (c) Could Matt and Donna enter into a valid marriage? The third question would not be answered for almost 1 year because the wedding date had been tentatively set for June 1995. Yet how were text and viewers answering the first two questions at this time?

Although textual efforts to convince viewers that Matt found Donna attractive and deserving of his love and commitment might have repudiated, if not convinced, those teenage girls who wanted their idol with a young woman, they did not address another group of viewers whose prejudices were differently skewed. As the historical/cultural background indicates, the gender/age double standard succeeds, in part, due to shared cultural assumptions about young men. Despite his mature behavior, there were still those in the audience—primarily older viewers—who could not buy Donna's love for Matt. Donna's resistance to the relationship was selectively enhanced and seen as valid by these viewers while Matt's efforts to persuade her (and them) otherwise were interpreted as an overstepping of bounds. "Is anyone else sick of Matthew lecturing her?" queried one fan in a magazine letter. "It was tiresome when Michael did it, but even worse when Matthew does it" (Another Look, 1994, p. 2). In fact Michael had lectured Donna on many counts and was sanctimonious about her brief affair although his behavior contributed to it. However, Matt's lecturing only addressed Donna's concerns about violating social convention. At one point Donna remarked that all her society friends would regard him as her "boy toy." Matthew countered that as long as *she* did not regard him that way, he didn't care.

Apparently for those women who feel that the double standard is "just the way things are" and do not fathom how it may contribute to their disempowerment, Matt's moralizing was uncalled for and worse than Michael's. Moreover, it was not seen in the context of screwball comedy's convention of feigned feminine protest—a convention that, particularly in this instance, inverts the soap opera/romance novel formula of the angry, cynical hero brought to his knees by the spirited, innocent young woman (see Barlow & Krentz, 1995). Related objections were also being voiced about another older woman/younger man romance just underway—Matt and Vanessa of GL. One older woman commented about 44-ish Vanessa: "She used to have so much class and now it's really stupid . . . he's just a kid." Several fans of that program agreed with one who remarked that Vanessa was "lowering herself" to be with this "boy" despite that he was played by an actor in his 30s.

Accordingly, Donna's reluctance allotted space for some to believe that her heart was not entirely in it, and those unable to identify with Donna in the framework of this love story were inclined to slide into that interpretive opening. The ongoing lightness of the story was also a factor as certain reactions—particularly those that would emerge along with the romance's next pivotal stage—hint. For some uninvested viewers, Matt and Donna were entertaining and fun as long as neither one of them had more promising and "realistic" options.

Logically, this duality of meaning was not part of the natural, unmanageable polysemy—the semiotic excess of the text (Fiske, 1987)—but quite intentional on the part of the creators. Because the romance's initial humor and frivolity were fashioned in contrast to the authentic love story envisioned for Matt and Josie, the storytellers were presumably confident that a majority of viewers would obey the text's directives and refuse long-term investment in Matt and Donna. Although many fans did not behave accordingly, others did. Because the course was adjusted in midstream and the creators had first tried to circumvent that eventuality through textual and meta-textual manipulation, they must have been somewhat cognizant of the ambiguity that initially permitted the resistive readings. Later, the belief that Matt and Donna's relationship was genuine and could lead to a legitimate marriage *and* the assumption that the duo was just for fun were *both* preferred meanings of the text— one counter to and the other consistent with the hegemonic status quo. In other words, the creators had decided to play along with those who loved Matt and Donna while maintaining the humor so that those who could not take the romance seriously would not be too alienated.

However, it is possible to answer the first two enigmas central to *and at* this stage of the story in the affirmative in the light of the negotiating room deliberately granted. For many viewers, Matt was an unusually mature young man who appreciated the multiplicity of things this woman of experience had to offer and who truly loved and was capable of committing to her. Donna also could be seen by many as sincerely and lovingly devoted, despite her anxiety about the social taboo.

Also crucial to this interpretive duality was viewers' ability to identify with Matt and/or Donna in the context of their love story. The desire for Donna to be portrayed as a role model indicates a strong identification with her character. Indeed several Matt and Donna fans on a bulletin board insisted that this story was the only reason they watched, and one woman threatened to "return her VCR" if *AW* ever split them up.

The identification process also works against this kind of story. The speculation that many young women would hate Donna with Matt was the main catalyst behind the writers' initial desire to end the story quickly and position Matt in a Generation X romance. Young women are not trained by the culture to project into the future and identify with older versions of themselves. The dearth of older women as adventurous, independent, romantic leads in Hollywood films is contributive. One cannot help but wonder to what extent this inability to identify can evolve, with age, into self-contempt. A young cyberfan listed Matt as her favorite male character and loathed this storyline and Donna, whom she referred to as "Miss Priss."

Young men, in contrast, appear to have less trouble identifying with Arnold, Sly, Clint, or Harrison, although these actors are at least a generation removed. For related reasons, many young male fans could identify with Matt Cory as he courted a relatively innocent soap babe, with all of the implications of power and authority that entailed, but were intimidated by the thought of going one on one with a Donna. Yet there appeared to be more young men than young women who loved the story. Several online participants were actor Stuart's biggest fans. "Age is all in the mind" one contended, adding a hyperbolic appraisal: "Donna looks like she's 20 anyway."

Still determining the ages of cyberfans can be problematic. I initially assumed that the woman who said she would "return her VCR" if Matt and Donna were split up was at least in her mid-30s. Surprisingly, she later revealed herself to be all of 19. Her views as well as those of some other younger women indicate that it is possible, even desirable, for them to be able to identify with someone like Donna.

These differing tendencies and creators' assumptions in this regard are fully considered and theorized in upcoming chapters. However, it became evident, even at this juncture, that coupling middle-aged female characters with young men in romantic, dynamic storylines might be one way to construct an audience of young women who are more inclined to identify with such heroines as future versions of themselves and to cultivate in them an affective sense of long-lived currency. Logically, the fact that older heroes in a variety of media texts are central, active, and often paired with young, attractive women is a key reason that young male viewers have no problem adopting their subjectivities and using them to fantasize a range of lifespan possibilities.

However, inveighing against the prevailing cultural assumptions in this fashion is not what the soap opera business is about. It is about making money, and it is much easier for soap creators to placate and satisfy advertisers by exploiting what are assumed to be the existing values and prejudices of the majority of the most desirable viewers especially when those values and prejudices are consistent with hegemonic aspirations in the bedroom as well as the boardroom.

"This is not a Frank Capra movie," Donna cautions her daughter in a scene occurring soon after a new head writer took the reigns in the fall 1994—a decision announced just as the previous head writer's promise that Matt and Donna would remain a couple appeared in one of the magazines (Fall Preview, 1994, p. 9). Alhough ostensibly made in another context, Donna's statement underscored a possible shift in tone and direction—from a wonderful midlife of new horizons to one of more traditional demarcations. Even fantasy worlds can have boundaries, and Donna and Matt transgressed those boundaries and ventured "over the rainbow"—a place that looks splendid and inviting, but where all might not be what it seems.

NOTES

1. An interview with Stuart reveals her dissatisfaction with the menopause story's telling: "They're writing that she's freaking out because it's a horrible thing. What I'd rather happen is to let Donna freak out, but then have Bridget point out that so many strides have been made . . . " (Allocca, 1994a, p. 46). Other articles praised *AW* and Stuart for doing a story that soap divas, such as Susan Lucci (*AMC*) and Deidre Hall (*DOOL*), would not have agreed to do (DeLacroix, 1994b; DiLauro, 1994). Several years later, *One Life to Live* (*OLTL*) had forty-something heroine Nora encounter early menopausal symptoms that led to marital issues. This story was watered down because, according to actor Hillary B. Smith (Nora), the network (ABC) "got scared" (Logan, 1998c, p. 78).

2. This eventuality seemed plausible to fans despite Donna's previous fertility problems and Matt's reassurances that it was not an issue. On *ATWT*, a quest for pregnancy via new reproductive technologies was incorporated into the intergenerational marriage of Susan and Larry. Susan's daughter donated an egg for in vitro fertilization and implantation, allowing Susan to give birth to Larry's biological child.

5 OVER THE RAINBOW . . . DREAMS BECOME NIGHTMARES

Writers don't have to . . . write only what fans want,
but they DO have to work
within the integrity of established characters.

NOSTALGIA VERSUS P.C.

The time-factored, multiperspectival analysis of Matt and Donna's journey resumes in this chapter as a shift in creator aims is detected. Inasmuch as ambiguity reduction is key to minimizing deviations from a preferred reading (see Lewis, 1991), textual alterations and related fan interpretations are pivotal.

The phase began with Donna devoting herself to her embattled daughter—Vicky—the soap's preeminent young heroine. In November 1994, a story arc promising to provide obstacles for Matt and Donna developed and then halted in midair. A magazine article predicted a "change of life" for many of Bay City's men, including Matt (DeLosh, 1994, p. 3). Additionally, over the next several months, the romantic comedy element faded, and Matt was portrayed less and less as the sophisticated match for Donna. No young women pursued him, and their one-on-one interaction was practically nil.

This state of affairs disturbed magazine editors and many of the couple's fans. *Soap Opera Digest* (Thumbs Down, 1995) bemoaned the duo's "romance interruptus" and blamed it on "apron strings" between Donna and Vicky once Vicky returned after her portrayer's maternity leave. In letters to the editor, one fan warned that if the new head writer decided to split the couple, it would be "sending a message to women over 40 that a story celebrating their sexuality and attractiveness is not worth telling" (Your Turn, 1994, p. 32), and another commented that it would make her "angry and sad" if the show penned "a 1950s ending to this very 1990s romance" (Keep the Love, 1995, p. 141). These sentiments indicate that nothing short of a continuation of the romance could have kept their empowering fantasy intact.

The saga continues in the spring of 1995 as a wedding date has been set. Donna reassures Matt that her ex-husband, Michael, is out of her system. Matt accepts Donna's promise of loyalty and gives her a horse as an engagement gift, comparing her free nature to that of the horse. Unbeknownst to them both, Michael has returned to his family's farm next to the stables. He encounters Donna there, re-creating the conditions under which they first fell in love as teens.

In the mid-1980s, thirty-something Donna and her siblings had been introduced before Michael, and his insertion into the show's history a couple of years later involved the prior machinations of Donna's cruel father, Reginald Love. Michael, the Love family's stable boy, had impregnated Donna in the stables and was subsequently banished by Reginald, who locked Donna in the basement so he could pass her child, Marley, off as his own. As the story unfolded in real time, this secret was revealed. Then when a young woman arrived in town looking exactly like Marley, Donna eventually discovered that she had borne twins and that Reginald had given this one, Vicky, up to the care of a surrogate. Michael had vowed to return after acquiring the assets needed to challenge Reginald, and his reappearance sparked a series of events in which Reginald was repeatedly opposed and ultimately defeated. By and by, a spoiled and manipulative Donna was redeemed, if tenuously, in the love of her family. Despite that its earliest events were related purely through recollection and flashback, Michael and Donna's backstory was rich. Consequently, having Donna and Michael reunite in a barn was designed to evoke nostalgic longing in viewers.

When Donna gathers herself and informs Michael about Matt, he mocks her. Matt confronts Michael and advises him that Donna has proved herself to be a woman of integrity and warns him to give her respect. Michael responds that he has known Donna a long time and that with her, "some things are genetic." Donna is delighted that Matt has defended her yet it is clear that she feels a connection with her first love.

Reacting to a new creative team, dearth of story for their favorite couple, and the imminent return of Donna's ex, cyberfans of Matt and Donna feared the worst. Worries were allayed when the new executive producer stated that Matt and Donna would marry, although his elaboration implied that strings were attached (Allocca, 1995a). Fans with no investment in this romance were elated to have their old favorite back, and viewers interested in any of these characters set up in three camps:

(a) Matt and Donna (M&D) supporters who wanted this couple to remain together, (b) Michael fans who never fully embraced Donna and Matt or who disliked them because of Matt's presumed unsuitability and who wanted Donna and Michael to reconcile in a reinvigoration of "history", and (c) Matt fans who wanted Michael and Donna together because of Donna's presumed unworthiness and because they preferred to see Matt romancing a young woman. Seemingly, M&D fans ranged in age from 25 to 49, Michael fans were mostly situated in the 35 and older demographic categories, and Matt fans were predominantly under 30.

From the perspective of this researcher, the prospect of a triangle was intriguing. Even if Donna were to choose Michael, it seemed inconceivable that the romance with Matt could be remembered as a stereotype, with the young man ultimately rejecting the older woman for fresher quarry or the older woman left in the cold. Moreover, Donna's new life meant that she would deal with Michael from a position of strength. Making the older woman the focus of a triangle between her middle-aged but handsome ex-husband and a gorgeous, devoted younger man was certainly a first and afforded the older woman agency seldom given her. Her evolution as a confident professional woman also meant that one of her options could be complete independence from either man. Donna's continued centrality and strength were anticipated by many of her fans regardless of whether they preferred Matt or Michael. Because Donna's romance with Michael had also been played in the romantic comedy style, the triangle promised a light-hearted touch.

In cyberspace, debate centered around Matt versus Michael as a match for Donna. Michael fans invoked the couple's history and family ties as reasons for them to reunite. The nostalgia element triggers a predictable response to the return of any beloved soap character; long-time fans yearn to see love stories rekindled, and the chemistry of the original couple is assumed to be superior to that of any subsequent pair. Similar to what occurred with the Billie/Bo/Hope triangle on *DOOL,* some Michael fans insisted specifically and repeatedly that they never saw any chemistry between Matt and Donna, although their previous posts, many meticulously saved by this researcher, indicated otherwise. This was not outright deceit on their part, but rather evidence of the elasticity of memory in the process of negotiating new input. The real issue is whether this elasticity can facilitate the hegemonic goals of the powers that be as much as it has the potential to resist them. Moreover, these fans argued that Donna deserved a bonafide romance with a "real man," as if age alone signals who is a real man.

M&D fans cited Donna's maturation in her 1990s relationship with Matt, who treated her like an equal. In response to one such fan disappointed that Donna was turning into a "wimp" who "hangs on her ex-husband's every word," a Michael fan shot back: "Oh my. Such vitriol on behalf of feminists everywhere. . . . Since when does love have to pass the political correctness test?" Still M&D fans used the "real man" label to describe Matt and contended that there were many more story possibilities for Matt and Donna because Michael and Donna's three marriages had exhausted most options.

Matt fans became more vocal than ever, repeatedly stating that Donna "could be his mother" in apparent disbelief that anyone could approve of their coupling. When such fans were accused of holding to a double standard, a spiral of silence functioned to temporarily minimize their polemic postings.

At this juncture, cyberfan sentiments and magazine polls slightly favored Matt as a match for Donna (Networks Are Listening, 1995; Readers' Notes, 1995; Terrific Triangles, 1995). Although unscientific, these numbers are remarkable considering the nostalgia factor and cultural double standard. Nonetheless, the contingent favoring Michael included younger Matt fans who would be of principal concern to producers.

Even before Michael's return was secured, actors Crane (Matt) and Stuart (Donna) predicted an end to their story (Allocca, 1994b). The aborted subplot might have been meant to accomplish this, but apparently the decision to reintroduce Michael had altered the means if not the ends. Despite his insinuation that Matt and Donna would marry, the new executive producer, John Valente, declared that Michael's role was a decidedly patriarchal one—to "make the Hudsons a family again" (DeLosh, 1995, p. 5). This was consistent with the show's well-publicized new tactic—"the multigenerational family that works" (*Another World Tries*, 1995, p. 1). The addition of Clara, Michael's long-absent mother, and the centrality of the Hudson homestead were further manifestations of the new theme.

ARRESTING RESISTANCE

"It Doesn't Matter How Old You Are . . . "

The next phase of the story, from June to October 1995, features the diabolical Justine, a doppelganger impersonating Matt's mother and the latest evidence of *DOOL*ification, hostessing a party for the engaged couple. Donna interprets the peculiar affair as a bad omen. After she observes that everyone at the party is crazed and jaded except for Matt, who is "so good," and Matt's young niece, who "hasn't had the time" to get crazy, Matt attempts to calm her foreboding. Amid a lovemaking and Chinese-food-eating session, Donna wonders what might have happened if Matt, who is allergic to scallops, had eaten those his mother curiously served.

Matt tells her not to worry—that he will be around a long time. He sweetly asks her to "trust in the universe" and suggests she examine her fortune. "It doesn't matter how old you are, it matters how much you love," reads Donna, realizing that Matt has surreptitiously inserted the sentiment. A purposeful polysemy rests here, as fans could and did take away whatever they wished. However, this analyst could only see an attempt to depoliticize whatever was to come–to make it a question of love, which they would have us believe transcends the political.

A few days later, after Vicky accuses Donna of softening toward Michael, Matt becomes agitated. Donna composes him by pegging Michael as a controlling, condescending rogue. She recalls awakening to her love for Matt when he trusted her to share his work and his dreams. After Matt remarks that he is honored to have her devotion, Donna reacts without hubris: "You should be. I'm wonderful." When Matt asks what would happen if she could have a similar life with Michael, Donna insists that she "can't imagine a universe" in which Michael might need her, trust her, or treat her as an equal. This scene sparked approval from M&D fans who viewed it as embracing the essence of Donna's growth and the couple's appeal.

At that moment, however, we cut to a scene in which Michael is stricken. Later he hides his condition at a family gathering, after which a drunken Vicky warns Matt that Donna "wants what she can't have" and will drop him when Michael "wags his finger." Matt admonishes Vicky for not seeing the accomplished woman her mother had become. Such scenes heartened M&D fans who fervently believed that Donna had matured and that Matt's faith in her was certainly not misplaced.

"It Matters How Much You Love"

Soon after Donna learns that Michael has leukemia and has undergone a bone marrow transplant from his newfound son, Nick, she immediately begins to ignore Matt and nurse Michael. Matt again requests honesty, but Donna only chides him for not having faith in her. After Vicky faces tragedy and amid repeated invocations of family, Donna treats Matt like an "annoying piece of naval lint," as one fan put it.

Michael's intentions toward Donna are not so clear. He has guarded his secret so as not to appear weak, and we are left to think that he has not pursued Donna because he expected to die. However, once given a clean bill of health, he quietly dates his doctor while assuming that Donna will marry Matt as planned.

Although there were many clues foreshadowing an end to Matt and Donna's coupling, including their meager air time together and the symbolism of the sham engagement party, there was ample room to interpret that they might still enter into a valid marriage until she began to treat him with indignity. Still some M&D fans stood firm, believing that Donna had become a "Stepford wife" around Michael. Soon, they speculated, she would have an epiphany. However, undecided fans were coaxed into Michael's camp on account of Matt's self-righteous attitude toward his newly reinstated brother-in-law, Jake. Pitting Matt against two beloved prodigals had some wishing he would eat scallops and rooting for Donna to run to Michael's side.

This phase commenced as rumblings at the network and P&G resulted in yet another change in the show's creative team, including the installation of the controversial Jill Farren Phelps, veteran of such soaps as *Guiding Light* (*GL*) and the defunct *Santa Barbara*, at the executive producer helm. More than ever, the show's mandate was to improve demographics by making *AW* harmonious with *Days of Our Lives* (*DOOL*). If they wanted to shift audience sentiment in Michael's favor, Matt's character had to be assaulted. Interviews asserted that a wedding would occur "despite the obstacles" (Cukor, 1995, pp. 25–26), but the new youth focus had negative implications for both pairs.

October 1995 to April 1996 proves to be a pivotal period. As the wedding draws near, the audience is made aware of Donna's clear preference for Michael and utter disregard for Matt. Although Matt gives Donna every opportunity to confess a change of heart, she keeps stringing him along, uncertain of Michael's feelings toward her. Matt's continued support for Donna despite her contempt is displayed as immature, unmasculine naiveté. In one scene, Matt offers to read her to sleep when she is distressed about her daughter. He sweetly tells her that Vicky is strong like her mother. Yet such uncommon attention is shown to be wasted on Donna, making Matt appear foolish. In contrast, there is a clear effort to associate Michael with the promise of wild, adventurous passion. If M&D fans fantasized about a man offering spontaneity and excitement, the show would make sure that his embodiment would be in (now) earthy Michael as a opposed to (now) earthbound Matt. Indeed the challenge of making a middle-aged woman's romance with a twenty-something young hunk seem mundane compared with one with her gray-haired, middle-aged ex-husband must have loomed as formidable. Realizing this, one magazine published a picture of studly Matt sitting back to back with Donna along with the caption: "Will Donna turn her back on *that*?" (Will Donna, 1995, p. 20).

The wedding date is moved up to allay Matt's anxiety, and Donna sees to it that Michael is kept in the dark. As the groom sings Donna's praises to his best man, Donna heads to Michael's farm to retrieve her grandfather's cufflinks to give to Matt as a wedding gift. She finds Michael in the barn, and when their song—an early 1960s tune evocative of generational solidarity—plays, they flash back to their first time. Soon they have relived it. Afterward Donna misapprehends Michael's postcoital murmurings and runs off to inform Matt that she and Michael have reconciled. By this time, however, Matt is boorishly tying one on at a local bar.

Unable to locate Matt, Donna packs a bag and, glancing backward only to comment, "I should have known better," heads to the farm, climbs into Michael's bed, and announces, "I'm never leaving you again." A startled Michael responds that there must be a "misunderstanding," adding that their bedroom harmony does not extend to day-to-day life. Donna is incredulous, arguing that a reunion was inevitable especially because his brush with death had surely changed his roguish lifestyle—an effect that he denies. When questioned about Matt, Donna responds that she "thought" she loved him, but that she cannot hide her true desire any longer. Michael contends that they have been in a "time warp" and begs her to remember their tryst fondly, but to go on with her wedding as planned. Donna informs him that she missed her wedding for their tryst and dismisses the task of notifying Matt as something she will "think about tomorrow." She also implies that Matt has never been able to satisfy her sexually. Michael mocks her "Scarlett O'Hara" pose and suggests she do what she does best to rectify the situation—lie. Reduced to crying and begging, Donna claims she does not deserve Matt, but rather someone "as awful" as she.

Although these events were disquieting to some, a similar scenario with genders reversed would be unthinkable in most any popular genre. Even in a soap, the younger woman in such a triangle would have to be profoundly wicked for an older man to prefer an immature but age appropriate ex-wife, and allusions to a gorgeous, devoted younger woman's sexual ineptitude would seem laughable. The show was methodically illustrating how the disparagement of young men contributes to the double standard while representing the stereotypical desperation and folly of aging women.

Donna does lie, parlaying a minor fender bender into a major ordeal that kept her from making her wedding. She embellishes this with a tale about a flat tire and a farmer who refused her assistance. As she imitates the farmer's cackling chickens in her hospital bed, Donna spies Michael listening at the door. On exiting, Matt apologizes to Michael for storming over to the farm in a drunken rage looking for Donna. Alone with Donna, Michael congratulates her for her fancy footwork. Later he shows up with the hospital chaplain and, as if to dare, suggests that the wedding commence. Donna tries to resist, but relishes calling Michael's bluff. "You made me believe in love again," vows Donna to Matt, as he pledges to never give her cause to doubt him. Donna is released, and her marriage to Matt is consummated off screen. On the morning after, Donna is shown fantasizing about Michael as Matt awakens her with kisses.

In a matter of a few days, Donna has been reinvented as a dependent, insensitive, exploitative child. The confident woman who described herself as wonderful had taken to seeing herself as awful with encouragement from her supposed true love. Michael had already been subjected to backstory alterations positing that he was never a sanctimonious family man. This Matt could no longer be read as a sophisticated charmer with his own philandering past, but as a self-righteous, pathetic dupe—a cuckold in the making. New aptonyms appeared for both Matt and Donna at this juncture—"DoorMatt" and "Donnasaur." All of the key enigmas of the original Matt/Donna story approached hegemonic closure. Thus, both the Michael and Matt contingents appeared to be constructed as preferred readers. Despite Michael's juvenile behavior, the inherently inequitable notion that young women (from everyone's perspective) and older men (from the perspective of all but the youngest women) should be the sought-after prizes in our cultural romantic sweepstakes was bolstered.

M&D fans were directed to realign their prior perceptions; Donna had not matured, Matt was not a real man who could satisfy her, his faith in her was completely misplaced, and the marriage was anything but valid. In short they were made to feel as gullible as Matt appeared. "I'm furious!" exclaimed one unhappy camper. Another lambasted the show for "toying" with its audience. A fan who previously embraced the authenticity of the romance adjusted her reading to observe that Donna always had reservations and that she should not have led Matt on. Immediately or gradually, viewers' negotiations of the story were affected by the ideological weight of closing arguments.

However, magazines tallied mail from disheartened M&D fans lobbying for their reconciliation. Claimed one: "If Matt Crane and Anna Stuart were reading a cereal box, they would be more exciting than some other duos masquerading as couples in love" (Mail Call, 1996, p. 41). Another observed: "Michael had three chances with Donna. She should put him in the history books and leave him there" (Viewers' Voice, 1996, p. 10). Objections to the story's evolution are evidence of polyvalence and not of the ability to glean something empowering from the text as received.

Although young women were experiencing pleasure and a certain empowerment as a result of these events, it was at the expense of more marginal viewers. As Feuer (1995) reasoned, hailing the resistance of readers when the empowerment of "one subordinate group . . . conflicts with the interests of another" (p. 5) renders the idea of marginality meaningless. In fact setting one marginal group against another in this fashion is nothing to celebrate. In this case the empowerment of young women coincided with that of middle-aged men, rendering their pleasure hegemonic.

Interestingly, however, the most telling reaction emanated from Michael fans, many of whom were also piqued. "Why can't Michael and

Donna have a mature relationship?" asked one, while another—the same fan who accused M&D devotees of being politically correct—was "appalled" at the wholesale destruction of all three characters, dismissing Michael and Donna's lovemaking as "wham, bam, thank you, mam." This suggests that Michael fans, too, were not the creators' first priority as a preferred audience when this textual turn was conceived.

What many fans did not fathom was that Michael's and, especially, Donna's immature behavior was necessary to create character development for Matt—the real prize in the triangle in terms of commercial imperatives. Now vested as a potential romantic hero through his romance with Donna, he would be recruited to entice the audience segment with the most currency. At this point, the tale was being told to whet the appetites of Matt fans who were no longer shy about expressing their feeling that Matt deserved a woman "his own age" who would treat him better. Several confessed to being "nauseated" by Matt and Donna all along.

Textually, things go from bad to worse as Matt notices holes in Donna's story and contrives his own plan to eavesdrop on her and Michael. Caught red-handed, Donna still pleads innocence and berates *Matt* for his machinations. Michael tries to take the blame and suffers a blow from Matt. "You two deserve each other," Matt comments in disgust, as Sarah McLachlan's music and lyrics hint that Matt is "at the crossroads" of a new and eventful future. Later Donna is reduced to groveling as he packs his bags: "Say that you want to hurt me. But don't leave me." Matt cannot forgive. In a heartbeat, he leaves her and the TV station for a newspaper partnership with his arch nemesis, Jake. Although Matt has not rejected Donna for a younger woman, the show insinuates that Donna deserves to be rejected. Matt's reputation as a faithful lover is preserved, whereas Donna's worthiness is not.

During this massive recontextualization of story and character, dress and makeup are employed in strategic ways. In his last incarnation, Michael had been a hotshot business tycoon in a three-piece suit, so retooling him as a humble farmer in Levis™ serves to make him appear more youthful and "salt of the earth." Just as Rock Hudson was the simple gardener as Jane Wyman's preferred *younger* man in *All That Heaven Allows*, this story renders middle-aged Michael as Donna's genuine and natural love. After their roll in the hay, Donna dons his flannel shirt, whereas she has worn only proper lingerie with Matt. When she crawls into Michael's bed in his pajama top and he mentions her suitcase full of peignoirs, she says pointedly that she prefers what she is wearing (Fig. 5.1).

Donna's look is relaxed and youthful during these scenes, but as she becomes more desperate in the face of Matt's suspicion, matronly big hair, heavy makeup, and clothing appear (Fig. 5.2). As he is being suckered by Donna, Matt sports ill-fitting sweaters worthy of Mr. Rogers (Fig. 5.3). As he wises up, however, he is buff and brawny at the gym (Fig. 5.4).

Fig. 5.1. *Another World's* Donna sports Michael's shirt as a sign of their "natural" love.

Fig. 5.2. As Donna becomes more desperate, matronly, "big hair" appears.

Fig. 5.3.   As Donna's dupe, Matt (left) dresses for
the part.

Fig. 5.4.   Wise to Donna's schemes, Matt is buff and
strong.

As the breakup occurred in late 1995, serious cancellation threats surfaced, and an abrupt shift to a youth orientation took shape. Matt's move to the newspaper put him in one of four downtown venues the producer had designated as centers of action. The TV station became completely irrelevant. Few of the older, veteran characters worked in any of the primary settings and had to wander in from the outskirts to become part of the story, giving new meaning to the concept of the satellite character. Matt averaged four appearances per week for the next several months, Michael about two, and Donna barely one. Matt got more action at the newspaper in a single day than he had at the TV station in the previous year, whereas Donna was never seen working. Clearly the task was to make Matt a featured player *sans* Donna.

Moreover, magazine reports intimating that Donna would find herself pregnant after her wedding night calisthenics (*AW's* Donna, 1995) and text foreshadowing this as well, Michael's paternity proved premature, as plots were altered to accommodate new imperatives. One of my students with medical knowledge pointed out that Michael could not have fathered a child in the first place because treatment for leukemia would have rendered him sterile. Still Donna's assertion that their lovemaking was a miracle from God suggests how they probably planned to play it. This would have given Donna more story and allowed her to confess her indiscretion with some dignity and be set on a road toward motherhood, maturity, and Michael in short order.

Although some M&D fans interpreted the change as a good sign, others worried that it would only prolong their agony. For months fans and this analyst had been wary of more ominous foretelling, such as Donna's constant references to Matt's goodness, her remark that she deserved someone "as awful" as she, and her allusion to Matt hurting her. Additionally, as Matt's suspicions grew, Donna endeavored to quell them by singing him a song from the musical *Jekyll and Hyde*. The song "Someone Like You" was apropos; it is sung by a prostitute, Lucy, about the redemptive love she might have with Dr. Jekyll. However, in this version of the story, Lucy is murdered by Mr. Hyde. The fear was that Matt and Donna were not through, but that he would turn to the dark side and become as awful as she. Having Donna suffer while Matt pined for another (younger) woman could have been the plan, followed by Michael's rescue of Donna and their miracle child.

Although a Matt/Donna affair and the prophesied "Whose baby is it?" subplot did not come to pass, the same cannot be said of Matt's metamorphosis. Awaiting an annulment, he rebounds with Blair, a slightly older femme fatale who surreptitiously involves him in her murderous plot. When she inquires about a popular jazz club, Matt mentions that he has been "out of the loop" for awhile, as if Donna has selfishly stolen his youth. Their tempestuous sex on the docks also implies that his newfound angst transformed him from wimp into hot-blooded lover. Additionally, Blair's death and the revelation of her deceit push Matt closer to cynicism. Another love interest was planned according to previews—and because she was also an imposter out to exploit him, Matt's villainization seemed inevitable.

Meanwhile, yet another change of executive producer portended story modifications. There was information that Jill Farren Phelps had not been conforming to all of the network's wishes and consequently was on her way out. One thing she supposedly refused to do was turn the character of Carl, recently redeemed of prior wickedness through a romance with Matt's mother, into a supernatural villain similar to Stefano DiMera on *DOOL*—a network preference later confirmed in the press (Logan, 1998d, p. 31). Rumors also circulated that the network might like to model Donna after *DOOL's* Vivian—the harridan infamous for burying young heroines before their time. Yet Vivian was not a character with a long and complex history or the devoted mother of a popular heroine. It seemed impossible that Donna could be revised to that degree. Fans expressed their displeasure with the network's apparent wishes, but still celebrated Phelps' exit on account of unwelcome changes in the program during her tenure.

Matt's previewed romance did not pan out, and there were rumblings in magazine previews that a well-loved character was to fall victim to a serial killer by the end of the summer. Because Blair was suddenly being written as the first victim of this killer and Donna was behaving like a jealous, drugged-out, desperate soul in an effort to regain Matt's affection, she became the prime suspect in the crimes. Her behavior at this time is characterized by Matt and many fans as "pathetic," and there are those who believe and want to believe that she is guilty. In one scene, a disgusted Matt tells Donna that he does not need another mother, and this prompted a cyberfan to comment that she would not be surprised if he called Donna an "old hag" next. Donna's fantasies reflect her desperation; in them she functions as Matt's moll while he reminds her that he can never love her the way he once did. Donna's "dumbing down," as some described it, coincided with other evidence of the soap's tabloidization, including the Felicia/John/Sharlene triangle and its incessant catfighting over the adulterous John. Cyberfans lamented that the "spine monster" was invading Bay City and absconding with any backbone its women once possessed. Meanwhile, Michael was shown falling for his former sister-in-law, Sharlene, and one new fan argued that Donna was expendable because she was "too old for anyone on the show."

It is at this point that some Michael fans began to realize the extent to which they had been suckered:

> I wasn't too upset when Matt and Donna were broken up, thinking as I did that there would be an ultimate payoff in the form of a beautiful, history-rich Donna and Michael reunion. Boy, was I stupid. . . . I never   dreamed that Michael would be . . . putting the moves on Sharlene, while Donna was . . . contemptuously rejected. . . . I never dreamed that Matt, who could not keep his hands off Donna for two entire years . . . would be . . . in love with a new, young, and criminal stranger within three months. . . . If you were to turn on AW today as that much-sought-after, mythical Gen-X viewer, you . . . might notice Matt swatting at an annoying mosquito—no, wait! That's Donna. . . . Never would you imagine that Matt and Donna were a groundbreaking soap couple, sizzlingly hot and refreshingly complicated. Never would you believe that Donna was torn between two men . . . neither of whom could resist her. Most of all, you would never believe that all this was going on just three months ago!

The text's implication was that Matt was not wise to the complexities of life when he loved Donna, and that the new Matt, fully integrated with his dark side, would know better. No simple breakup was possible here because they had to remove the taint of his having loved Donna so that young women identifying with Matt's new love would be sufficiently flattered and have no doubt about his preference. Matt was now the beast waiting to be saved by an unsullied beauty, and neither Donna nor Blair fit the bill. Although the innovative twist of having an optimistic young man successfully redeem a jaded older woman was rendered invalid, the innocent younger woman does retain this power over the angry older man even if it is her only power and comes at the expense of who she will be in the future.

What innocent young woman stood poised to rescue Matt? When Sofia, a virginal, 18-year-old convent girl who was to be the apple of Michael's son's eye first appeared on the program just after Michael and Donna's tryst, she cast a fascinated glance in Matt's direction as he furiously quizzed Michael about events on his wedding night (Fig. 5.5). Even then I suspected that the glance was scripted. When I mentioned the prospect of a Matt/Sofia romance to other fans at that time and a few months later, they thought it completely nonsensical that Matt would be placed in the teen interest story after his involvement with the likes of Donna and Blair. This attempt at poetic justice was precisely what evolved, however, although they did SORAS Sofia to 21 before pursuing it. If all this upheaval was meant to please young Matt fans, what better way to exert the text's interpellative pull on these viewers than to have him worship sweet Sofia? Matt/Sofia/Nick, and not Matt/Donna/Michael, must have been the front-burner triangle creators truly envisioned as the ultimate payoff resulting from Michael's return to the canvas.

Fig. 5.5. Virginal Sofia's backward glance foreshadows a romance with Matt.

Donna's fate was not so clear. Why did they reconsider the midlife pregnancy story if the plan was to eventually reconcile her with Michael? Near the end of Phelps' tenure as executive producer in the spring of 1996, as the magazines hinted that a long-time character would be sacrificed to the stalker, there were clues that Donna was a prime candidate. She peers prophetically through cemetery gates as Matt anguishes over Blair's casket. Later she admonishes Matt that when he comes to his senses and wants her back she will not be around. When Matt encounters her on the docks one evening she is in a deep melancholy, returning his engagement ring and lamenting that she no longer believes in fairy tales. Led away, she bobs her head and stares forebodingly into the water. Fans were initially prompted to see this as evidence that she could be guilty of the latest killing at the dock. Yet as it became obvious that she had been drugged and framed by the real culprit, the backward glance recontextualized as suicidal. However, once backstage power changed hands, it was announced that Frankie Frame, another female Baby Boomer, would be the sacrificial lamb.[1]

For all the disintegration of Donna's character, it seemed as if Phelps could have had a reifying closure in mind. There had been enough ambiguity in Matt's behavior after the split for Donna and some fans to remark that he was not yet over her and, consequently, caught in what Donna called a "rebound spiral." Michael's rejection of Donna and his pursuit of another woman were framed as callous and dismissive. Donna's blackouts during her ordeal with the stalker foretold the possible presence of an ailment that might have explained her bizarre behavior over a period of months—perhaps even predating her indiscretion with Michael. Donna could well have expired with both men realizing that she had indeed reformed and that they still cared deeply for her. Guilt might have propelled Matt into a bitter vendetta against the Hudson men, leading to his pursuit of Sofia.[2] The price of Donna's redemption and exaltation as a true heroine, however, would have been her extinction. Had this closure occurred, the story would have been counter-hegemonic in terms of the original enigmas, but not in terms of broader lifespan issues.

With the decision to eliminate Frankie, Donna is immediately vindicated through the efforts of Michael and her daughter, Vicky. Marley was absent from the canvas for some time, but the latest actor to portray the twins had just returned from her second pregnancy leave and was playing Vicky only. With her beloved daughter in town, it seemed implausible that Donna could remain in her downward spiral, and her part in the stalker story halts abruptly with no effort to follow up on the pills that had supposedly caused her blackouts. She confesses to Matt that "it never would have worked," and a dance with Michael at a party in her honor seems prophetic.

However, the newly appointed executive producer, Charlotte Savitz, had honed her skills in positions at both *DOOL* and NBC. Cyberfans suspected that her appointment was a condition of contract renewal by the network, and the Michael/Donna story did not materialize.

Meanwhile, on a rampage against his stepfather, Carl, Matt collides with Sofia's car as she careens down a slick road after discovering that her betrothed, Nick, has cheated with a young vixen in the infamous Hudson barn. Although it is clear that Nick adores Sofia, and that he dallied with the conniving Maggie only after what he thought was a breakup with Sofia, the situation is obviously meant to parallel the Michael/Donna/Matt triumvirate.

Soon fans noted that the two victims of infidelity had much in common. Efforts to sell this romance were not half-hearted as they had been with Matt and Donna. For instance, actor Crane's sculpting skills were deftly written into the story, with fair Sofia posing as his subject. This was a scenario M&D fans had envisioned for their couple. Sofia's internship also had her working for Matt at the newspaper, and the work/play context that spawned the Matt and Donna romance was replicated. Still Matt's ongoing sanctimony with respect to his stepfather caused many fans to dislike him and suspect that his vindictiveness would eventually spell trouble for the blossoming romance. Thus, the triangle differed from the Michael/Donna/Matt circumstance in that it was even-handed and the woman in the middle was portrayed as deserving. Although many in the older contingent of fans saw Matt and Sofia as nauseatingly cute and/or lacking in chemistry, the anticipated following of mostly younger enthusiasts did emerge. One reported being "delighted" that Matt finally had a "real love story."

At that point, however, Crane decided to exit the show to pursue his artistic ambitions. Initially, Matt was sent away. When a highly touted new head writer, Michael Malone, was hired, Matt was recast and brought back to pursue Lila, a slightly older Southern Belle, as Nick and Sofia's romance flourished. Lila was a younger version of classic Donna—manipulative and insecure. Yet the story stalled. Donna's once-a-week appearances during this period depicted her as a snobbish busy-body who dismissed Vicky's working-class beau. One poster, in an obvious reference to *DOOL*'s Vivian, wondered: "What next? Donna getting a European manservant to follow her around and call her Madame?"

As 1997 wore on, only one mature couple—Carl and Rachel—continued to be active, having become the beneficiaries of the midlife pregnancy story once planned for Michael and Donna. Meanwhile, Baby Boom actors and characters were falling victim to a strategic weeding process (Logan, 1998d). The Emmy-winning actor playing Sharlene, Michael's former sister-in-law, was axed first. Kale Browne, the actor portraying Michael, was then taken off contract and placed on recurring status. At about the same time, Michael's brother John abruptly departed when his portrayer refused to take a pay cut. Michael's demotion actually served to elate many of Matt and Donna's fans because scuttlebutt suggested that Donna was in line for the chopping block herself and because they had been encouraged by head writer Malone's statement that Donna might be paired with Cass (Fig. 5.6), the popular, fortysomething widower recuperating from the loss of his wife, Frankie Frame. As the two long-time characters began tenuously and lightheart-

Fig. 5.6.   Some fans insist that middle-aged Cass
is too young for Donna.

edly dating at year's end, Malone's dismissal was announced. Again rumors flared that he had not acceded to network demands. Incredibly, although many fans were excited at the prospect of a Cass/Donna romance, and although the two actors are the same age, some protested that Donna was not good enough and/or that she was too old to be Cass' paramour.

Malone was replaced by Richard Culliton, who wrote for the program in the early 1980s. No sooner did this transition occur than Donna and Cass' budding romance fizzled. Another older character, and the promised love interest for fiftyish Felicia, was eliminated. As Michael and Donna suddenly rekindled their romance, the final exit of Kale Browne was divulged. Long-time fans were livid about the wholesale eradication of Baby Boomers, but those looking forward to a Cass/Donna love story were pleased that the path would be unencumbered for them once Donna emerged from her bereavement. However, if this were the plan, there was no logic in having Michael and Donna reconcile before his departure. Such a course of action only necessitated a longer period of stasis for the surviving partner. So although many of Donna's fans remained optimistic, this researcher was apprehensive.

The new management wasted no time in making additional changes. A second Matt recast was declared. In a surprise move, the first actor to portray the twins was drafted to play Marley only, leading fans to speculate about how the program would explain identical twins who were no longer identical. Yet the most controversial announcement was that Charles Keating, the Emmy-winning and popular actor portraying Carl, had been handed a pink slip. Because it now appeared that middle-aged Cass would be romantically linked with young Lila, Carl's departure threatened to leave the show devoid of romantic heroines over the age of 35. Fans were outraged at the decision, especially at what they viewed as the presumptuousness of the program's official statement. In it the powers that be explained that Carl, "like all villains," needed a rest when, in fact, Carl had been redeemed several years earlier. Later an article in *TV Guide* (Logan, 1998d) claimed that the network, in the person of West Coast President Don Ohlmeyer, found Carl and Rachel "stomach churning" as a romantic couple. If fifty-something Carl could not be typecast a villain due to the resistance of his faithful fans, he was out.

Fans on the Internet mobilized in protest of Keating's ouster and the youthification of the show. Moreover, many were annoyed that Matt, who was suddenly preferred by innocent Sofia, seemed destined to be proved right about his stepfather. A mysterious new character, Scott, emerged as Carl's surrogate. After staging Carl's demise, he was issued malevolent orders from afar. Without having to pay the actor, the creators had managed to have their way by reinstating Carl as villain in absentia.

On Carl's departure, only six characters over 40 endured. One of the two remaining men, Grant, was a villain married to one younger woman and in love with another. The second, Cass, was poised for a romance with the thirtyish Lila, now pregnant with Matt's child, who had purloined Donna's Scarlett O'Hara mantle as well as her men. Among the women, Rachel was positioned as the matriarch figure. Fiftyish Felicia—another character some fans hoped might be paired with Cass—was installed as his comic sidekick. Etta Mae, a recent addition, circled around her own daughter and Vicky, whose children she had once cared for. Vicky needed a surrogate mother because, although Donna's love of family was incessantly invoked to convince viewers that she belonged with Michael, it was just as handily undermined to thrust Donna into her next stage of evolution.

Because Michael meets with a fatal accident after venturing out on a wintry night to retrieve his daughter, Donna believes Vicky to be responsible. Although married to Jake, Vicky had gone to a secluded cabin to deliver some vital information to her former boyfriend, Shane, at which time the two nearly made love. Thinking better of it, they headed back to town on icy roads, colliding with Michael's car. A dazed Vicky was thrown clear and collected by Donna before Michael's involvement was discovered. Then Donna orders Vicky to lie about her whereabouts because Shane had been killed in the mishap, while Vicky contends that lying is not only wrong, but unnecessary.

When Michael's car is found in a ditch, his death revealed, and the engagement ring he was saving for Donna delivered to her, something snaps. Explained by the head writer as a descent into madness due to grief, Donna's free fall leads to unforgivable acts. Vicky eventually admits the truth, and Jake splits with her for keeping it from him. As they inch toward reconciliation, Donna comes across Shane's diary, which has been altered to indicate that Shane and Vicky had made love on that fateful night. In a fit, Donna impulsively hits the gas instead of the breaks when she sees her daughter in a tete à tete with her ex-husband, Grant. However, the daughter in question turns out to be the prodigal Marley, who is only slightly injured. A subsequent hospital fire necessitates the cosmetic surgery that would alter Marley's appearance. Donna accuses Lila of the hit-and-run accident, not suspecting that she and Grant are responsible for the forged journal. "Mommie Dearest," as fans began calling her, then proceeds to brainwash a burned and bandaged Marley, who confesses to still being in love with her ex-husband, Jake. Donna wants Marley to save Jake from her treacherous twin. The catch is that Marley had once been raped by the same man she and Donna are now placing atop a pedestal—a fact conveniently forgotten in the ongoing narrative. After discovering the truth about the journal, Donna is blackmailed by and enters into a conspiracy with Grant. Donna's wits and history are swept under the rug because Lila's skill at forgery and Grant's machinations to gain custody of his son were well known to her. Twice Donna had gone to jail to protect her progeny. Now to avoid jail she would manipulate one daughter into hurting the other and sell her own grandson to the devil in the process.[3]

Reactions to Donna's metamorphosis illustrate the creators' power to pervert fans' appreciation of the show's history for demographically lucrative ends. Some preferred readers viewed the story as a homecoming for Donna, harkening back to her earliest incarnation. Asserted one fan: "I don't defend Donna's action, but this . . . has given Anna Stuart a storyline and back to the same Donna I know and love. I don't want Donna to be strong. I want Donna to be needy and insecure . . . like in her olden days with Reggie Love. . . . " Younger fans unfamiliar with this history and who were now the show's privileged audience labeled Donna as a "witch," and hegemonic representations were thereby preserved.

A second preferred reading—one in which fans refused to accept that Donna was becoming an unredeemable miscreant—exploited a polysemy that was perhaps intentional. As one perturbed poster stated:

> . . . this is really bugging me. Donna is not the villain. . . . Lila is the villain. The reason Donna is behaving the way she is two-fold: 1) She read this faked diary that makes Vicky look like she lied . . . and 2) She has not fully grieved and mourned the loss of Michael. These two things have been played out so obviously and so overtly . . . that I'm simply shocked that anyone can simply dismiss Donna as being a villain. . . .

Other posters countered that grief does not excuse criminal acts, especially against one's own children, and that Donna should not be throwing stones at anyone considering her track record. It is significant that Donna's defender in this instance was upset by the polyvalent views and declined to accept the possibility that the opposing stance was intended by the powers that be. If he were not on the Internet, he would have happily watched and believed that the writers were simply giving a good story to a favorite character. Of course the show benefits from such negotiative leniency. Although his view was counter-hegemonic in that it resisted seeing Donna as an unredeemable harridan, it also allowed creators to have their cake and eat it too.

Even an oppositional reading rejecting Donna's actions as cartoonish and out of character could not be seen as unanticipated. Creators might not have preferred such a reaction, but they must have considered it as part of a calculated risk taken in the hope that they could recoup any losses by enticing newer, younger viewers. Such readings demonstrate distance from the text and comment on the motivations of those in charge. One fan was

> appalled by the way Donna has been pared down to a cartoon. I guess those people decided that to make sure the characters stayed one-dimensional, they would get rid of one actor able to rise above lousy material (Keating) and mire another in such . . . ill-conceived material that she could not possibly get a grasp of motivation and/or subtext. . . .

In response, another long-time viewer and poster observed: "As much as I love to watch Anna Stuart, this is *too* painful. . . . Donna may be snobbish and self-centered at times, but she would *never* run down her own child with a car. . . . The woman we are watching . . . is not Donna . . . it's PodDonna!" A third fan acknowledged the *DOOL*ification of Donna and the program:

> When I stopped watching *DROOL*, part of the reason was that nothing was ever subtle. Reilly wanted to smack you in the face and drive his points home. . . . There was always the hint that TMFIC at NBC wanted *AW* to be more like *DROOL*, but I never felt it was actually happening. . . . Donna is morphing into Kristen. Wacko from the word go.

Still other cyberfans mocked the soap's tabloidization by creating *Jerry Springer* topics out of its plots: "Episode #8: 'I want the Truth.' Donna Love gets her turn to confront her 'slut-of-a-daughter' Victoria Hudson about her passionate nights with Shane Roberts. The ghost of Shane Roberts, in the form of Big Bird, settles the dispute." As distance from the text increased, objections to other fans' criticisms of Donna became more subversive and dedicated to laying blame where it belongs:

> Donna's "transformation" is . . . the responsibility of writers. . . . This blatant disrespect for one of the basic foundations of Donna's personality (her ferocious love for daughters) is an insult. . . . Writers don't have to . . . write only what fans want, but they do have to work within the integrity of established characters. If they want to create new characters, either add them . . . or leave and write for the movies.

These latter negotiations entail opposition to the creators' hegemonic preferences even if such opposition was foreseen. However, beyond the

satirical play, there appeared to be more pain than pleasure in their
protest as public fantasies sanctioning a sense of long-lived currency
were repeatedly and brutally rescinded. The upcoming examination of
the insights and interactions of avid followers of Donna in her story with
Matt acquired through e-mail correspondence contributes additional
data with which to flesh out these issues.

NOTES

1. Foreshadowing of Frankie's demise had also been apparent, so it is
    likely that the show had been debating for some time which of the two,
    Donna or Frankie, to eliminate.

2. In fact there was much foreshadowing of such a vendetta. Matt's angry
    confrontations with Nick before he ever spoke to Sofia, and Michael's
    admonishments that Matt should not seek to hurt his family, seem out
    of place outside of this context.

3. The text hints, ever so subtly, that Donna was really angry with herself.
    She compares her own tawdry misdeeds to Vicky's. She sees them as an
    impediment to true love, but still advocates lying to cover them up.
    Anyone familiar with her history knew, however, that it was always
    the coverup that caused the insurmountable problems between her and
    Michael. It was not Donna's true love who had been the latest victim of
    her duplicity. Infrequent references to Matt and Donna's romance at
    this time recalled it as a fling initiated by Donna who, they now wanted
    fans to believe, always had a penchant for shamelessly pursuing
    younger men.

6 PLAYING (WITH) FAVORITES

We have imagined what might be going on . . .
when scenes ended. . . . If only everyone
could have seen what we saw and run with it,
we would not be left to dream. . . .

As Donna and Matt's story peaked and began to unravel, another approach was added to the study's ethnographic repertoire—e-mail. Key pals and groups devoted to particular actors, characters, or couples spring out of conversations on the public forums. After taking note of some of the most avid Matt and Donna enthusiasts on various bulletin boards, I invited them to engage in small-group discussions via e-mail.

Over a period of 4 years, five e-mailers participated in the group with some degree of regularity and interactivity, if not total simultaneity. Although this would be considered too small a number for a traditional focus group, the advantages and disadvantages of virtuality, and the desire to maintain a mostly noninterventionist approach (except for the initial invitation), warranted a modification of standard. There is no way to ensure that participants will remain in an ongoing virtual group or interact with other participants for periods sufficient to designate them as official members. Moreover, their decision(s) to linger or depart can be telling and, consequently, should be as unprescribed and unhampered as possible. Therefore, this portion of the ethnography is just that—a facet of the overall, naturalistic approach. The terms associated with established focus group procedures, including the focus group designation, are not applied in the strictest of senses.

The five official members are identified with pseudonyms and demographic information as follows: (a) Sonia, a single, 19-year-old, Black Hispanic college student when her involvement began, eventually entered graduate school before losing interest in the show and the group; (b) Lisa, a married White mother in her early 40s, worked and attended college part time during her participation and slowly drifted away on account of lack of enthusiasm for the program; (c) Kathryn, a single White graduate student in her mid-20s as she joined our discussions, also withdrew gradually from our talks; (d) Rick, a single White graduate student and teacher in his mid-20s, entered our conferments relatively late, but survived until the end; and (e) Priscilla, a married White mother in her early 30s, studied part time, signed on to the group comparatively late, and then bowed out close to the end of the research period.

My position as group facilitator and participant was a delicate one. All e-mailers were fully aware of my research objective, but accepted me as an authentic fan. Consequently, they did not appear to defer to my opinion of story development and, in fact, disagreed with my perspective in many instances. The questions and probes I submitted to the group reflected my personal interest in the story and the show as well as my professional one, as the latter had been motivated by the former. Additional analysis of the intricacies involved in virtual ethnographic methodology occurs in the concluding chapter.

CONDITIONS OF LOVE

The first to participate was Sonia, who engaged this researcher in a one-on-one conversation before others joined in. She was the surprisingly young fan who claimed that she would toss away her VCR if Matt and Donna's story ended. Her first e-mail explained her devotion to the story at its height in 1994:

> Most older men/younger women pairings on TV and the movies do not appeal to me. . . . We're supposed to take it for granted that an older man and a younger woman would get together without worrying about the age gap, so a lot of these stories are not developed to the point where I can believe. . . . I see what Donna would find attractive in a younger man. He is impetuous and leads with his heart. I also understand the attraction Matt has for Donna. I would like to think that I have a few more decades left before I reach my prime. . . . Matt is not a typical twenty-something. He's the adult in the relationship a lot of the time. It's about unconditional love. It's well-written . . . funny. . . .

Sonia displays interest in the show's efforts to deal with the age difference, but also with its message that this gap can be bridged if the coupling is right. She is also annoyed by the assumption that older men and younger women need not deal with generational difference, and she reveals her need for a sense of long-lived currency when she envisions her prime in middle age. This indicates that it is possible to cultivate such an impulse in the preferred audience of young women if a program has the desire, rather than playing to a contempt for aging that some fans can and often did display. Still the latter approach facilitates the creation of audiences primed for the purchase of cosmetics and other products supposedly designed to minimize the effects of aging, so it would be the expected tactic.

Sonia was also inclined to reflect on Matt and Donna in the context of similar stories on other soaps with which she was familiar—in this case, *As the World Turns* (*ATWT*). Early in 1995, just after Michael's return was announced, she considered Donna's presumed infertility as an obstacle for her and Matt:

> It's the whole idea of making sacrifices for true love. On *ATWT*, I understand Lyla and Casey may have come to terms with the fact that they may never have their own children, and they went on to have a daughter. Larry and Susan went through the same thing.

At this juncture, Sonia's continuing optimism about Matt and Donna was based on two rare cases of older woman/younger man romances that were treated seriously well into marriage.

Sonia was incredulous as Matt and Donna's romance disintegrated. At first she was perturbed with Matt, thinking that it was his paranoia about Michael that was causing the problem long after this researcher and others in the group criticized Donna for not being honest about her true desires. Once Matt and Donna's sham marriage burst this bubble, and the implication was unavoidable that Donna had never fallen out of love with Michael, Sonia bristled: "Although I wasn't familiar with the old Donna, I assume this is her. She's fickle, spoiled, jealous, and immature. I think I'm at the point where I don't care any more what happens to them. I'll start weaning myself off the show when I get a chance." Most likely this reaction from a fan in the preferred demographic was not anticipated by the powers that be. Sonia had been attracted by the new Donna in her relationship with Matt and did not care to remain for a romance between Matt and a young woman. She no longer viewed Donna as a character who allowed her to envision her future positively. Although this turnabout was a preferred, hegemonic reading, the hope was that it would flatter younger women. For many it worked. Nevertheless, Sonia's devotion to the Matt and Donna story demonstrates that other tendencies might be cultivated. Sonia did indeed terminate her viewing after the advent of the Matt/Sofia romance. She found it excruciatingly boring and, at the same time, regarded the intermittent, screwball-style interludes between Michael and Donna as degrading. The key difference between these interludes and those that typified Matt and Donna's early story was that the former featured Donna's pursuit of Michael and his repeated rejection of her, whereas the latter were based on Donna's feigned resistance to Matt's heartfelt advances. Clearly, Sonia's identification with Donna had been intense but was no longer, and the character's regression was key.

REALITY CHECKS

The only Baby Boomer besides this researcher to have participated in these e-mail discussions was Lisa. Her devotion to the Matt and Donna story can only be characterized as fierce. However, Lisa stated forthrightly that the age difference had little to do with it. Unlike me, she was flummoxed by the notion that younger women might have had anything in particular against them, feeling that a soap opera love story should be judged on its romantic aspects. However, in considering the double standard at my request, she reasoned:

> When an older man nabs a younger woman it's . . . "ata boy." Women, on the other hand, are cradle snatchers. People in general feel that a woman is stealing a man's youth if he is much younger. . . . I also think most people . . . do not feel that a man in his forties could stay faithful to a woman in her sixties because so much emphasis is on beauty and youth in this country. We are a judgmental bunch. The pledge should end with: "With liberty to stereotype all. . . . " I believe that if you're an adulterer, you will cheat no matter what age your partner is, no matter what their appearance is.

This suggests that Matt's morality—his ability to be faithful regardless of the age difference—was, for her, a key element in the story's appeal. So indirectly the age difference may have had more to do with Lisa's appreciation of the romance than she was willing to admit. It is also evident that she saw this story and, by extension, all soap opera romances as fantasy projections that exist apart from realities such as the double standard and that they, consequently, should proceed relatively unconstrained. Indeed while not objecting to the idea of other women doing it, she insisted that *she* would not want to be with a younger man and would find Matt's doting hard to take in any case.

Still Lisa's focus on Matt continued to be evident during the romance's downward spiral. As Donna became more cavalier toward him, Lisa despaired that he could eventually snap and, perhaps, become an abuser. Although she confessed to having liked Michael and Donna previously, Lisa was adamantly against a reunion, feeling that Michael never respected Donna. Her intermittent pessimism about Matt and Donna's future was fueled by the magazine tidbits she consumed: "I read that Donna will view Michael as she did when they first got together as teenagers. Another reason I feel there is no hope." Lisa drew similar conclusions from textual omissions, such as the fact that during the holidays before Michael's arrival there were no scenes of Matt and Donna surrounded by family, exchanging gifts, or cheerfully anticipating their future—scenes that are *de rigueur* for favored couples.

Of the e-mail participants, Lisa was hit hardest by the fact and manner of their breakup. When I asked why she kept watching, she replied: "I watch because . . . I like being depressed about things that are fictional better than I like getting depressed about the reality that surrounds me." The answer lends credence to Ang's (1985) theorization of melodramatic identification, although it is not nearly the sign of pleasurable empowerment evident in the responses of Ang's subjects to Sue Ellen, the melodramatic heroine on *Dallas*. Sue Ellen's melodrama was characterized by her inability to cope with a husband who controlled, belittled, and cheated on her. Donna, in contrast, was the architect of her own agony and ceased to be the subject of any emancipatory identification for Lisa or other female fans. Neither was she remodeled in the devious but powerful image of *Dynasty*'s Alexis. Lisa's comments also speak to the issue of fantasy versus reality in the text and viewing experience—and whether romantic fiction provides a distraction from tedious domesticity and/or potentially constructive political action. These issues are elaborated later, but in this case Lisa's escape into soapland was the lesser of two evils. She was not motivated into overt political action by frustrating realities *or* fantasies. On the contrary, Lisa seemed most energized about the outside world—her family, classes, and work with the elderly—when her favorite story was going her way and, conversely, most daunted when it was not. Here she offers a heart-wrenching description of her daughter's empathy with her distress over the breakup: "My poor [daughter's name] comes running in. . . . 'It will be okay, Mom. I know it will. Please stop crying!' And people wonder why I like to be alone to watch the show."

As we see shortly, Lisa was one of two e-mailers who enjoyed creating their own stories when the given text disappointed them. Because Matt and Donna's sexual relationship had been an especially gratifying element for her, Lisa became incensed by the show's implication that it was not for Donna. "I'll never believe it wasn't real," she insisted, and sexual encounters, as opposed to relational *rapprochement*, were to become the focus of her own creative efforts. Undoubtedly, Lisa's use of the term *real* is, in this instance, a reference to the authenticity of the character interactions she had perceived within the context of fiction. However, she experienced a sudden, angry realization that she may have been supplying her own fantasies all along:

> When it comes down to it, no PTB that were in place at any time during the M&D storyline were ever really committed to it. Most of the romance . . . really only went on in our imaginations. . . . Maybe that's what separates us from non-M&D fans. We have imagined what might be going on (what we hoped would be going on) when scenes ended . . . especially when they were not seen for weeks. If only they could have seen what we saw and run with it, we would not be left to dream. . . .

This indicates a preference for publicly sanctioned fantasies over privately fabricated ones. It also demonstrates the limits of what reader-response critics refer to as *gap filling*—a process which Allen (1985, p. 78) recognized as regulated by the soap opera text and which is, therefore, only partially malleable according to viewers' "frames of reference." Lisa had come to believe that inveighing against the pressure of the given text is more demoralizing than diverting.

Indeed her resignation was somewhat more thorough than that of other e-mailers, to the point of discerning, after some initial skepticism, the spirit of Matt and Donna's story in the Matt/Sofia pairing. The text's insinuation that Matt was bolstering Sofia's ego after Nick's infidelity was clearly intended, and the fact that Lisa focused on this element demonstrates her attachment to the same aspect of Matt and Donna's tale. When others in the group, myself included, argued that, unlike Donna, Sofia had everyone's love and respect and Nick's adoration of her had never been in doubt, Lisa still clung to the hope that Matt would be rewarded with an equal relationship regardless of the woman's age.

Although Lisa had not cared for Matt before his story with Donna, despite his sanctimony, she was now more devoted to his character than to Donna's. It was as if Donna betrayed Lisa when she betrayed Matt. When Donna was suspected of being the serial killer or his future victim, Lisa stated her wish that Donna commit suicide as a consequence of her folly. When actor Crane exited the show and the Matt/Sofia story fizzled temporarily, Lisa's enthusiasm for all things *Another World* waned, and she dropped out of the group. She had begun detaching herself after Matt and Donna's split, withdrawing from the public bulletin boards and confessing to e-mailers that her "heart and happy disposition" could abide no longer. Afterward I received occasional e-mails and instant messages from her expressing disapproval of the second Matt recast, remarking that Donna had become an "asshole," and waxing nostalgic over taped highlights of Matt and Donna's romance.

At first Lisa behaved as the creators probably hoped the fans of Matt and Donna might after the split. She dismissed Donna and followed Matt's coattails into what is, for creators, demographically desirable territory. However, in that her viewership dwindled with the departure of one actor, the scuttling of Lisa's favorite romance, Matt and Donna, had taken its toll. As she lamented: "We will never see another couple like them."

FUTURE PROJECTIONS

Kathryn joined the group at the time of Matt and Donna's counterfeit wedding, although she had been a devotee of the couple on public bulletin boards. Here she grapples with my suggestion that some young women may have been resistant to Matt and Donna because of competitiveness with their mothers:

> I'm a fairly young woman (Matt and Donna got engaged on my 25th birthday—nice present!), and I haven't had any boyfriend anxiety, but then my mother looks nothing like Anna! I think the age difference plays a role in why I got into the story. Donna is much older, so I can't really compare her situations to my life. Sometimes . . . with heroines my own age, I can all too easily put myself into their shoes. It can spark a bit of "competitiveness"—like, "here's this woman . . . with this life that's much more exciting than mine. . . . " It may not make me hate them . . . but I would not adore them like I do Donna.

This response is intriguing because, although Kathryn suggests that she does not identify with Donna, her conjecture is dependent on age. Her enjoyment of Donna seemingly springs from projecting herself into an unmapped future, implying a desire for long-lived currency. However, knowing that she shared the experiences, but not the thrills, of her character contemporaries, she was apt to see them as rivals and refrain from adopting their subjectivities.

Like many fans, Kathryn resisted my suggestion that politics may have affected the show's treatment of Matt and Donna. As discussed in the next chapter, her view is associated with a narrow definition of that term. Accordingly, she reasoned that the message of the story at the point of the couple's breakup might not have been discouraging to older women:

> . . . while TPTB are wrecking a successful older woman/younger man story . . . one could look at it this way: Here's an older woman trampling on the affections of a devoted young man! Rather than saying "older women can't 'get' and keep younger men," they are actually saying that "older women can have relationships with men of any age."

Indeed the fact that Donna rejected Matt and not the other way around might have allowed some space for the previous reading. Still Michael and Matt's subsequent brushoffs, further deterioration of her character, reification of the romance as a fling initiated by Donna, and the absence of other, similar pairs would strain counter-hegemonic decoding for Kathryn and others in the long haul.

In discussing why the writers endeavored to make Matt seem the guileless cuckold in scuttling the story, which I construed as an effort to reinforce older women's traditional preference for mature men, Kathryn commented perceptively:

> Usually our society would guess that the young man would be discontented sexually with the older woman rather than the reverse. I'm not saying that this is good. . . . I don't think that most people consider who the older woman *should* prefer. . . . The approach is more along the lines of: "Be realistic. This young man is not going to stay with you." So, it's not that given a choice, an older woman should choose an older man. Rather, it's given that she doesn't really have a choice, an older woman should choose an older man.

Kathryn deftly identifies mistaken cultural assumptions about middle-aged women's sexuality. However, there are many older women who do, and did in this case, view a young man as a fallback option or consolation prize. It is the hegemonic standpoint that, in concert with prevailing myths about older women's desirability (or lack thereof), benefits mature men. As Kathryn recognizes, its consequence is to limit women's romantic choices as they age. Even if an older woman prefers a younger man, as some certainly might, she dares not risk it. She remains, therefore, in fallback position for men her age and convenient to those who are older still. In believing that older men are not the automatic, sought-after prizes for mature women, Kathryn also denaturalizes young women's attraction to mature men in her response. Many young female fans expressed a distaste for older man/younger woman duos during the study period. Yet creators do not feel obliged to cater to this particular audience bias.

Like others in the group, Kathryn was an active person who often discussed her life outside of soap opera fandom in her e-mail messages. She described the M&D story as "therapeutic"—a useful escape that allowed her to "wait out a problem-laden period." After the story's unraveling, she and Lisa were to share scenarios for how it might reignite. They also attended the show's Fan Club event in April 1996 just as Donna was pining after Matt. However, unlike Lisa, Kathryn was more dismissive of Matt for his treatment of the lonely, besieged Donna. She looked to Donna's future and hoped she would regain her independence. When I remarked that the writers were painting Michael and

Donna as a couple who would have to be together because nobody else would want them, Kathryn answered: "[W]hat makes me unhappy is that this may well be true of Donna, but not of Michael. He is still presented as Mr. Superstud."

After realizing that the writers had, in her words, "pressed reset on Matt's life," Kathryn's desire to observe and deliberate the program faded. Within weeks of Lisa and Sonia, she bowed out.

ALIENATIONS OF AFFECTION

Rick entered the group shortly before the departures of these women. His devotion to the couple emerged from a long-time dedication to its female half. His initial e-mail raved about the talent and beauty of Donna's portrayer, Anna Stuart, and half-teasingly pondered how his mother might react if he brought a woman like Donna home to dinner. His attraction to Donna was not unique among younger male fans of the program and implies that prevailing representations of older women help shape assumptions about their desirability. He also seemed especially sensitive to Michael's effect on Donna, characterizing him as "kryptonite" to an otherwise strong, spunky, and autonomous heroine.

By far Rick was the most enthusiastic and optimistic fan in the group, always ready to doubt that the worst would happen or, if it did, to claim that amelioration would ensue. When I predicted Donna's disintegration after Michael's death based on narrative trajectory and other clues, Rick replied that they would not make her into a "cardboard cutout" villain like her father, adding:

> To be a long-term villain, she would have to have axes to grind with a lot of people. . . . Right now, they are making her more sympathetic than mean-spirited, and fans would not let the writers do such a metamorphosis on Donna. Fans tend to be quiet when things are okay, but if something starts "stinking," they really start bellyaching. So many people like Donna that the writers would never want to alienate them by pulling such a switcheroo.

Up to the point of the hit-and-run accident, Rick's focus was on the expanded air time his favorite was getting. However, he soon realized that the writers had crossed a line. Although his prediction about fans was borne out, his belief in the unwillingness of the writers to estrange these and like-minded viewers was another element revealing a spurious empowerment endemic to cyberspace fandom.

Based on his own experiences, Rick questioned the basis for the creators' view that younger characters attract younger fans:

> I have *never* heard a soap viewer say that he/she didn't watch a soap
> simply because it was "all old people." Most younger people I know
> like the older characters more, since soap teens are always so un-
> real. My thirteen-year-old niece just *adores* Carl and Rachel, but
> turned her nose up at Sofia when she first came on the scene.

However, I observed numerous fans stating or, at least, implying their
distaste for older characters. Some might not articulate this preference,
but still act on it. Yet there is an element of truth to Rick's assertion.
Many teens do follow older characters, but primarily when they are in
their 20s or early 30s. Teenaged devotion to middle-aged couples is,
however, a rarity at least insofar as such couples serve as their main
inducement for watching. So the powers that be do not anticipate forfeit-
ing these fans when they expel characters over 40.

Amid Donna's downward spiral, continuing speculation that she
was in line for the chopping block, and after other group members had
thrown in the towel, Rick simultaneously reaffirmed his optimism and
disclosed his limits: "They are forever mentioning her as the 'ax victim,'
so it's a little like the boy crying wolf. And if she is finally let go, that
will be an excuse to stop watching once and for all." Inasmuch as Rick
was the only e-mailer who never had been or would be in the show's
target audience, his status as a fan who was bruised, battered, but still
game is intriguing. Although the Matt and Donna story prompted him
to wonder about dating older, there is little evidence of interpellative
involvement in his savoring of the characters or the show. The majority
of his comments pertained to the performative aspects of *AW* and other
soaps—actors' expertise, dialogue, evocation of history—as if a willing
suspension of disbelief was not essential to his enjoyment. Indeed Rick
mentioned his participation in online discussions for other TV genres.
From observing other young male fans on the Net, this concentration on
technique appears to be typical and, perhaps, linked to their posture
toward culturally masculine genres. For instance, action movies inspire
commentary of this sort from young male cyberfans exhibiting remote-
ness from the narrative and an emphasis on technique and production
processes. Because identification with one or two male protagonists is
unproblematic, it is a technique that arouses scrutiny. As soaps begin to
emphasize form over content, they are apt to collect viewers who are
loyal without being profitable.

FEASTS OF BURDEN

Priscilla joined our shrinking band of e-mailers after the other three
women opted out. She had been an ardent supporter of Matt and

Donna, but subsequently remained devoted to Donna and fervent in the hope that she would declare her freedom from Michael once and for all. Priscilla focused along with this researcher on the prospects for a Cass/Donna match, thinking that it might return Donna to the relative maturity she exhibited with Matt.

Although she was disturbed by the show's marginalization of Michael and Donna, observing that they "don't even need names" because they might "just be referred to as 'Vicky's parents,'" Priscilla stated that she would not mind it if Michael departed because it would leave the door open for Donna to dally with Cass. Yet even before Michael's exit came to fruition, she was hopeful:

> I read a spoiler last night from a *very* credible source that said Cass will have an exciting summer with a new love interest. . . . So, we must conclude that this is what we've been hoping for, unless TPTB would dare to put our sexy, charming, funny, wonderful Cass with that . . . Scarlett O'Hara wannabe. Surely, they won't go there!

Of course although it took another year of wavering, they did pair Cass with Lila. In the meantime, Priscilla's desire for Donna's maturation persisted: "Last week's Cass/Donna scenes were great!! I just hope there was no significance to the fact that he caught her encouraging Nick to lie in a relationship. . . . But it seemed to be in fun." Because the show's pursuit of this story was clearly tentative, Priscilla's wishes were intermittently quashed: "I'm so disappointed. The Cass/Donna flirtation scenes were so good. I think we got our hopes up and these awful scenes lately have dashed them. . . . " Then seesawing back to elation based on a single day's interaction, she exulted: "I'm still in shock after yesterday's show. Even we, Donna's biggest fans, couldn't have asked for anything better. The fact that he's pursuing her is beyond my wildest dreams." After Lila was positioned for a romance with Cass, Priscilla quixotically hoped for a triangle, seeing the accident as a perfect opportunity for Donna to hire him as her lawyer. However, she was disheartened when Donna did not admit her wrongdoing and continued her regression. Despite Priscilla's seemingly unflappable faith, her exit was sudden and definitive:

> Are you sitting down? I've been *AW* free for a week! I feel like I should go to a meeting and say . . . I'm a soapaholic. . . . I've decided that I've been spending too much time and energy on a show that's not worth it. . . . As a working mom and student, I need to manage my time better. I feel relieved—no setting the VCR, no more disappointment. It's like a burden's been lifted.

Priscilla's farewell, along with the similar remarks and retreats of other group members, suggest that uplifting public fantasies can quickly degrade into time-consuming, labor-intensive travails when they cease to enchant and empower. Commiserating with like-minded coworkers does not, in the long term, adequately offset this negative outcome. Upcoming discussion considers whether such disengagement can in fact be a potentially positive step or whether the loss of encouraging fantasies reduces the psychic energy with which women meet the challenges of their everyday existence.

POACHED PLEASURES

Textual poaching, as introduced by DeCerteau (1984) and elaborated by Jenkins (1992), is a form of reader negotiation in which fans can appropriate conventions, characters, situations, and/or settings of a given mass culture text in the creation of their own fiction, often incorporating counter-hegemonic traits lacking in the original. Prevalent in science fiction fan cultures such as that of *Star Trek*, *fanfic*, as it is often called, has emerged with respect to other genres, including soap opera. Because women are the primary participants in this activity even when males are targeted by the primary text, it is not surprising that a female-oriented genre such as soaps might give rise to such an enterprise. However, although the poaching of *Star Trek* developed without benefit of online fandom, the Internet has been the primary impetus and medium for dissemination of soap opera fan fiction.

Fan Web sites offer opportunities for such creative endeavors, either through special fanfic bulletin boards distinct from those earmarked for discussing the given text or by devoting their entirety to alternative storylines.[1] Episodes on the alternative *Days of Our Lives* site known as "Alt-Days" appeared to be authored solely by the site's proprietor, whereas the originator of "Folly World," an alternative site based on *Guiding Light* and inspired by the much maligned couple, Fletcher and Holly, encouraged other fans to contribute.

The fanfic boards do not reflect nearly as much participation as those devoted to the given text perhaps because the daily dose of story is satisfying enough for many viewers. Although *Star Trek* fan activities blossomed in the post-cancellation absence of the original program, soaps do not provide huge gaps ready for the filling. When events surrounding the arrest of O.J. Simpson resulted in the preemption of the daytime schedule for a couple of weeks, satirical role-playing games positing humorous exchanges between present and absent characters did develop on Usenet, demonstrating the significance of gaps in stimulating fan creativity. One such game, FAWC (Favorite *AW* Character), featured this post purportedly from Matt's ex-girlfriend Lorna to Donna:

"I just wanted to congratulate you on your recent engagement to my old friend Matt. I hope you're enjoying every inch of him. Remember, I taught him everything he knows. I guess you owe me one, huh?"

Otherwise, despite a smattering of playful satire while the program is in full force, the poached fiction that emerges on bulletin boards provided for this purpose appears to be mere elaboration of ongoing, traditional love stories. For instance, an *AW* story entitled, "Forbidden Desires: A Matt and Sofia Romance," dreamed up another encounter for the front-burner duo without indicating why the coupling of this young, unattached, beautiful, healthy pair of racially homogeneous heterosexuals was viewed as forbidden. However, based on a cursory look at the fan-authored material displayed on alternative Web sites such as "Folly World," a nostalgic longing for the reappearance of absent characters clearly emerges and is, consequently, oppositional in challenging youthification and the ousting of a program's veteran performers.

In the e-mail group, Lisa and Kathryn began exchanging "what if?" scenarios featuring Matt and Donna after the show scuttled the story. This occurred spontaneously without prompting by this investigator. Initially, their messages proposed ways to undo or undermine backstory so as to portend a rekindling of Matt and Donna's romance. Lisa suggested the following:

> I would love for Matt to hit his head and get amnesia. He would not remember he and Donna got married. Mike can yearn for her from afar and she can remain loyal to Matt from that day forward. They can have a big wedding that he can remember. At that point she could go on like nothing happened and live in wedded bliss until he remembers, say, five years from now!

Similarly, Kathryn consciously introduced the notion of sharing original fiction in positing an alternate ending to the romance:

> We've all speculated on different scenarios which would have been preferable, but I'd like to really flesh one of them out. I've never been a fan of "fanfic," but this is M&D. My current favorite idea would take place before the unfortunate events of November (obviously). . . . Something would happen to snap Donna out of "the place of Michael" and she'd plan a surprise wedding, just as Matthew was about to give up on ever getting to marry her.

To this Lisa responded that she would rather fantasize about what could happen at that point to modify the story to her taste instead of reinventing the past. Kathryn agreed that she liked doing that too, but wanted to "make use of some wasted resources," such as Matt's lovely wedding vows:

I want to see the same words, but write them into the story so that they'd be appreciated. It'd be nice to have Donna sing to M when she wasn't being desperate and to "see" the joy it would give him. Along the way, I could stick in something like Michael pining (!) and trying to stop the wedding, and Donna tells him "if we did that there'd be three very unhappy people in Bay City tomorrow."

After this exchange, Lisa attempted to remake her own fantasy as fiction:

> Donna picks up her phone and calls Matt just as he is having a flash of making love to her. He answers the phone and she does not say a word. He says, "Donna?" She says "Goodnight, Darling," and hangs up. She cries herself to sleep . . . in one of his old shirts. He tries to sleep and cannot. . . . He dresses and goes to make love to a sleeping Donna. She awakens in an . . . amorous state and says "Matthew?" He puts his finger to her lips and says "Shh!" and continues to envelop her. . . . When the deed is done . . . he gives her a sweet kiss goodbye and says softly, "I love you forever. . . . " When Donna awakens, she . . . remembers his parting words. She is relieved that the wall between them has broken down, although she knows there is no more of a chance of reconciliation than before.

This passage hints that Lisa was willing to accept a breakup as long as the romance—particularly its sexual aspect—was no longer remembered as fraudulent. She even poaches the given text's evidence of Donna's genuine love for Michael—the need to wear her true love's garb—and inserts it as a sign of Donna's enduring desire for Matt.

Not to be outdone, Kathryn articulated her own fantasy:

> Matt dropped Blair off at her apartment and drove home, if you could call it that. He was still staying in the suite at the Bayview and needed to get himself a new place. Still couldn't believe he wasn't living in Donna's suite any more. . . . He was still so furious with Donna, but she was still a huge part of him. . . . He turned the key and went inside. . . . He focused again on Blair as he changed his clothes for bed. Generous, flexible, and easy to get along with. . . . He reached into a drawer. . . . The shirt he wound up pulling out was a lovely, soft cotton one which had been a birthday present from his wife. In typical Donna fashion . . . she mentioned how "I love the way it feels against my cheek." He'd smiled, tried it on, and held her close. . . . If only his wife had really loved and wanted him. . . . Throwing the shirt aside, Matthew sat on the bed with his face in his hands. . . . The future stretched out hopelessly ahead of him. There was nothing to do but sleep and pray for dreams of past illusions.

As the prior analysis indicates, Kathryn's allegiance remained with Donna and Lisa's with Matt as the given text evolved beyond this juncture, and their fictional creations appear to coincide. Although each uses Matt's shirt as a symbol, Kathryn seeks to reassert Matt's adoration of Donna, whereas Lisa's emphasis is on Donna's residual feelings for Matt. Neither fan scripts an actual reconciliation, but in both instances the stage is set. Most important, the scenarios reestablish the romance as a legitimate and consequential event in the soap's history. If their beloved story had to be relegated to memory, they wanted it to be remembered well. In essence, they acted to rewrite the story's closure and, thereby, answer its narrative enigmas so as to preserve its counter-hegemonic tenor.

These activities are resistive, but are they empowering? Fleetingly, yes. Yet the trading of fanfic halted as the program's narrative steered Matt and Donna beyond a point of repair. Possibilities for resurrecting the romance receded as frustrations multiplied for Kathryn, Lisa, and Sonia, prompting their withdrawal.

The positive force these e-mailers brought to their exchanges when the show delighted them does not expose a need to escape the challenges of the outside world, but rather an emotional vigor with which they might confidently meet them, including those attendant to pursuits outside the home. Affirmative comments about the program were often accompanied by personal information about work, school, family, and/or other activities rendered in similarly optimistic fashion. Negative reactions, in contrast, became more succinct and less habitual before ceasing altogether.

Educated and uncommonly articulate, these e-mailers may not be representative of many soap opera cyberfans or viewers in general. Yet they appeared to be somewhat typical of Matt and Donna devotees. It is significant that the member most demographically similar to Donna was the one least forgiving of her. Lisa's sentiments indicate that she may have felt the pressures of being a middle-aged woman in a beauty- and youth-obsessed culture. The kind of devotion Matt offered Donna was, therefore, not to be rebuffed.

Rick's singular status as what he later termed a "bitter ender" is also noteworthy. Because appreciating performances from a distance rather than substantially adopting subjectivities seemed to be his pattern, the annihilation (symbolic and otherwise) of favorite stories and characters did not seem to plague him as much as others in the group.

Overt politics do not appear to correlate with devotion to this story. Of the three e-mailers who indicated their political proclivities, one—Sonia—embraced liberalism, and two—Rick and Priscilla—voiced their devotion to the conservative cause.[2] Intellectually, they all realized that the imperatives of commercial TV contributed to the marginalization and/or eradication of characters and stories they loved. However, they did not leap to discussing alternatives to such a system or the existing system in light of liberal or, more significant, conservative politics. Moreover, although the two conservatives expressed displeasure with the feminism of Hillary Clinton, they did not explicitly acknowledge the feminist implications of Donna's initial liberation or of Matt and Donna's romance at its pinnacle. Yet they loudly and repeatedly applauded these highlights and mourned their ruin. Any connection to broader political contexts, however, seemed to evade their notice.

The previous subheadings in this chapter enact additional conclusions. "Conditions of love" and "alienations of affection" are significant in that soap opera fandom is shown to be fragile when favorites are discarded. Although soaps are designed to involve fans with an array of characters and actors so that the loss of some will not disrupt their viewing habit (Allen, 1985), widespread taping and time shifting allow viewers to fast forward through stories and characters they dislike, and online fans are quite vocal about those to which/whom they give the "F-F" treatment. There is more of a gaze allowed by soap opera than Modleski (1982) and others performing textual analysis alone have surmised based on the genre's propensity for multiple protagonists. Singular identifications are no longer rare at least among cyberfans. Their love and loyalty are conditioned on certain characters/actors continuing to be played, featured, and/or involved in the story/romance they prefer. If not affection ebbs and alienation flows freely.

The "future projections" subtitle refers to the desire for that all-important sense of long-lived currency demonstrated by Sonia, Kathryn, and Priscilla—younger women who all present evidence of looking forward to a vital future through Donna. Along with a face-to-face focus group participant, mid-30s, who stated that she gravitated to the story because it communicated that she could and should be loved when she is in her 40s and beyond, these e-mailers suggest that aspirational identification linked to a sense of long-lived currency might be nurtured by cultural texts.

"Reality checks" accompany reader negotiations of the genre, although the application of the term *reality* differs depending on whether soapland or the real world is the measure. Although Lisa embraces engaging, empowering soap opera fantasies regardless of their real life verisimilitude, others check these realities and claim transgression when soap opera's hegemonic conventions are violated. The next chapter clarifies this tendency in light of relevant theory.

Although "poached pleasures" provide a temporary respite when the given text is disagreeable, they soon develop into "feasts of burden" as the possibility of widespread realization of their key ingredients fades. As Priscilla's input implies, quitting a show might be the only way to lift the time-consuming burden of taping, negotiating, and unrequitedly pining for satisfying but elusive public fantasies. Yet their previous existence offered instant stamina—a shot in the arm that allowed her and other e-mailers to greet their everyday lives with a positive energy that ongoing negotiative labor or, logically, the mere absence of viewing and interactive play are unlikely to yield. The rest of the chapter elucidates many of these arguments and assesses the broader implications of the case study.

THERE'S NO PLACE LIKE HOME

The case of Matt and Donna reaffirms that soap opera, like all commercial TV, operates primarily on tried-and-true formulae and economic imperatives. The initial plan to feature Matt and Josie and the overall tendency to downplay Matt and Donna's story were motivated by the sponsors' and network's preference for younger viewers and their unwillingness to cultivate the audience's taste for such an uncommon tale. Just after the head writer who conceived the story was ousted, executive producer Terri Guarnieri sidestepped a question about whether Matt and Donna would marry, pointedly adding that the show needed to get its "demographics up" (You'll See, 1994). Of course this means catering to a younger audience.

However, realizing that a large segment of viewers were reading Matt and Donna as a genuine couple, the powers that be initially felt secure in going ahead with the story within certain parameters. Those who simply could not buy such a romance seemed able to tolerate it as long as it retained its humorous tone and only went so far. Allen (1985) observed that such *pluri-signification* is anticipated by the soap opera text. However, with Michael's return, Donna's opportunity for a real romance outweighed the amusement provided by Matt and Donna in the eyes of many of these fans.

The liberal feminist notion that having women behind the scenes will result in texts that seriously defy patriarchal values is challenged by this study along with others (see e.g., Dow, 1996; Ferguson, 1990). Although many of those closest to the *AW* product have been women, it is established modi operandi that have governed their actions (see Caploe, 1994). Still a low-rated soap is more apt to take risks (Cantor & Cantor, 1983), and when permitted to make Matt and Donna a bona fide love story, the writing staff tackled the task with relish, snatching what they probably expected would be a short-lived opportunity.

It is also noteworthy that many Matt/Donna fans were steps ahead of the storytellers in wishing that the story would be told without regard to age. A young woman in the focus group wanted to see them have light-hearted adventures. A cyberfan was "disappointed that every obstacle those two face is related to age."

Despite that the creators did not try to bolster support for the romance, it achieved surprising popularity, with fans constantly begging to see more of them. Instead of regarding this as a happy accident and testing the waters to see how huge the story might become with greater emphasis and promotion, the show seemed to do everything it could to contain it. Creators retained a standard interpretation of the "least objectionable programming" axiom in fearing they might totally alienate dissenters if they overplayed the story. At the intersection where patriarchy meets profit, the profit motive would seem to warrant this testing of the waters despite preconceptions about what does and does not appeal to the younger set. The two would also seem to be in league when it comes to "the underlying, inherently conservative value system of the soap opera," which Allen (1985) claimed is "expressed most directly through the commercials" (p. 174). Although one can envision skin cream advertisers cringing on hearing Matt tell Donna that he loved her wrinkles, few of them would deplore a similar sentiment in a text targeted to men if the genders of the intergenerational couple were reversed. So motives other than profit operate.

In the end, those behind the scenes understood the story's appeal all too well and attempted, through sleight of hand, to turn it inside out. If an older woman wanted sexual satisfaction, sweetness, sensitivity, adventure, and optimism in her lover, she was told that she is more likely to obtain gratification from some reasonable facsimile of Michael than from a young man like Matt. She was told that fantasizing about an ex-husband returning to her side after many years and romances with younger women is her best bet—without such a miracle, she could remain lonely and bitter. As long as the packaging fits, the absurdity of the fantasy is no obstacle. Therefore, embodiment is a critical tool of ideology.

Matt and his younger love interests were subsequently granted more action and air time than Matt and Donna ever had and more than Michael and Donna would likely have garnered if a reunion story had been pursued. Moreover, their reconciliation would have minimized story options and rendered the thrift of sacrificing at least one member of the middle-aged couple all the more tantalizing. Consequently, the relative invisibility of older characters contributing to the need for this sense of long-lived currency in the first place remains. Affirmation of this affective desire is furnished sparingly to older female enthusiasts of the genre regardless of whether a younger or older man is their fantasy. Moreover, the currency granted younger women is ephemeral. It relates primarily to their romantic ambitions and can logically dissuade them from spending too many years in pursuit of nonromantic goals. It can cultivate contempt toward older women and dread of becoming one.

Begrudging women of all ages a sense of long-lived currency serves patriarchy.

For older women seeking such currency, there are few places to look. Matt does not resemble the "couch potatoes" from whom some feel the need to escape in fantasy because as even the quiet life with him seemed a rebellious adventure. Most were not fooled by the text's insinuation that Matt and Donna's sex life had been lacking, with one woman offering to "comfort Matt in his hour (or two) of need" after Donna's rejection. "I miss Donna and Matt *being* together" was another response. Although the couple was ignored for months before the breakup, there was still room to embellish their relationship with "imaginings," as Lisa put it. However, with the insistence of closure, those imaginings became ever harder to imagine.

The imperatives of commercial TV limit women's fantasies in specific ways. A story that was seen as refreshing and devoid of stereotypes in its midlife was re-created to conform to the worst of clichés. It is also significant that, in campaigning for the Matt and Donna story and against the status quo, fans did not do so proactively but reactively. Initially, they had to be offered something to rally around.

As previously noted, *AW*'s creators might not have been fully cognizant of how the transitional tidbit they first provided led to its interpretation, by some, as a romance with long-term prospects. In fact Allen (1998) acknowledged that soap opera viewers "oriented toward the text by assumptions other than those of its author . . . frequently produce aberrant readings" (p. 82). In this case the screwball comedy aspects of the story played a role in generating these assumptions.

It is possible, however, to construct an audience of young women who might readily identify with older characters and stories of this kind,[3] but it is not expedient to do so. *AW*'s much sought-after new recruits were given little reason to want Donna on the show at all. It is no wonder that attention is shifted to the younger heroines who often exhibit more maturity, dignity, independence, and currency than their older counterparts. Moreover, limiting the older woman's romantic options sends the message that youth and beauty are a woman's only currency and the products that supposedly provide them are all the more vital.

Moreover, the much-heralded soap opera form only increases the ability to reinstate the ideological status quo—nobody would have accepted this total and utter recontextualization of character and backstory in a 2-hour narrative. When I present a condensed, edited version of the story to others, they find the turnaround laughable.

The study suggests that the affirmation of long-lived currency is a right in of itself and one that precedes a feeling of power and energy in other pursuits. It is an ideological articulation of affect that is dependent on embodiment and largely denied to women even in a feminine genre such as soap opera. This cautionary tale, traveling across genres from screwball comedy, to film noir, to horror, warned women against venturing over the rainbow even in their fantasy worlds and asserted once again that there is no place like home.

In a query posted long after the tale had been forgotten in the ongoing text and featuring the subject heading, "Matt and Donna, Yuck!", an incredulous young cyberfan begged to know the reasons anyone could have liked this romance. One reply stood out, offering reminiscences of scenes and dialogue, a description of Donna's positive metamorphosis during the relationship, and a sample of the operatic duet she had composed for the pair, including the following reflection in Donna's voice:

> I knew from the moment I saw you
> that your lips were calling to me.
> Blonde, handsome and young,
> we were destined for fun.
> That was all it could ever be.
> It was only a brief flash of passion
> as swift as a bird on the wing.
> No lifetime romance,
> just a beautiful dance.
> It was a lovely fling.[4]

NOTES

1. Official soap opera Web sites and forums do not provide spaces for fan fiction. This is perhaps for the same reason that some of those devoted to other popular TV programs, such as *Star Trek* and *X-Files*, specifically prohibit such activity. They do not wish to discourage the participation of creative insiders who theoretically risk intellectual property lawsuits by exposing themselves to fans' story ideas.

2. At one point Rick and Priscilla teased me about my liberal leanings, saying they "still loved me" despite them.

3. Even the best-selling, fictional diary of thirty-something Bridget Jones (Fielding, 1996) has her "checking out everyone's ages in a desperate search for role models" (p. 62) over 40 to imbue her with the spirit of future possibility. Chagrined that her mother might be seeing a younger man, she is both repulsed at the idea of "demi-parental sex" and filled with "selfish optimism at an example of another thirty years of unbridled passion," which, she adds, is "not unrelated to frequent thoughts of Goldie Hawn and Susan Sarandon" (p. 53).

4. Printed by permission of the author, Rena Singer.

7 PLEASURE PRINCIPLES

If you want to post something political go to a political
folder. Soaps have offered an escape from everyday life
and when these issues are raised I want to scream.

ALL THE NETWORK ALLOWS

This chapter illuminates exceptions to the age/gender double standard
in soap opera, explores the multifarious influences of magazine meta-
texts and backstage personnel, and details the implications of viewer
perceptions of and attitudes toward generic verisimilitude. The ramifi-
cations of Internet gossip, "netiquette" rules, and other factors—particularly in terms of the genre's potential for motivating explicitly political
expression and/or action in and beyond online forums—are also
assessed.

Love and the "Geritol" Soap

The investigation has uncovered evidence that the strategy used by soaps
since the late 1970s to hook viewers while they are young and count on
their loyalty in later years had lost some efficacy by the late 1990s. With
competition from talk shows (Kennedy, 1993), a proliferation of channel
options, and more and more women in the workforce, the gainful viewership of daytime drama dwindled. Despite an elevation during the
1993/1994 season, which was soon to be eclipsed due to competition
from the O.J. Simpson trial the following year (Torchin, 1995), the aver-

age soap rating decreased from 5.3 for 11 soaps during 1990/1991 to 4.5 for 10 soaps during 1995/1996 (Waggett, 1997). Moreover, the appeal of daytime soaps to college students no longer translated into guaranteed patronage once these viewers completed their education (A Matter of Degrees, 1995). The formula presumably responsible for revitalizing *Days of Our Lives (DOOL)* beginning in 1994, enhancing its youthful demographics (The Other Survey, 1995), and setting the latest generic trends proved to be less dependable when it came to retention as ratings for the upstart show took a downturn in 1997. Although the program's producers seemed to attribute the slide to the departure of innovative writer James Reilly, cyberfan commentary suggests that *DOOL*'s camp tenor, perpetual triangles, and cartoonish villains had become tedious. As previously argued, postmodern detachment could be inimical to the investment necessary to hold viewers as they mature. Many online fans assert that their soap has changed for the worse, but this could be as much the result of their own evolution as the soap's. Regardless, they come to a realization that something that once catered to their sensibilities no longer does. Online messages such as "bring back so and so" reflect this disenchantment, as do the occasional criticisms unspecific to particular soaps or networks in the soap press (see Kape, 1987). Ironically, it is this yearning for the past that abetted the producers of *Another World (AW)*, allowing them to finesse their way out of the Matt/Donna romance on a wave of nostalgia for Michael and Donna. By the time fans understood that there would be no follow-through, it was too late.

Still many soaps persisted with a youth orientation as *AW*'s trajectory during the course of the decade attests. The powers behind TV soap opera maintained this conventional wisdom to the point of some of them gearing focus group research to the 18 to 34 female demographic preferentially (Kelley, 1995). In 1994, Megan McTavish (Loving Lucci, 1994), then head writer for ABC's *All My Children (AMC)*, responded to an insider's comment about the back burnering of older soap characters in an *Entertainment Weekly* article with the following claim: "The last thing baby boomers want to see on TV is women their age relegated to having coffee and discussing their teenager's problems." However, by 1997, the president of ABC Daytime, Pat Fili-Krushel (Gauging the Value, 1997), was forced to backpedal from her own harsh but honest comments alluding to the soaps' devaluation of older viewers by explaining, in a follow-up letter to the editor of *TV Guide*, that "households do not watch TV; people do." In other words, when viewers are counted individually, they are valued differently according to demographics. What Fili-Krushel deemphasized in her statement is that household ratings are dismissed by advertisers because they cannot be treated in the same discriminatory manner.

This does not mean, however, that there are no distinctions among ongoing serials in terms of the number and centrality of older characters. In fact although mincemeat was being made out of the Donna and Matt story, another soap was proceeding positively with a similar couple.

Guiding Light's (*GL's*) Matt and Vanessa paralleled Matt and Donna in time and in several other respects, not the least of which was the fact that they were never intended to be a long-term story. *GL* fans were aware that the newly conceived character of Matt was to be an eventual love interest for the young, virginal Lucy. However, to revitalize Vanessa's character and establish Matt's hunk credentials, an out-of-town fling was contrived as a prelude to his arrival in the soap's home base of Springfield. While snatching R&R on a secluded island, mid-forty-something divorcee Vanessa Chamberlain Lewis encountered the enigmatic, late twenty-something Matt Reardon, whom she later learned was the biological uncle of her adopted son, and sparks flew.

A fan following soon developed as reflected in magazine letters, online messages, and eventually, a Web site devoted to the couple, and the program altered course and pursued the unconventional romance with conviction. Although the screwball comedy antics characterizing Matt and Donna's early story were not prevalent here, polyvalent readings of "Mattessa's" relationship occurred with comparable frequency and intensity. As previously noted, many younger fans regarded it as ridiculous and hoped at first that Matt would turn to Lucy and, later, to Vanessa's daughter and, later still, to a third younger heroine. Additionally, there were older women who found Vanessa's relationship with this "boy" embarrassing although *GL* was, at the time, replete with older man/younger woman pairs. In fact once such fan bemoaned the latter reality while disparaging Matt and Vanessa, revealing a qualified rejection of the double standard that still embraced the tenet that older men are singularly desirable. Matt was considered second string— a poor substitute for any of the middle-aged males who might romance Vanessa, but were instead with younger women. When Vanessa's ex-husband, Billy, was brought back in a noncontract role, many fans jumped on the "Vanilly" bandwagon seeking nostalgic respite from "Naptessa"—the duo they thought of as boring.

Why then were Matt and Vanessa allowed to progress into marriage (see Fig. 7.1) and parenthood as an authentic, long-term couple while Matt and Donna were mercilessly invalidated? Both soaps were Procter and Gamble properties, so the explanation must lie elsewhere. CBS, often mocked as being the *Geritol* network (Secret Rules, 1994), was more apt than other networks—NBC and FOX in particular—to target its prime-time schedule to Baby Boom and older audiences in the 1990s. This tendency appeared to transfer to its daytime lineup, in which all

Fig. 7.1. *Guiding Light's* Matt and Vanessa wed and
gain legitimacy as an unlikely pair.

four soaps, including *GL*, possessed large numbers of older viewers
(Kelley, 1996).

NBC's faith in the *DOOL* formula and its ability to draw younger
viewers is also a differentiating factor. Indeed even in prime time, NBC's
"eleven commandments of programming" set the standard (Thou Shalt
Program, 1998, p. 39). Commandment #1 declares: "Tried and true =
dead and buried—not!" Commandment #8 asserts: "Everyone was
young once." Apparently, the Peacock Network was committed to the
strategies of imitating successful shows such as *DOOL* and populating
these programs with younger lead characters because it is supposedly
easier for older folks to identify with younger folks than the reverse.[1]
Although research shows that it is therapeutic for seniors to reminisce
(see Buchanan & Middleton, 1993), it is doubtful that it is emotionally
healthy for them, much less for midlifers, to restrict their intake of public
fantasies to those that situate them in the past as opposed to the present
and future. Nevertheless, NBC's devotion to these principles seemed
unshakable, and the Matt and Donna story was likely a casualty.

Textually, there was a scarcity of favored romances on *GL* when
Matt and Vanessa's began generating excitement, whereas *AW* featured
several other immensely popular couples along with Matt and Donna.
GL's Matt, unlike *AW*'s Matt, was a new addition, and younger female
fans had not yet been interpellated by a young heroine in his orbit.

Most important, once the decision was made to stick with Vanessa
and Matt, the writers endeavored to specifically refer to and discredit

the double standard responsible for much resistance to the couple. In one episode, members of the Board of Directors of Lewis Oil threaten to fire Vanessa as CEO when they discover her affair with the youthful Matt. Vanessa confronts them, politely but sternly suggesting that the older woman standing in judgment of her is jealous of her good fortune, and that one of the older males had not hesitated to pursue his happiness by marrying his much younger secretary. Despite a retort of "that's different," he and Vanessa's other accusers eventually back down. Although not all fans holding to the double standard were chastened by this episode, the efforts did at least frame the romance in terms of true love conquering an unfair prejudice and thereby rallied its fans.

GL's higher ratings and the buzz surrounding Matt and Vanessa as the soap's sole electrifying couple at their advent may have led to greater attention by the soap press than was provided to Matt and Donna. Although one of the magazines, *Soap Opera Update*, was distrusted by Matt and Vanessa enthusiasts for seeming to promote a romance between Matt and Dinah in a couple of articles (Daytime's Forbidden, 1995; GL to Pair, 1996), and although evidence indicated that GL creators were, at minimum, testing the waters for such a romance, letters to the editors of several publications were quick to label such a prospect a "stereotype" and campaign for more and better Mattessa fare (Taking it to the Matt, 1996; Viewers' Voice, 1995). When Vanessa's portrayer, Maeve Kincead, left the program temporarily, Vanessa was presumed dead, and fans of the couple feared that the show would endeavor to soften and feature the bereaved Dinah in her mother's stead (Damning Dinah, 1996). When Matt's portrayer, Kurt McKinney, mentioned that Matt should have succumbed to his desires and kissed Dinah in a particular scene, he received many letters from unhappy fans (Coons, 1995b). During Kincead's absence, executive producer Michael Laibson fielded questions about his plans for the duo, stating: "Matt will never love anyone the way he loves Vanessa" (Michael Laibson, 1996). The response sidestepped the issue of whether there would be any involvement between Matt and another woman in Vanessa's absence, but such a story did not materialize. The intensity with which fans in "Matt and Vanessa's Love Cult," as soap columnist Marlena DeLacroix (1997b, p. 37) dubbed it, supported their story to the exclusion of all others on GL may have influenced the show to keep it afloat.

Coincidentally, Jill Farren Phelps was both GL's executive producer at the time of Matt's arrival and story turnabout with Vanessa and AW's executive producer at the time of Matt and Donna's annihilation. Hence, the difference was most likely the network. However, an occasional older woman/younger man story cannot make a substantial dent in the taboo. The overwhelming message of soap opera and the culture in general is that there are, and should be, many more older man/younger woman couples than the reverse.

Serealities

The case study and other analyses herein expose a need to explore standards and mechanisms of and attitudes toward verisimilitude in soap opera. On the surface, it appears that viewers condemn unsatisfying characterization or storytelling as unrealistic while defending favored stories against similar criticism by asserting that soaps are not meant to reflect the real world. Yet this seeming contradiction is more complex because the former appears to occur more frequently when the text in question is counter-hegemonic, as with older woman/younger man couples, and the latter when it is hegemonic, as with the redemption of rapists. Additionally, as is elaborated later, the widespread feeling that soap opera viewing should be treated as an escape from the mundane affects the ability of the genre to prompt overt political action.

The issue of realism in soap opera and other feminine texts has been theorized by several scholars. Considering the tendency of postmodernity to decenter the subject, destabilize identity, and question the existence or significance of unconstructed reality in the first place, Heide (1995) disputed the claims of the serial drama *thirtysomething*'s creators that the program served as mirror of real life for its audience. However, she confirmed that her subjects' ability to identify with particular characters and situations was a key factor in their devotion to the program. D'Acci (1994) argued that, despite the prevailing judgment of 1970s feminist media research, "mainstream realist texts" such as *Cagney and Lacey* do not necessarily buttress patriarchy. Citing Kuhn's (1982) views on realism in the "new women's cinema," D'Acci concurred that such texts might actually serve to invigorate feminist identifications in terms of "whose point of view organized scenes, whose voices enunciated the plots, and whose desires motored the narratives" (p. 173). Gledhill (1988) also anticipated counter-hegemonic pleasures when female identity is found to "ground the drama in a recognizable verisimilitude" (pp. 76–77).

Longhurst's (1987) allusion to soap opera realism is based primarily on British serials such as *Coronation Street* and *Emmerdale Farm*, in which "the action concentrates on the behavior of ordinary people coping with everyday problems" (pp. 638–639). Barbatsis' (1991) analysis of soap opera form reveals that both British and America soaps communicate realism through their compositional patterns, but that British soaps contain fewer camera flourishes and other "aesthetic manipulations" and are, consequently, truer to the sensibility of social realism Longhurst (1987) described. It is perhaps this relative degree of the ordinary and everyday, socially constructed as they may be, that may not only distinguish British soaps from their American counterparts, but some American soaps from others. Soaps that consistently feature overtly supernatural plots are accordingly labeled as *unrealistic* when compared with their comparatively earthbound rivals.

However, counter-hegemonic, real-world situations such as older woman/younger man romances are atypical in soap opera and deemed unrealistic by many fans. Conversely, some highly hegemonic scenarios, such as the potential redemption of former rapist Todd Manning on *One Life to Live* (*OLTL*), are occasionally defended as appropriate to the fantastic/escapist quality of the genre—a quality cyberfans often acknowledge with the acronym IOAS (it's only a soap). When Todd began abusing his wife, Téa, an enraged fan of the couple reasoned that the show's creators were dead set against redeeming him of his past sins and protested that "so called principles and political correctness have no place in soaps."[2] Although controversial, rape redemption stories have become realistic conventions of soap opera along with distortions of nature such as resurrection and SORAS, whereas stories subverting the hegemonic ideologies of class and embodiment are considered unconventional and, consequently, unreal.

Some who thought Matt and Vanessa ridiculous wanted Matt to turn to his stepdaughter, Dinah. Many who campaigned for Matt and Donna to "get back to reality" supported ex-rapist Jake's romance with Paulina and, eventually, with the twin of his victim. The criticism that "romances like Matt and Donna's never last" appears to reference "real life," but might instead have soap reality in mind. For instance, an argument against them was that Matt had a right to children and Donna probably could not or would not have them. However, there was no reason such a story could not be penned, whether it involved a conflict over the issue of children, surrogacy, and/or new reproductive technologies. These were built-in story options with a degree of verisimilitude, unlike the many outrageous obstacles contrived to thwart idealized and perfectly matched couples. Yet the matter of children was, for some, one that made Matt and Donna seem unrealistic.

If soap reality were not the standard, romances between former in-laws or step-relations, or those featuring characters with criminal pasts, sundry marriages, and other baggage endemic to the genre, would provoke criticism to the same extent. Yet they do not. In short, *sereality*, rather than the everyday, becomes the model for verisimilitude in much fan negotiation. Hegemonic fantasies are ample and often acceptable. However, truly rebellious flights of fancy *or* relative reality remain beyond the generic pale. Under such conditions, the feminine subjectivity of soap opera sheds some of its subversive, catalytic force.

META-TEXT AND MEDIUM MATTER

I'm Not an Older Woman But I Play One on TV

The disposition of and audience support for Matt and Donna, Matt and Vanessa, and other soap opera stories may be influenced by the meta-textual discourses of soap opera journalists, actors, and others behind the scenes. For instance, *AW*'s Amy Carlson, the actor hired to play Matt's once and future sweetheart, Josie, instigated a firestorm of specu-lation and fomented fan animosity when she appeared to campaign for a Josie/Matt romance long after the decision was made to alter that plan (see *Another World* synopsis, 1995). In an NBC-sponsored chat on America Online (Amy Carlson, 1995) conducted while Donna and Matt were engaged and as Josie was embarking on a new and promising romance with the popular new character, Gary, Carlson responded to a question about whether Josie would eventually marry by tendering, quite plainly, her hope that Josie and Matt would have a huge wedding. Not only did this miff Matt/Donna fans, but the legions of Josie/Gary fans as well. Scuttlebutt circulated by e-mail and bulletin board post. Did she have a thing for Matt Crane, the actor playing Matt? Was she trying to get fans to crusade for a story she wanted? Did she know something they did not? In fact the issue of soap actors attempting to use fans to lobby for their preferred stories has been deliberated online, in magazines (Keene, 1993), and in scholarly assessments (Harrington & Bielby, 1995). The consensus is that it is an inappropriate, exploitative tactic. Matt and Donna enthusiasts were already worried about Michael's return to the canvas, and regardless of whether she was lobby-ing, Carlson's comment demoralized them further.

A more encouraging air was communicated by Kurt McKinney and Maeve Kincead, Matt and Vanessa's portrayers on *GL*, who remained positive about their characters' ongoing love story despite the former's faux pas in intimating that it might be intriguing for Matt to lapse a trifle with Vanessa's daughter. Still McKinney defended Matt's romance with Vanessa by saying that, "to have a set formula that you're supposed to marry someone from your own age group and social status and your race is old hat" (Let Love, 1996). When Kincead prepared to take her leave, she expressed sensitivity to the concerns of Matt/Vanessa fans about how her decision might affect their favorite tale (Haines, 1996) and elsewhere likened Vanessa's journey with Matt to "a battered woman escaping into the kindness and the light" after marriage to a "domineering" ex-husband (Maeve Kincead, 1997).

In stark contrast to the prior passage, the skepticism of the actors portraying Matt and Donna on *AW*, Matt Crane and Anna Stuart, was palatable. This may have been due, in part, to their knowledge of the limitations of the network and/or specific backstage bargaining. In fact sculptor Crane, whose life-sized nudes reflect a creativity unencumbered by advertiser concerns (see Allocca, 1995b), indicated that he was quite cognizant of the artistic constraints on commercial TV in an interview for a college newspaper (Ward, 1995). It is not surprising, then, that he acknowledged that the Matt/Donna story had to be "snuck in on the side" because of network resistance (Allocca, 1994b) and later, after Michael's return, that it was "nice how they've kept us together as long as they have" (Cukor, 1995, p. 25).

Stuart's comments were even more dismissive of not only the story, but the very idea. It is understandable that she would downplay the romance when the creators still planned to shift to a Matt/Josie coupling. Yet in stating that Donna, as an older woman, must realize that a young man will eventually "walk on by her" (Cukor, 1994a, p. 68), she naturalized such an outcome. Later, when the text hinted that Matt and Donna's story was phasing out, she freely admitted: "I'm not secure enough to be with a younger man" (Allocca, 1994b, p. 55). Stuart's expression of inadequacy did not embolden her contemporaries in the audience, many of whom considered themselves less attractive than she. Later Stuart implied that it might be the appeal of young males that was truly at issue: "I, for one, have never been drawn to young men. Never." She went on to explain that the story "touches on a particular fantasy" in which women dream of "somebody out there who can save me from my terrible marriage," reasoning that "if Donna can do it, so can I" (Bonderoff, 1995b, pp. 55–56). However, she failed to indicate how the elements of this fantasy differ from those attendant to any idealized soap opera love story, including and especially those in which the age disparity is reversed. Although some fans of Matt and Donna's story interpreted her comments as reassurance directed to the older looking, white-haired beau with whom she was often pictured, others were disheartened by them.

In seeming to disparage the maturity and sophistication of young men, Stuart unintentionally affirmed the hopes, expectations, and privileges of older men. The few who participated in online conversations concerning Matt/Donna or Matt/Vanessa communicated reactions similar to those of one in their ranks who could not fathom what "a woman like Donna" could possibly see in a "kid" like Matt, even as Matt seemed to display unusual maturity. When asked what specific behaviors made Matt a "kid," and what it could have been about Matt's mother, Rachel, that appealed to her much older future husband when she was a mere 25 year of age, he could only generalize that Rachel's children were "immature." A student of mine in her early 40s related an approximating experience. When she revealed to her sixty-something casual date that she was also casually dating a man of 28, he told her to "grow up."[3]

Until it was clear that the show was going to scuttle Matt and Donna, the soap press backed the couple. In fact Matt and Donna were the very first dynamic duo featured in *Soap Opera Digest*'s monthly column of the same title (Love Is a Many, 1994). The only exceptions to this rule appeared to be two male editors of *Soap Opera Now!*, Michael Kape and Don Wagner. Fans complained that Wagner could not resist editorializing about the pair in his weekly plot summaries. After *Soap Opera Now!*'s demise, when answering a fan's query in a Q/A column on the *TV Guide* website, Wagner (1998) confessed that he "detested" the story.

Kape's disapproval revealed itself in, among other things, stinging barbs:

> We always suspected Donna . . . was still carrying a torch for ex-hubby Michael. Now that he's headed back to Bay City, will the pair pick up where they left off? And . . . where will that leave poor Matthew? Do we care? Hmm. We'll have to think about that one. (Kape, 1995a, p. 4)

In another issue (Kape, 1995b), he answered a pro-Matt/Donna letter by contending that Michael and Donna's history and children were inescapable bonds. This fan followed up (Kape, 1995c) and accused Kape of a double standard, pointing to his preference for pairing *DOOL*'s Marlena with Stefano, an older, rotund arch-villain, rather than with hunky hero and fan favorite John, with whom Marlena shared a marital history and a minor child. Kape defended himself by expressing distaste for *GL*'s coupling of fiftyish Roger and twenty-something Dinah, although this was only one of many older man/younger woman couples on this soap and others at the time and one of few that was never intended to be taken seriously. He added that Marlena and Stefano provided for dramatic conflict, thereby implying that Matt and Donna did not. In an earlier issue (Coons, 1995c), however, Kale Browne (Michael) observed that Matt and Donna had an atypical romance and it might be "more interesting for them to marry and for Michael to pine from a distance." Browne echoed the mantra of fans who felt the taboo romance had inherent, rather than contrived, plot possibilities.

Browne appeared to be the only older male in the business who publicly supported the Matt/Donna pairing. Indeed Marlena DeLacroix's (1994a) column on the older woman/younger man trend quoted an unnamed male soap journalist on the subject: "Soaps do this kind of thing to give those old-bag viewers on the couch something to dream about" (p. 34). The derogatory characterization aside, is this fantasy fundamentally different from male fantasies fed by older man/younger woman media romances or, for that matter, professional football and action/adventure yarns? It might be, but only because, as turnabout, it functions as fair play.

When members of the soap press single out a story for unusually venomous ridicule, it is all the more noticeable because the general rule for soap publications is to lay off specific elements on specific shows. As I mentioned, press support for Matt and Donna ceased once it was crystal clear that the show had no intention of continuing the story. As *AW*'s cancellation woes intensified in the summer of 1998, the fact that the magazines avoided the negativity dominating *AW*'s online message boards when, undoubtedly, they were receiving volumes of similarly critical mail is noteworthy. Ultimately, it does not serve the magazines' interests to provide a platform for such audience unrest.

The study indicates that the participation of soap pundits, performers, and other insiders plays a pivotal role in multifaceted fan culture. Although average viewers who do not read soap magazines or take their fandom online might not know or care what a journalist, actor, or writer has to say about a show they happen to patronize, the ways in which these creators' public comments are interpreted and internalized by avid fans says much about the reading process as well as the depth of their investment in favorite characters, stories, and fantasies. Such discourses also illuminate the imperatives and constraints of various players in the soap opera business.

Lies, Damned Lies, and a "Cybergossip"

The emergence of online fandom has had an impact on soaps and the soap press as well as fans. The speed with which information—whether rumor or fact—is transmitted through cyberspace has perhaps undercut the ability of the magazines to offer exclusive and timely news. Additionally, because of cybergossip, the soaps have become concerned about spoilers ruining the surprise element (Does Knowing, 1995). Although the previews they provide to magazines and online sites are sketchy, cyberfans' postings and e-mails are often detailed and particular and have an impact despite the good manners of warning readers of upcoming "spoilers." Occasionally, when speculations are erroneous, but nonetheless assumed by fans to be valid, the programs can find themselves addressing the mistaken plot in some aspect.

Developments in the Matt/Donna story and its reception illustrate this latter situation. Before Michael was set to return, the program was already taking steps to unravel the Matt/Donna romance. It began when the actor playing Jake, the husband of Matt's slightly older adoptive sister, decided to take a sabbatical. Magazine stories indicated that Jake would exit Bay City and be presumed dead. As the story unfolded, Jake's secret dealings with a loan shark put him and his wife in danger.

By this time, Matt had begun to exhibit a seemingly unmotivated hatred of the man. Soon he is seen running out on Donna to comfort his distressed sister, Paulina, in a secluded cabin. In the meantime, Jake has fingered Donna as his paramour for the benefit of a hit woman who would otherwise target Paulina. He then lures Donna to a hotel room under false pretenses. Donna tells Matt about her ordeal and, in need of comfort herself, moves in for an embrace. However, Matt can only stare straight ahead and rant about how Jake is destroying Paulina.

Stoking the embers was the fact that a magazine story spotlighting the changes in store for several male characters had the head writer hinting that Matt's hatred of Jake would lead to problems with Donna (DeLosh, 1994). This seemed plausible due to Donna's previous affair with Jake. Yet Matt's animosity toward Jake did not center around Donna. Matt is holding vigil with Paulina when she receives word that Jake has died in an automobile accident. After speaking privately with the officer on the case, Matt cannot wait to tell Paulina that Jake seemed to be leaving town—and her—when the accident occurred. She then banishes him from her life, creating an unfamilial sort of tension between them and eliciting a poignant "I love you" in reply.

Before these events there was increased activity among Matt/Donna fans on the silent Internet—the e-mail grapevine. Most were sure about and saddened by the story's dissolution and speculated about Matt's future. They listed the available women on the show, including Paulina. I found this curious and didn't think it could happen until the text insinuated it. E-mailers informed me of each clue as it surfaced, and I was amazed by their skill at textual reading. Matt, they surmised, hated Jake because he was jealous. However, he was not jealous because of Donna, but rather due to subconscious romantic feelings for Paulina. Meanwhile, public postings about this possibility appeared independently.

Some fans resisted this interpretation. One noticed that Matt had taken to referring to Paulina as "my sister" instead of by her name and that this would not be happening if *AW* were going to take such a course. However, another thought this was quite consistent with the Matt/Paulina prediction—that it was only Matt trying to convince himself that a sister was all she was to him. At this juncture, a fan announced that he had called the network and asked them point blank about a Matt/Paulina romance. They responded that there would be no such story and it was only a "vicious rumor started on the Internet." It was clear that his inquiry was not the first on the matter. Of course they were referring to public postings on Usenet when the rumor actually took hold through the e-mail grapevine. Moreover, it was hardly vicious, but just one speculation among many that are bandied about in cyberspace.

Once the show anticipated Michael's arrival, Matt's hatred of Jake and devotion to Paulina subsided, convincing me, at least, that an adoptive sibling romance was never intended. However, the fear that Matt/Paulina were indeed in *AW*'s future briefly reemerged when *Soap Opera Digest* (Cybergossip, 1995) published a snippet about cybergossip ruining the fun for fans of an unnamed soap in which an explosive story was being kept under wraps. Although the piece was probably about the upcoming storyline on *General Hospital* (*GH*), in which young Robin Scorpio was to discover that her boyfriend, Stone, had AIDS and that she was HIV positive as a result, a few Matt and Donna fans still worried that it was about a Matt/Paulina romance. In fact fans of several soaps mistook the blurb to be about a storyline they had prophesied. The piece provided an opportunity for cyberfans to accuse the magazine of "sour grapes" because news and gossip now spread faster via cyberspace than through the soap press.

So did they ever really plan such a story? The answer is most likely, "no." Although some cyberfans had little objection to the scenario, observing that Matt and Paulina did not even know about one another until they were grown, the majority of reactions—"how do you spell I*cest?", "please make it go away"—would certainly have given conservative P&G pause. The misreading can perhaps be chalked up to bad writing. In their effort to set a context in which Matt might link Donna with her former lover, Jake, and suspect her of cheating, the writers simply altered Matt's character without sufficient motivation. For fans the Matt/Paulina theory supplied the absent motivation, and the rumor took off.

Evidence that the writers may have been trying to quash the rumor could be seen in an episode in which Matt first encounters Paulina after their falling out. Matt conspicuously and often refers to her as "my sister," and Donna is present to defend Matt and, later, frame the quarrel as a family feud for him and us: "Paulina's not angry at you, she's angry at Jake. He abandoned her. He died. Paulina knows that no matter how angry she gets at you, you will always be there for her. . . . She's lucky to have you, and so am I." Finally, the text pointed to another romance for the widowed Paulina, and the rumor ran out of steam.

As the investigations herein demonstrate, online fans display a sense of ownership of their favorite soaps (see Harrington & Bielby, 1995; Jenkins, 1992) by keeping abreast of shifts in the power hierarchy and reacting to alterations in story, character, cast, and tone, which depart from what they see as a soap's established tradition. Although lately soaps have challenged the dictum to its breaking point, Allen (1985) noted that incoming suds creators cannot "do violence to the expectations generated on the basis of this history without also risking the loss of that audience" (p. 50). When well-liked John Valente was abruptly replaced by Jill Farren Phelps as executive producer of *AW*, fans posted the addresses and phone numbers of both P&G and NBC on various boards and encouraged others to protest Valente's ouster as well as Phelps' planned focus on youth. In part they were forewarned by *GL* fans who were displeased with Phelps' tenure on their soap.

In another instance, cyberfans of *GL* perceived that a rape story was planned for virginal Lucy. Because they were tired of "seeing women victimized," they organized a letter-writing campaign to halt the story. The soap probably should have taken heed because ratings suffered after the rape, and one soap publication reported being barraged with negative phone calls in response to the crucial episode (The Debate Begins, 1995).

The spread of the "vicious" rumor about Matt and Paulina also suggests that cyberfandom can be a thorn in the side of commercial media. The fact that the speculation could be discussed immediately and en masse allowed it to take root and become a potential problem for producers regardless of whether the plotline was intended. As for the soap press being unnerved by cyberfans predicting and reacting to soap stories, one *GH* fan noted that the speculation about Robin and Stone was "no different from what I've always done verbally with family and friends." Yet the ease, coverage, and swiftness with which this occurs on the information superhighway does make it novel. The soaps and soap press are saddled with unanticipated glitches in their plans even when the gossip is gospel.

In response to the cyberboom, the magazines quickly adopted an "if you can't beat 'em, join 'em" attitude by establishing their own Web sites and/or loaning out journalists to participate in online chats, Q/A columns, and the like. They now routinely publish columns and articles on the activities and views of cyberfans (see Champagne, 1994; Fishman, 1996; Soaps Enter, 1996), and this is additional evidence that they have exploited the technology to their advantage.

Although the soaps deny using information gleaned from the Internet in their market research, arguing that online fans are not representative (Wendy Riche, 1997), they are believed to observe these data (Ask Logan, 1997) and perhaps float trial balloons to gauge audience tastes. The fact that fans must register and provide demographic information to participate on network and some other "official" bulletin boards evidences ongoing attempts to evaluate the resulting input accordingly. However, despite hearsay and some glaringly suspicious posts, and although soap actors have been known to lurk and/or participate online using actual or pseudo-identities, I am unaware of evidence that representatives of programs and/or their creative personnel act as shills by posing as fans and posting messages that attempt to drum up support for their efforts.[4] Yet there are other pressures exerted on cyber-space discourse.

No Politics Here

"There is no race. There are no genders. There is no age. There are no infirmities. There are only minds. Is it Utopia? No, it's the Internet." So posited a 1996 commercial for MCI. In fact the information superhigh-way has been characterized by some as a panacea providing for poten-tially empowering and open exchanges of information and opinion and by others as another communication technology to be commodified by "the powers that be" and used to protect and extend their vested inter-ests. Interrogate the Internet (1996), an interdisciplinary group examin-ing the implications of cyberspace, hesitated to automatically equate information with emancipation. They argued that, beyond the "structur-al barriers that keep many voices from being heard" (p. 125), there is a tendency for Usenet newsgroups and similar forums to "reproduce and reinforce" existing hegemonies through a "pastiche in which new media refer to old, and vice versa" (pp. 126–127). They also maintained that, although cyberspace travelers are not "collections of cultural dopes," resistance should not be merely assumed, but rather "understood as a function of reflexivity and communication" (p. 129).

Despite these warnings, many scholars studying computer-mediat-ed communication (CMC) in discussion groups equate power with free speech and free speech with lack of government regulation, ignoring the likely reproduction of hegemonic values imported from the larger cul-ture. For example, MacKinnon (1995) content analyzed newsgroup post-ings for indicators of deference to a single power such as a newsgroup moderator or author of *netiquette* guidelines as if such entities were the only sort of barrier to potentially subversive discourse. Although these researchers glossed over finer issues of cultural hegemony and opposi-tion, those who have studied the collective activities of soap opera fans have not. The social, collaborative contexts of soap opera reception and interpretation have been theorized for more than a decade. Brown (1994) studied soap opera fan friendship networks in which oral gossip allows women to attain pleasure through the construction of collective insights that acknowledge their subordination. Collectivized empowerment is also stressed by Condit (1989) in maintaining that private pleasures are ephemeral and minimal in their potential for social impact.

With cyberfandom, the opportunities for collaborative negotiation of soap texts have proliferated. Baym's (1993) study of the soap opera newsgroup on Usenet identified it as a site populated primarily by women, whereas more than 70% of Internet users overall were male (see Interrogate the Internet, 1996). Baym (1995) saw within this "primarily female subculture" (p. 142) opportunities and strategies for critical resistance and appropriation. Moreover, she argued that a certain egalitarianism prevails because "gender, race, rank . . . and other features of cultural identity are not immediately evident" (p. 140). So the sentiments of the MCI commercial are being rearticulated in much of the research. Similarly, Harrington & Bielby (1995) contended that an assumption of equality and relative anonymity results in freer participation, and they valorized cyberspace as a place where fans' "mattering maps converge" in a way that both "celebrates and validates their knowledge" (p. 168). Yet they observed that some voices emerge as more authoritative than others, just as Baym (1993) acknowledged the potential for cliquishness and tension between established participants and newcomers.

Thus far, the use of cyberspace to investigate audience readings of particular, contested popular texts has been limited. Studies of soaps and cyberfandom would appear to affirm the existence and, in fact, the extension of a "critical gaze" (Brown, 1994, p. 181) within soap opera fan collectives. However, Baym (1993) warned that "the voicing of multiple interpretations" can degenerate into flame wars, the effects of which were illustrated earlier in this inquiry.

These quandaries raise a number of other issues. Are online meanings complicit with hegemonies in operation beyond the cyberspace playground? If so which meanings gain acceptance and which are explicitly or implicitly discouraged? Does anonymity in cyberspace increase the likelihood of political debate or make it seem unwelcome, unnecessary, and/or irrelevant?

Although this investigation concurs that kibitzing on Net bulletin boards can be an empowering pleasure in and of itself, it goes beyond the previously mentioned audience studies to address these issues and examine such kibitzing in light of ideologies inherent in the producers' commercial imperatives. Next, I elaborate the politics of the public and private spheres as they relate to the text, the economics of its production, and the conundrum of public cyberspace.

That "the personal is political," soap opera researcher Charlotte Brunsdon (1995) reminded us, is "the most resonant and evocative claim of 1970s Western feminism" (pp. 58–59). This belief that "the oppression of women as women is most consensually secured" (p. 59) within the private realm has been, according to Brunsdon, a primary impetus for feminist study of media culture generally and of soap opera particularly.

Indeed Mumford (1996) theorized the genre's focus on the "private sphere of intimate relations" (p. 47), arguing this sphere's predominance even when such relations are exposed, as they often are, within public settings. She reasoned that because personal matters are made public in the soap opera narrative, one is tempted to celebrate this "destruction of the private realm" as a generic feature that is implicitly, if not explicitly, feminist. Still she recognized that this destruction tends to depoliticize personal issues, much as patriarchal ideology instructs us to relegate politics to the public arena. The peculiar tendency of popular culture is, as Mumford echoed other scholars (see Elaesser, 1987), to display politics in terms of its private, emotional impact while denying that the private sphere can be a site of political struggle. Thus, she acceded: "There are no politics—and there is therefore no feminism—in the soap opera community" (p. 66).

So the question arises, is this also true of the soap opera cyberfan community? Scholars have variously considered cyberspace in terms of conventional notions of space, with most acknowledging the novelty of accessing and interacting within a public forum from the privacy of the bedroom or study (see Beniger, 1995 ; Strate, Jacobson, & Gibson, 1995). Clearly then it has been the potential for noncommercial individuals and groups to address large numbers of people through CMC that has been most praised as an egalitarian and empowering potential of the technology. Accordingly, it is all the more crucial to determine the extent to which the depoliticization of the soap opera text—its insinuation that the personal transcends the political—is reproduced in discussion groups devoted to the genre.

The genre's focus on younger, female viewers believed to spend more on the products soap sponsors advertise says much about the inherent politics of the genre. Thus, when Matt sweetly reassured Donna that "it doesn't matter how old you are, it matters how much you love" and counseled her to "trust in the universe" just before their 2-year long romance unraveled irretrievably, the depoliticization of the private realm, and of soap opera generally, was evident and acquiesced to by many cyberfans. Even for many who embraced the story, if an older woman/younger man romance could not survive into marriage, it was merely a function of destiny and the strength of their love. It had little to do with the soap's well-publicized ultimatum to get demographics up or be canceled, the fact that a minority of fans thought that this kind of couple was nauseating, or even that the writers had stated that they were concerned about snubbing young female viewers by keeping this hunk with an older woman (Cukor, 1994a). Years later, even after the opportunities for a Donna/Michael reunion had long since past, many fans still insisted that the writers opted for a Matt/Donna breakup to facilitate such a reunion. The relative acceptance of the breakup as an artistic decision made in the service of true love, rather than one designed to flatter some fans and marginalize others in the service of profit, reveals a key impediment to meaningful empowerment.

In assessing the amenability of Internet forums to resistive fan activities, netiquette guidelines are yet to be considered. Network etiquette, or *netiquette*, evolved out of early cyberculture (see McLaughlin, Osborne, & Smith, 1995) ostensibly to compensate for the lack of nonverbal cues and preserve open and respectful communication (MacKinnon, 1995). Yet rules of netiquette have the potential to reproduce the larger culture's hegemonic inhibitions (see MacKinnon, 1995; McLaughlin et al., 1995). They can be particularized within a given site (see McLaughlin et al., 1995) and according to individualized notions of proper social behavior.[5]

Although policies prohibiting explicit advertising and the posting of private e-mail correspondence are *de rigueur* on Usenet and forbidden on sponsored boards, sanctions against "flaming" have received the greatest scholarly attention.[6] Thompsen (1995) listed more than a dozen publicized meanings of this term all dancing around the notion of intentionally heated, incessant, or rude communication. However, he observed distinctions based on whether one is sending or responding and/or being hostile or merely emotional.

Because we are considering soap opera forums, it is useful to localize our notions of flaming to the Usenet soap opera newsgroup(s), where Baym (1995) noted that the activity is strongly discouraged. Curiously, the "Frequently Asked Questions" advisory on "Inappropriate Posts" (Gibbs, 1996) periodically disseminated on these newsgroups does not explicitly define or prohibit flaming. Instead participants are warned against responding to trolls whose only purpose is to "start trouble even if the troll him/herself gets immolated in flames." Trolling then can be understood as a hostile, provocative post intended to invite flames—thereby conceived as belligerent replies—and "challenge the long-standing traditions of the group." A poster who declares that "soap operas suck" is clearly a troll, the advisory explains, before admonishing participants to resist the bait.

Such interpretations are liquid, however, and this can be appreciated when posts dealing with representational issues are scrutinized. For instance, a poster who blatantly announced his or her "Asian-American rage" in the subject heading went on to lambaste soaps for their treatment of Asians. Those who responded did so primarily to designate the poster as a troll, thereby short-circuiting any serious discussion of minority inclusion. Yet was this poster only trying to make trouble and invite flames?

Similarly, on America Online (AOL) bulletin boards, an African-American fan who repeatedly censured *AW* for its under-representation of African Americans was automatically castigated and labeled a racist. Although her language was uncompromising, she appeared to be sincere in her opinions and not merely baiting. Nonetheless, even the most courteous responses warned her that unless an overtly discriminatory message was purveyed on the show, racism was an unfair charge. Because this viewer posted on no other topic, she was considered a traitor among true fans and told to cease and desist. Occasional carefully worded posts of this ilk are tolerated as long as the poster is clearly interested in, if not favorable toward, other facets of the soap. Even so, they are few and rarely generate extensive deliberation compared with those tackling lighter topics.

In terms of age and similar issues, this loose interpretation of trolling can be even more problematic. On the Usenet soap opera newsgroup, *DOOL* fans were serious when implying, in one case, that a fortysomething character was too old to "play the young couple in love" and, in another case, that the sight of two midlifers in bed was "gross," and some did politely challenge their assumptions. Yet when an *AW* fan on AOL proclaimed that she was "going to be sick" just thinking about how "adorable young Matt" once preferred a woman "old enough to be his mother" when he is "cute enough to be with any woman he wanted," only one or two very gentle, self-effacing reproaches followed. The result is that hegemony-reinforcing messages are aired without sufficient rebuttal and their underlying politics remain unexplored. The assumption that such viewpoints are aberrations and not taken to heart can play right into the hands of those who reproduce them in the culture. Clearly, in the case of Matt and Donna, the attitude expressed by this fan was taken seriously by the powers that be. Gradually, many of the names and Internet handles of those who had been vocal devotees of the unconventional couple became less visible on several of the bulletin boards. Some retreated to e-mailing groups and conversed primarily with one another while their viewpoints faded from public display.

Similarly, when fans realized that *AW* was being pressured to emulate *DOOL*, fans vented by criticizing *DOOL* fans, with one noting how she hates "weeding through subject headings" from the *DOOL* contingent, such as "Sami is a big fat whore." Later when a troll labeled an actress who returned to *AW* after her maternity leave a "planetoid," those who seized the opportunity to begin a dialogue on the politics of appearance and gender were scolded for taking the bait.[7] "This newsgroup is about *AW*," a poster responded vehemently. "It is not about weight, it is not about gender, it is not about race. . . ."

On AOL the assumption that politics and soap opera are mutually exclusive was echoed when some posters alluded to feminism in connection with the relationship of Josie and Gary. "If you want to post something political go to a political folder," they were warned. "Soaps have offered an escape from everyday life and when these issues are raised I want to scream." Although a few begged to differ, the debate tapered off, and the use of words such as politics or feminism continued to be regarded with suspicion.

The quarrel between escape and politics is omnipresent even in the magazines. *Soap Opera Digest*'s "Love it/Hate it" feature often pits the views of fans mindful of a storyline's political implications against those preferring escapist fare assumed to be nonpolitical, but that is in many cases hegemonic. Its focus on the reconciliation story of middle-aged Eric and Stephanie on *Bold and the Beautiful* (CBS) is a case in point (Love It, 1997). One letter supports the story based on the fact that it was Eric's womanizing that caused Stephanie to become a harridan. However, a negative letter argues that seeing Stephanie squirm is far more delightful and Eric should move on to "yet another younger woman." A third magazine letter (DeLacroix, 1997a) spotlights the age-related signifi-cance of the story for many fans:

> Stephanie and Eric became engaged . . . but there was no romantic bedroom scene to go with it. It is a downright insult to women over 40 that the producers . . . will not allow our faithful Stephanie to have sex scenes. I'm sure younger people think Stephanie is a witch who should not get back her ex-husband, but there are a million middle-aged women who have been dumped for 20-year-olds! We deserve a sexy love scene.

The thirst for age-related interpellation, the assumption that younger women—and younger female fans—are the enemy, and a potential for active politicization are reflected in this letter. However, when others favor ageist stereotypes in the name of formula entertainment, marginal pleasures and their associated politics are imperiled. Thus, a subject's particular articulation to a text is paramount.

The poster warning people to seek out a political folder if they wish to discuss politics employs the term *everyday life* in a manner that is intriguing in light of its significance in the empirical analysis of lived experience advocated by the project of cultural studies. Its characteriza-tion as something that warrants escape is also pertinent to key debates concerning the implications of women's uses and interpretations of romantic, fictional texts such as soap operas and romance novels. As previously discussed, Ang (1996) took Radway's (1984) germinal study of romance novel readers to task for its theorization of the pleasure derived from reading as merely compensatory for personal satisfactions women seek, but are unable to achieve under patriarchy. She countered with the argument that the fantasies provided by such texts might be, in and of themselves, empowering. One could interpret the poster seeking refuge from politics to be buttressing Radway's claim that engagement with romantic fiction is an escape from the drudgery of everyday life or use it to illustrate Ang's contention that the fantasy play it offers is key to envisioning a better world. Either way the apparent need to contain debate to accommodate the gratifications of some fans at the expense of others is noteworthy.

Although Baym (1995) argued that sensitive personal issues are addressed on the Usenet soap opera newsgroups, this study observes pressure to avoid linking these issues to larger political contexts. This pressure mimics that which is exerted on soap opera creators who are often sanctioned against dealing with socially conscious topics to avoid offending segments of viewers (Intintoli, 1984).

This brings us to a consideration of the apparent effect of discord and the polyvalent readings it reflects. The ignominious end to Matt and Donna's story on *AW* left little room to read this relationship as authentic or viable, therefore differing attitudes toward the story's resolution reflect polyvalence rather than polysemy. Although the creators did allow (if not privilege) an interpretation of viability at points before the story's decline, realization of opposing interpretations and evaluations in cyberspace stood to diminish whatever limited and inconsequential pleasures individual readings might have bequeathed. Moreover, the pleasure of younger fans in seeing their hunk say good riddance to Donna is in conflict with that of more marginal viewers who reveled in the subversive quality of the original story.

Either way the emphasis is on defending one's interpretation or evaluation rather than relishing it. The defense cannot become too political because that too is discouraged. Accordingly, the celebratory postures of soap opera scholars who have studied face-to-face fan groups (Brown, 1994), as well as those who have assessed fans' online conversations of brief duration and/or without corresponding examination of specific content or institutional practices (Baym, 1993, 1995; Blumenthal, 1997; Harrington & Bielby, 1995), must be reconsidered.

Based on this look at the impact of netiquette rules, the larger investigation's study of conflicting readings and evaluations of soap opera stories, and the influences of the industry on soap opera discussion groups, it is plain that the vision of a public cyberspace where all are represented and the assumptions of cultural producers can be effectively redressed is perhaps too optimistic. The feminist dictum that "the personal is political" seems not to be significantly advanced by the soap opera text's reception and negotiation in these forums. The escape from the politics of everyday life sought by some viewers and catered to by creators mitigates against the satisfaction other fans derive from situating their interpretive pleasures within a more explicit political framework—such contextualization being a stimulus for social action. Netiquette rules, such as those against flaming, appear in practice to sanction the first gratification and constrain the latter. As previous analyses indicate, industry infiltration on the Net and the deference of some vocal fans to industry imperatives can also work to inhibit political activation.

Ironically, the soaps' brief hiatus during the networks' initial coverage of the O.J. Simpson affair stimulated overtly political comments related to class and consumer culture on the bulletin boards. Of all things the comments centered around the possibility of extended preemptions during the trial. One *AW* fan identifying herself as the mother of an 18-month-old baby wrote:

> I'm sure that OJ is not making the BabyButtWipesUltraDryBabyButt HuggersFeminineButtHuggersLaundryDetergentsFloorDetergents BodyDetergentsHeadacheZapperETCETC. . . . Fly off the store shelves!! Geez!! You'd think that the daytime advertisers want us to spend all our waking hours CLEANING!!! (But they DO, they DO!!!!)

A second fan remarked:

> America. Land of the free and brave . . . the rest of the world is probably having a good laugh. There is no freedom, just oppression by the rich. They own the TV and newspapers, the courts, the judges. Notice the makeup and scarf on OJ's judge. . . .

Such observations were rare and short lived in their indictment of TV's commercial imperatives and their implications for women. They demonstrate a simmering discontent that might be tapped and directed toward political mobilization if such efforts were not contraindicated by those same imperatives.

The foregoing assessments of soap opera's political agency are distinct from, yet related to, the notion that empowering fantasies about private concerns can cultivate an affective sense of long-lived currency— a feeling that one can make a difference—that is logically a prerequisite for overt political involvement. Although the currency effect would not require a conscious acknowledgment of the genre's political dimension, such acknowledgment could prompt political aspirations rendered imaginable through currency.

NOTES

1. Unfortunately, this logic does not work for many backstage personnel in Hollywood, who still find youth an advantage despite that an older person, having experienced various life stages, might be able to write

more effectively for an array of characters. The case of Riley Weston (Rich, 1998), whose writing career was imperiled when it was discovered that she was 32 and not the 19 she pretended to be, is but one testament to this.

2. The creators of *OLTL* may have found a way to redeem a rapist without violating such principles. Although it turned out to be a charade on Todd's part, it was briefly suggested that rapist Todd was not the real Todd at all, but an alternate personality who first appeared when, as a child, he was sexually abused.

3. Men's responses to other, similar cultural texts also reproduce the double standard of aging in all its imbalance. When French filmmaker Brigitte Roüan (1997) released *Post Coitum,* her autobiographical account of an older woman's adulterous affair with a young man, she was lambasted in conservative French newspapers and confronted in a restaurant by a fiftyish male who chastised her for her "disgusting" effort to "turn the world upside down." His young dinner companion later confided to Roüan that she was his mistress and that he was "outraged because it could happen to him" (Riding, 1998, p. II-15). The outrage occurred despite the fact that *Post Coitum* is, ultimately, a cautionary tale portending heartbreak for women who might imitate its heroine.

4. In early 1999, posters on several *GL* boards referred to themselves as shills and were known for responding to criticisms of the program with glowing praise. It is not possible to know whether they were, in fact, associated with the show.

5. Newsgroups overseen by a moderator are generally subject to stiffer constraints than unmoderated newsgroups. Bulletin boards on online services often enact their own, somewhat more restrictive rules. AOL's controversial "Terms of Service," for instance, clearly prohibit vulgarity and personal attacks on penalty of expulsion. Particular AOL sites, such as *Soap Opera Digest's,* also warn against straying off topic. Excessive off-topic posting of a personal nature caused friction on various bulletin boards during the study period. Various Internet sites provide separate boards for such posts and/or encourage the use of a prefix in the subject heading such as "OSP" (off subject post) or "TAN" (tangent) to indicate messages that are not strictly on point.

6. What also might be the impact of prohibitions against "spamming"—in this usage, the posting of "long and verbose" messages (see Strate, Jacobson, & Gibson, 1995, p. 12)? Is the inclination to communicate a cogent, well-supported argument squelched by such sanctions?

7. Chiming in on the weight issue, another fan declared that she watched soaps to experience a fantasy of "beautiful people," and that if she wanted to see average-looking people she would simply "look out the window." To this a poster who had previously established himself as an insider and defended the show's youthification policy commented that this fan was just the kind of viewer the network was seeking and

sarcastically asked whether she might be available for a focus group. The actor in question, Judi Evans-Luciano (Paulina), and a surprising number of fans discussed this postpartum weight gain as if it was undoubtedly a temporary state of affairs that was, consequently, excusable. The issue was written into Paulina's story, in which she became addicted to diet pills after her pregnancy. Like many women, however, Luciano had not reclaimed her pre-pregnancy figure after 2 years. In another case, *DOOL*'s plumpish Sami Brady (Alison Sweeney) developed bulimia in an apparent public service story, but the upshot was that she became the evil interloper desperately scheming to steal her slimmer sister's beau and acquiring the Internet nicknames "Spami" and "Scami" in the process.

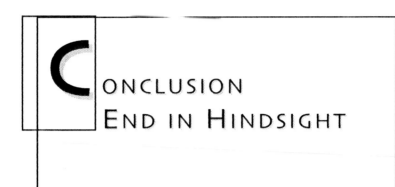

CONCLUSION
END IN HINDSIGHT

The investigation concludes with reflections on its use of virtual ethnographic methodology, a summary of its findings and contributions, and suggestions for further inquiry. Emergent theoretical understandings of gender, lifespan, romantic fantasy, and power manifested in evolutionary production practices, generic conventions, and audience readings of soap opera are advanced.

EGO TRIPPING ON THE INFORMATION SUPERHIGHWAY

The issues surrounding ethnography as an approach to audience analysis are numerous and, when virtuality enters the picture, doubly so. The ability to traverse virtual space with alacrity and, many times, anonymity can cultivate in Internet users, including ethnographers, a sense of power *sans* risk. This further complicates issues inherent in naturalistic ethnography.

Speaking on behalf of the other as an ethnographic subject has been a widely debated problematic. Although accounting for researcher subjectivities through self-reflexive scan has been offered and practiced as a remedy, Bird (1992) cautioned that such an exercise, if taken to an extreme, can "have the effect of reinscribing the voice of the ethnographer as the central focus" (p. 257) and render irrelevant ethnography's ability to encounter and observe subjects/readers empirically. Moreover, scholars such as Modleski (1986) pointed out that audience research in which the ethnographer becomes too involved with subjects and habitually raises their pleasures to the level of resistance lacks the critical distance necessary for valid inquiry. As I broke new virtual ground, wearing the hats of both fan and scholar, and walked the fine line between an impenetrably self-reflexive posture and an overly presumptuous voice of the other, I attempted to tread softly and map the pitfalls one is likely to encounter in such an approach.

First and foremost, the lack of nonverbal cues in CMC can create antipathy and misunderstanding. Smileys, emoticons, and acronyms (see Fig. C.1) are designed to help compensate for this deficiency, but are inconsistently employed and occasionally ignored. Consequently, careful and precise wording, redundancy, and clarification by example are additional recommendations for maintaining fruitful and mutually respectful online relationships.

Without such care, it is easy for straightforward claims and opinions to come off as pushy and arrogant. Moreover, because prior research (Harrington & Bielby, 1995) has shown that soap fans can gain a sense of achievement from establishing themselves as authorities in online discussion groups, creators of Web sites, and so on, the mere presence of an interloper engaged in scholarly investigation, and who might be regarded by other fans as a competing authority, can be perceived as a threat. Most cyberfans did not react to my participation in this manner and, in fact, had no difficulty maintaining and asserting their equal status as fans. However, two individuals who were active on several boards and otherwise highly invested in claiming special expertise were sensitive to my interjecting comments about the commercial goals and possibly manipulative intentions of creators. Although other *Another World* (*AW*) fans expressed disagreement with my suggestion that Donna could be

SMILEYS, EMOTICONS, AND ACRONYMS	MEANING
: -)	happy/no offense taken
: - (	sad/disappointed
; -)	winking/sarcastic
(VBG)	very big grin
(BG)	big grin
(g)	little grin
LOL	laughing out loud
ROFL	rolling on floor laughing
IMHO	in my humble/honest opinion
IOAS	it's only a soap

Fig. C.1. Smileys, Emoticons, and Acronyms

left completely without a story after Michael's reappearance—an assertion made pursuant to the fact that the meta-textual evidence I had amassed gave me reason to believe that Matt, rather than Michael and Donna, was the show's real motivation for Michael's return—these two superfans reacted to the hypothesis with outright hostility at separate times and online locations.

When such responses occurred, I took care to avoid intervening in message threads initiated by these fans and, in a couple of cases, refrained from active participation for a time. This proved to be an effective way to calm the waters and uncover the number of persons who felt the online forums were becoming far too hierarchical and cliquish. These fans, many of whom had relegated themselves to the anonymity of lurking—that is, eavesdropping without participating—bombarded me with empathetic e-mails on the few occasions that I took a "breather," providing further confirmation that cyberfan power relations can function to intimidate and, consequently, marginalize.

Although some might recommend restricting data collection to lurking so as to avoid poisoning the pool of the experiment, the data gleaned through actually but honestly interacting as both fan and scholar have been exceptionally illuminating. I could not have understood the ego involvement of super-cyberfans by observing from a distance, nor could I have realized that my role as a researcher, which I announced periodically on boards to which I was a frequent visitor, did not seem to affect my interaction with the vast majority of fans as long as my comments sprang primarily from my fandom and did not focus exclusively or stridently on stories or characters especially crucial in the study. However, anonymously eavesdropping on other sites served to corroborate data gleaned from those in which I was actively engaged.

That is not to say, however, that my natural mode of participation did not have to be adjusted. As a White, middle-class, and educated Baby Boom female, there were characters and stories I would have normally favored as a fan. Characters of my gender and generation such as Donna, Sharlene, and Frankie on *AW*; Vanessa and Holly on *Guiding Light* (*GL*); and Nora on *One Life to Live* (*OLTL*), as well as the age-related stories in which many of them were involved during the research period—Donna and Vanessa's defiant romances, Nora's perimenopause, Holly's midlife pregnancy and Downs Syndrome infant—all inspired special investment on my part. Sometimes this meant that I gave less attention to characters in their 50s as well as their fans, exposing myself to the charge that, as a Baby Boomer formerly indulged by and in consumer culture, I had not been concerned about this issue until *my* generation was affected. Indeed Banner (1992) acknowledged her sudden motivation to explore issues of gender, aging, and sexuality once she reached a certain age, perhaps neglecting the plight of those women who preceded her. If this is the case, I can only offer the defense that characters much over 50 were not generally given much story for me to analyze, and that I have attempted to make that point throughout. Still, as an investigator, my decidedly political frustration about the backstage biases contributing to the disposition of stories involving Baby Boomers tended to alter the tone and content of my posts. This caused me to question the propriety and tenor of my participation and, in some cases, temper it or back off.

Additionally, had I not engaged in posting, I might not have received telling responses to my pessimistic and, perhaps, overly politicized prognostications, including that of a woman who declared simply that she preferred to "go with the flow." This indicates, among other things, that the resistive impulses of many fans, to the extent they exist, are not typically proactive.

I must also consider the warnings of Ang (1996), who maintained that the pleasurableness subjects derive from reading cultural texts should be assessed apart from feminist and other agendas of the researcher. As a fan myself, I was not setting myself above the text and other fans in the manner Ang decried. Nor do I minimize the importance or resistive potential of pleasure. In fact, if anything, the conduct and conclusions of this investigation address the containment of pleasure articulated to counter-hegemonic elements linked to embodiment precisely because fantasy and its delights *are* construed as vital. However, there was the danger that I might dismiss pleasures I did not share and, as I already mentioned, elevate corrective measures gleaned from my scholarly, feminist arsenal. To this I must plead guilty, at least to the degree that I have labeled soap opera's privileging of some pleasures and denial of others as hegemonic. In other words, I continue to maintain that not all pleasures are created equal. Such a conclusion should answer some of the criticisms of those who dismiss ethnographic audience research as inevitably poised to discover resistance at every turn.

THE PLOT THICKENS: A SYNOPSIS

By early 1999, the older woman/younger man trend in soap opera had tapered off or evolved. The trend had inspired numerous magazine articles (Best Trend, 1995; Cukor, 1996; DeLacroix, 1994a; In Praise of Younger Men, 1995; Martin, 1996; May/December, 1997), which neglected to point out inequities between prevalent representations of older woman/younger man and older man/younger woman couplings. Matt and Vanessa of *GL* appeared to be drifting toward a potentially permanent breakup after a long period of neglect. A highly proscribed situation on NBC's *Sunset Beach*, in which married and fortyish Olivia Richards and her daughter each suspected they were pregnant by the latter's young beau, had played out, leaving Olivia on the back burner. Middle-aged Monica's adulterous affair with a younger doctor on *General Hospital* (*GH*) had come back to haunt her when he sued her for sexual harassment and then turned up dead. The romantic liaisons with fortyish newcomers developing for fiftyish divas Viki Lord (*OLTL*) and Felicia Gallant (*AW*) were resisted by those long-time fans weary of seeing veteran male performers replaced by younger hunks. Interestingly, Felicia's portrayer, Linda Dano, subsequently reprised a previous *OLTL* role, Rae Cummings, and was again paired with a forty-something suitor. Along with Erika Slezak's Viki Lord Buchanan, she went on to conventionalize the 21st-century variant of the older woman/younger man soap couple (i.e., as long as both parties are over 40, and the male half is a relatively new character with no backstory to foster his idolization by younger fans, it is not considered too risky).

In prime time, made-for-TV movies portended stiff penalties for older women venturing over that rainbow. In *Her Costly Affair*, Bonnie Bedelia plays a professor whose trysts with a young graduate student lead to stalking, while in *Lady Killer*, Judith Light is a married woman whose fling with a young charmer places her daughter in danger. In comedy, Murphy Brown's postmastectomy romance with a twenty-something admirer was engaging but short-lived, and the affair between *Ally McBeal's* thirty-something attorney, Richard, and a fifty-something judge played by Dyan Cannon was colored by postmodern dizziness and Richard's neurotic desire for female domination evidenced in, among other things, his paramour's moniker—Judge Whipper.

As for Hollywood, a spate of films pairing older leading men with much younger love interests, including *As Good as it Gets* (1997), *The Horse Whisperer* (1998), *Bulworth* (1998), *Six Days, Seven Nights* (1998), and *A Perfect Murder* (1998), inspired a series of articles in the popular press (Aging in Hollywood, 1998; Frerking, 1998; Gilchrist, 1997; Haskell, 1998; What's Age Got, 1998) and a piece on MSNBC's *Weekend Magazine* (8/15/98) questioning this practice.[1] Only Haskell's entry adopted a critical perspective, whereas the others quoted female casting directors and agents denying that their choices had anything to do with an age bias and/or naturalizing the older man/younger woman configuration. *People Magazine's* cover story (What's Age Got, 1998) generated a companion bulletin board on its online site asking visitors to propose older woman/younger man film couplings. Some took this opportunity— Demi Moore/Leonardo DiCaprio and Matt Damon/Susan Sarandon were two ideas—but others simply chastised Hollywood for age disparities of any kind. One woman admitted that as a 28-year-old she finds the thought of a romance with a man over 35 distasteful. It seemed clear that beyond the token exception, such as the older woman/younger man love story in *How Stella Got Her Groove Back* (1998), Hollywood would consider Stella's brand of romance, but not the reverse, less than tasteful for some time to come.

I had been witness to profound changes in American daytime drama during the course of the study. The decline in viewership and overall interest was evident in the elimination of E! Network's *Pure Soap* program, CNN's weekly, 15-minute interview with *Soap Opera Digest's* editor, *Entertainment Weekly's* brief but dependable "Soap Box" feature, and the weekly publications *Soap Opera Now!* and *Soap Opera Magazine.* However, *Soap Opera Digest* went from a biweekly to a weekly publication, and two new publications—*Soap Opera News* and *Soap Operas in Depth*—emerged. The former did not survive for long, but the latter hoped to beat the odds by concentrating on a single network's soaps in alternating editions—a strategy that piggybacked on each network's strategy to carry the same viewers from one of its sudsers to the next. Eventually, however, this magazine's NBC issue was dropped presumably for lack of readership.

Aaron Spelling's *Sunset Beach* premiered on NBC while ABC's *Loving*, after revamping and becoming *The City*, folded. It was replaced by a *GH* spinoff, *Port Charles*. The soap I followed and studied most vigilantly, *Another World* (*AW*), was marked for extinction by June 1999 after 35 years on the air. This occurred despite the threat of P&G pulling its advertising from the network in retaliation and the fact that *Sunset Beach* was rated even lower than *AW*.[2] Greater success in attracting teenage girls, part ownership by NBC, and overseas popularity made the Spelling creation a better candidate for retention at that juncture (Logan, 1999), although it was later axed after *Passions*, an audacious soap created by *DOOL's* former head writer, James Reilly, premiered. Fittingly, it might have been Spelling's abandonment of multigenerational prime time soaps such as *Dynasty* in preference for youth-oriented offerings such as *Beverly Hills, 90210* and *Melrose Place*, which eventually encouraged daytime to follow suit.

Even before the cancellation announcement, *AW's* ratings dipped and long-time viewers jumped ship, with some of them establishing e-mailing groups for disgruntled fans. Actor Matt Crane returned to play Matt, who was now the father of Lila's baby and competing with Cass for her affection. The triangle that might have been for Michael/Donna/Matt had been reformulated, but with Lila, Donna's younger incarnation, as the heroine. Although many fans rushed to suggest a Matt/Donna reunion on Crane's return, there was nary a word between them.[3] Donna, rarely seen, was inexplicably bound to a wheelchair. As the marginalization of veterans continued, Generation X characters became the older generation through SORAS and instant child stories and a *DOOL*ish tale about a disfigured, time-traveling villain dominated.

Once the program's demise was imminent, Matt and Donna fans continued to hope that there would be a *rapprochement* in store for their favorite couple in the closing episodes because sentiment favored the Cass and Lila match. However, Matt and Donna were the only long-term characters not paired off with someone in time for the series finale. By not allowing them to share a scene, the show denied viewers any reminder of their past and, perhaps more significant, the slightest hint of a future together. However, Donna did mention her long-dead ex-husband Michael in the last episode.

Kale Browne (ex-Michael, *AW*) had acquired a second life on ABC's *OLTL* as Sam Rappaport, whose introduction generated story for two other midlifers, Bo and Nora (see Fig. C.2). Browne's good fortune was credited to the program's new executive producer, Jill Farren Phelps, who was providing much air play to mature characters while not ignoring the younger set (Logan, 1998e). This suggests that NBC might well have been tying her hands while she was at *AW*. Long-time *OLTL* fans were still miffed, however, when several other older males were eventually dismissed from the cast in favor of younger actors, and this was to be Browne's fate three years later after Phelps moved on. Still *OLTL*, along with the other established ABC soaps *All My Children* (*AMC*) and *GH*, seemed to be devoting more attention to Baby Boom characters than soaps on the other networks, although the Baby Boomers in question

FIG. C.2.   *Another World's* ex-Michael (Kale Browne)
gets a second life on *One Life to Live*.

Attitude/Perspective	Production	Text/Metatext	Audience/Cyberfandom
Age, Beauty, & Romance	Older characters/actors minimized due to expense and preference for female viewers 18-49, 18-34, and under 18 who are potential, longtime fans. Beautiful characters in idealized romances considered vital to attracting young viewers.	Most older characters are villains, revolve around young characters, and/or placed in outrageous plots. The soap press values them in statements but, as do official websites, neglects them overall. Less attractive characters are evil and/or insecure.	Some young fans value older charaters as symbols of a show's history but tolerate their neglect. Others denigrate them online. Older fans won't blame the "system" for their devaluation. Unattractiveness impugned mostly by younger fans. Cyberfandom exposes older fans to younger fans' rejection of their pleasures.
Intergenerational Couples	Older man/young woman okay but soaps fear that the reverse alienates young female fans. They may exploit fan nostalgia by bringing back ex-beaus for for older women so young men are not "wasted" on them.	Many serious older man/young woman pairs but reverse situation rare. When reverse exists, plot evolution or closure tends to reify couple as a sham. Press favors older woman/ younger man when shows do, but not some male editors.	Older man/young woman okay but reverse unacceptable to most young female fans due to their devaluation of older women, and to older male fans and some older female fans due to their devaluation of young men. Rifts between these groups unavoidable online.
Politics & Controversy	Socially relevant stories considered too risky and alienating. If outrageous but not political, risky tales viewed as appealing to young fans. Otherwise, they are avoided or contained.	Issues of class, race, age, and gender mostly avoided in text while simmering in subtext. Rape redemption a convention; gay stories avoided or relegated to "gayness as problem." Black man/white woman romances abruptly ended. Press covers issues but won't take stand on individual cases.	Some fans reject rape redemption stories but others accept them as a "fantasy" convention. However, unconventional fantasies resisted. Gay and black man/white woman stories resisted in viewer mail but seldom online. Explicitly political discussions considered taboo in many cyberfan forums. Explicit connection to public or private politics discouraged.

Fantasy & Reality	Postmodern, "camp" tone, outrageous and/or supernatural stories considered the key to attracting the younger generation. Putting older characters in these plots makes these characters palatable to younger fans while, theoretically, satisfying older fans.	Abrupt character changes and supernatural plots with fairy tale good/evil, thick-headed, third party schemers and their foolishly trusting victims, and older characters prevalent. Rape redemption, rapid aging, and other distortions of reality also present. Press questions use of outrageous plots, but primarily when they do not work to increase viewership.	Younger fans tolerate or prefer outrageousness and conventional distortions of reality such as rapid aging, resurrection, and rape redemption, but reject realistic, unconventional plots such as older woman/younger man. Older fans tend to reject many realistically unconventional and outrageous plots, preferring comparatively "realistic" romantic stories. Relegation of older characters to "camp" gives pleasure to young fans at expense of older ones.
Nostalgia/History	Used strategically to boost ratings and facilitate story changes, especially those seen as "demographically correct." Ignored when demographically counterproductive.	Characters who are static and unchanging can result. Longtime or "supercouples" reduced to repetition or backburnered if story ideas exhausted. Older women's romantic possibilities often limited to former loves. Magazine features remind fans of backstory, especially if relevant to current story.	Being true to history sometimes means fans resist character evolution, especially if the character is not a true hero or heroine in their eyes. Longtime fans fall in line behind previously established romances that they feel represent the ideal of "one true love."

Fig. C.3. Table of Key Results

were mostly late Boomers—clustered more around 40 than 50. Anna Stuart (ex-Donna, *AW*) would enjoy villainous stints on *AMCs* beginning in 2002.

Although not suffering the "slash and burn" of their P&G sister soap on the Peacock Network, CBS' *GL* and *As the World Turns* (*ATWT*) also experienced the erasure of many veteran performers from their cast rosters. *GL* fans complained that one older heroine, Reva, was getting the lion's share of story and air time to the detriment of the handful of others still remaining on the show. Holly had been stripped of her baby and both her potential romances and temporarily "Donnafied" into a drunken criminal.[4] Matt and Vanessa fans were convinced that their favorite story was on its last legs as news circulated that Vanessa's portrayer was not re-signing her contract and would be placed on recurring status.[5] Indeed both characters were relegated to the back burner as a prelude to dismissal a year later.

The Bell family soaps on CBS, *Young and the Restless* (*Y&R*) and *Bold and the Beautiful* (*B&B*), still exhibited their trademark of desperate divas and harridans pining for former loves who had repeatedly dismissed them in preference for younger women. *B&B's* Stephanie and Eric had an uncertain future while *Y&R's* Nikki Reed still yearned for her significantly older ex-husband Victor Newman even after his multiple dalliances, including a marriage to a delicate, even younger, sightless beauty named Hope Adams.

Based on key categories derived from vetted and emergent issues pertaining to gender, lifespan, and romantic fantasy, the evolutionary tendencies of soap opera reflected in the study's analyses of production, text, and audience are summarized in Fig. C.3. Across the board, hegemonic positions clearly predominate, but they along with their nuances and theoretical implications require further explication.

The influence of the *DOOL* formula, including and especially its youth-orientation and camp, postmodern sensibility, endured into the next century despite declining numbers. No network wanted to relinquish the younger generation of viewers to its competitors, having learned lasting lessons 20 years earlier when some shows seized the day and cornered the Baby Boom influx. Consequently, that generation's children, Generation Y, Boomlets, or Echo Boomers, had emerged as the new and elusive golden egg and the postmodern, MTV world they had inhabited since birth as their nurture and their nest.

As Harms and Dickens (1996) noted, "the postmodern sensibility shifts emphasis from purposeful politics to playful gaming" (p. 212). The playful gaming does not, however, impede representations of embodiment articulated to ideologies of gender, race, age, appearance, and, to the extent that the latter is facilitated by obedient and conspicuous consumption, class. If such gaming were truly antithetical to politics and, consequently, hegemony, as some postmodern theorists assert, it would be a simple matter to substitute other, diverse embodiments at will. The study indicates, however, that this is not by any means a simple matter. As Shugart, Waggoner, and Hallstein (2001) contended, postmodern flourishes in purportedly feminist texts can be merely appropriative, serving to "reinforce a dominant, patriarchal discourse" (p. 207). Consequently, although characters' identities, personalities, and faces often metamorphose in soap opera, the changes do not often defy conventional expectations of attractiveness, sexual orientation, age, or race. The relative constancy of beauty and age appropriateness, then, magnifies their perceived significance as criteria for deciding who belongs front and center, and with whom, on the soap opera canvas. In fact it appears to be those viewers most steeped in a postmodern perspective who resist the infrequent violations of these canons more so than traditionalists. The celebration of subaltern voices supposedly privileged in postmodern culture appears not to include all the bodies from which such voices might issue. Because women's bodies are more integral to their identities, the exception of age is especially noteworthy and surprisingly underresearched.[6] Although rare attempts are made by fans and/or cultural texts to address and refute these politics, the postmodern posture frustrates these efforts, maintaining instead the preference for and illusion of apolitical escape.

Grossberg (1992) admitted that pleasure is not always positive or resistive and can, in fact, be "articulated to repressive forms of power," but he also contended that almost nothing is "unthinkable" in the vast panorama of consumer culture (1995, p. 75). This investigation appears to concur with the first claim and challenge the latter. Certain representations of embodiment are so rare as to be inconsequential. Moreover, some consumers seek more than their own, localized instances of "rearticulating such practices to escape, resist, or even oppose particular structures of power" (p. 76). To a large degree, it is the shared, public fantasy—the "in your face" communication of their transgressive hopes—that is sorely lacking and most pivotal in arousing affective involvement and a sense of long-lived currency. If *AW* rebuked Matt and Donna fans with unrelenting, public, mass-communicated impunity, these fans seek no less in desiring to reaffirm their vision.

As a scholar and a fan, I searched for the rearticulations Grossberg valorized in various nooks and crannies of fandom. Although some efforts exist and are, here and elsewhere, worthy and illuminating objects of study, they seem not to engender outpourings nearly equivalent to those inspired by the given text. In postmodern culture, images are powerful. Alternatives to prevalent representations of embodiment beg to be as widely and viscerally available. Research on *Star Trek* fandom (Penley, 1991) noted that blatant violation of the given text manifested in the homoerotic, "slash" fan fiction pairing male characters romantically is the source of true enchantment for many fans, whereas it appears to be the mass-communicated message that has an unmatched power to excite and embolden most soap opera enthusiasts. This is due, in part, to fans' desire to bear witness as expressions of their long-lived currency are preached to those not already in the choir.

It is precisely when such a subversive, public fantasy is briefly granted only to be callously revoked that this requirement is most glaring. Try as they might to compensate through various coping strategies, the absence of the fantasies fans truly desire looms. Seiter (1999) challenged researchers to do more than uncover the readings of TV texts and stories already available to viewers, but also to "investigate the unfulfilled desires of the audience." This study has moved purposefully in that direction and found that many profoundly oppositional dishes still are not on the menu or are taken off far too quickly. Remedies might include policies that discourage the use of public airwaves for discriminatory casting, programming, or storytelling practices; well-funded public media open to creating counter-hegemonic variations in popular genres such as soap opera; and a greater range and diversity of feminine texts as well as motivations for, and mechanisms of, their existence.

The prior conclusions might strike some as unjustifiably pessimistic in that I have discussed numerous resistive activities throughout the investigation. Yes, soap opera fans enjoy the genre's focus on culturally feminine domains and subjectivities. They recognize the gendered reasons their pleasures are devalued in the larger culture. Especially if they congregate online, many are aware and outwardly critical of the advertisers' enslavement to age, race, and gender discriminatory demographic imperatives. Fans are also occasionally successful in getting short-term, counter-hegemonic stories expanded once they have been given a taste of them.

However, it seems as if most fans ally themselves with particular actors, characters, and/or stories, bemoaning their marginalization or erasure above all others and remaining willing to re-enter the ranks of loyal, contented viewers should their favorite be revitalized or reinstated. Moreover, cyberfans' penchant for blaming head writers and/or executive producers for youthification and other alterations in their programs serves as a mechanism for avoiding the critical issue. Even when networks are identified as the source of the problem, it is individual executives who take the heat. Fans look to the next change in backstage personnel as a possibility for recovery despite repeated disappointments; consequently, inherent problems with the system are not the primary targets of their ire. The system remains naturalized—that is, a given beyond their perceived capacity to influence. Morley's (1980) classic study of the audience for the British TV news magazine *Nationwide* revealed a similar phenomenon, in which trade union officials who objected to what they saw as the program's anti-strike stance in relation to particular disputes still accepted the hegemonic notion that strikes in general were a destructive force in British society. So like these intermittently piqued soap opera fans, their reaction was actually more negotiated than oppositional.

Indeed media literacy education might exploit the microscopic connections consumers have with cultural texts such as soap opera to illustrate macroscopic, systemic tendencies as this research has intended to do. Motivating citizens to action based on such enlightenment remains, however, a daunting challenge.

I have also observed a divide-and-flatter strategy taking shape not only in texts, but in the online audience's polysemic or, more frequently, polyvalent readings. The analyses indicate that when women and womanly things are inherently privileged in a text or genre, the most clearly articulated divisions seem not to be between men and women, but between and among women of differing racial, class-based, and, especially in the case of soap opera, lifespan identities. In fact the fondness of many fans for catfights, especially those involving older women, is a testament to this. As anticipated by the two hypothetical cases presented at the beginning of this volume, fantasies contributing to affective currency for older women are regularly supplanted by those catering to younger women's sensibilities. However, the boost these younger women consequently derive is precarious, convincing them, perhaps, to satisfy their romantic goals in advance of other ambitions before it is too late.

I have noted the profound disappointment of more marginally situated fans when their desires are downplayed or dismissed entirely—whether by the text or other fans. The mere fact that soap opera creates an opportunity for women to gather around a common interest does not mean that they share the same desires or that all their desires are necessarily resistive. The study disputes this seemingly essentialist assumption underlying some feminist cultural studies such as Brown's (1994) analysis of face-to-face soap opera fan groups. The fantasy orientation of the genre does not appear to facilitate the truly subversive and unconventional; such pleasures are held to standards of realism not demanded of other, patently outrageous content. There does not appear to be lasting pleasure in commiseration; riding against the tide is frustrating, time-consuming, hard work. When they do occur, counter-hegemonic stories violating hegemonies of gender and lifespan are constantly threatened with elimination. As exemplified by the introduction of

Michael into the Matt and Donna story, creators exploit the nostalgic longings of long-time viewers to wean them off of demographically questionable storylines, only to leave them unsatisfied. Additionally, the age-related biases of the genre, its production, and the culture at large create a condition by which the pleasures of older viewers are denigrated by other fans. Rather than facilitating resistance, fan collectivity on the Internet can exacerbate dissatisfaction. Even when fans argue that older viewers should be valued, they do not fault the idea of valuing viewers based on demographics. The issue merely shifts from a question of age to a question of class. Older viewers should not be marginalized because, after all, they can afford more things.

There is little suggestion that soap opera, as a form, is necessarily resistive, but rather that the content communicated via the form is crucial. Mumford's (1995) theory of storyline closure is supported by audience study. In fact soap creators utilize the flexible character of both format and audience reception to facilitate their hegemonic goals. When storyline closure does occur, it tends to recast previously emancipatory elements in a hegemonic light.

However, the findings of this study do not entirely buttress political economy's critique of cultural studies. Dissection of the structures of media power is not adequate to fully understand the intricacies of media culture and hegemony. Audiences can be studied empirically without losing sight of those structures, textual power, or the specific intents of producers. Such examination can reveal when audiences, although not dopes or dupes, are apparently duped and when they are not. It can reveal the conditions under which these outcomes occur. It can discover, for instance, that the observation of some soap opera scholars (see i.e., Lovell, 1981) that the genre actually challenges monogamy and forever afters because its penchant for serial romance is far too simplistic. Long-term observation of fans clearly leads to a conclusion that the ideal of one true love is reproduced despite the relational musical chairs. Nor does the investigation suggest that soap opera and similar genres are merely compensatory or that fantasizing vicariously with popular culture is a waste of potentially subversive, political motivation. On the contrary, it claims that such fantasies can prime and energize social actors for activity in other areas of life, including politics. Hence, the content of the fantasy becomes key.

This study's assertion of the significance of romantic fantasies might read as hegemonic. After all women should want and expect to see female characters whose lives are full, exciting, eventful, and purposeful without a love interest. Certainly, as analyses in this study have shown, many fans do lobby for such women on the soaps. Yet as long as the primary storytelling vehicle on American daytime drama is romance, to single out women of a certain age for independence from love is to also relegate them to comparative invisibility. The message to female viewers is that the value of female characters—and, by extension, their own value—stems primarily from marketable attributes of youth, beauty, and reproductivity.

Moreover, the connection between the private and public spheres should not be so readily minimized. Much critical literature suggests a hard separation between public and private activity and devalues the latter by associating it with self-indulgence, avoidance of civic life, and the paralysis of left politics, as Gitlin (1983) did in the concluding remarks of his book, *Inside Prime Time*. He lamented that the private sphere is valorized in popular culture; in certain respects, he might be correct in doing so. Should we then applaud, rather than wince, as conservative pundits contemptuously describe the outpouring following the death of Princess Diana as indicative of the feminization of our culture because her popularity may have had more to do with overcoming relational turmoil than with public achievement in her own right? Should we suggest, as Barker (2000) did, that soap opera fosters a sense that relational contentment is more important than public sphere concerns? Interestingly, the doctrine of separate spheres contradicts Gitlin and Barker's claims in linking, de facto, the public, masculine sphere with individualism and self-interest and the private, feminine sphere with interdependence and commitment (Coontz, 1992). Therein lies the basis for the right's disdain of the culturally feminine even as it gives laudatory lip service to women's work as long as it is performed without monetary gain or public acknowledgment and, of course, mostly by women. As we challenge the separate spheres arrangement, might we recognize that the private domain could be a place in which motivation to public service and civic life based in interdependence, nurturance, cooperation, sensitivity, and commitment might be cultivated?

Accordingly, we might also ask whether interpersonal relationships are essentially trivial or if it is evidence of our culturally constructed, gendered power relations that some persons, but not others, have the luxury of thinking so. With the economic disadvantages that marginal groups often face, should we concern ourselves with how many friendships they have or how romantically viable they feel? Perhaps it is because prosperous men of whatever political bent benefit from a cultural double standard, sensing that their success in public pursuits will naturally facilitate their relational goals, that they are often able to focus on the public and casually devalue the private. Yet are they less concerned about relationships because they do not need or want long-term intimacy or because they are already empowered by the culture to perceive more options in this arena than women particularly as they age? The more interpersonal choices one has throughout the lifespan, the more easily she or he can take them for granted, make them a second priority, or postpone indulging them indefinitely. This is a key aspect of the politics of the private sphere, and studying which privately oriented fantasies gain public expression speaks to such politics. Most important, as Haskell (1987) observed, "the emphasis in the women's movement on domestic arrangements is not a trivializing of 'larger' issues," it is "the recognition that the essence of salvation is not in the single leap of the soul, but in the day-to-day struggle to keep the best of oneself afloat . . . " (p. 157). Confidence in meeting those everyday struggles can aid in making civic life feasible.

In maintaining that private politics do not register in fan activities, I am not claiming that the hegemonic values negotiated and often reproduced in fandom are not political but, rather, that the cultures of soap opera and cyberspace mitigate against fans recognizing them as such. As a result, efforts to steer debate in any explicitly political direction seem to halt prematurely. The myth that personal issues, including those pertaining to soap opera characters and stories, somehow remain outside the purview of true politics is perpetuated.

I realize, of course, that this investigation will be cited partly for what it has *not* done. Perhaps class has not been adequately considered as a demographic variable. The relatively unobtrusive, virtual ethnographic approach made direct questions or even allusions to class differences among fans seem out of place and potentially silencing.[7] I also neglected to extensively scrutinize fan Web sites for examples of textual poaching or in terms of their design, use of visual imagery, and other significant content.

However, what I *have* accomplished is to raise heuristically valuable, intriguing questions and offer parameters for ongoing study. Those interested in exploring class difference through virtual ethnography can refine and refocus their strategies accordingly, utilizing the findings of this effort to articulate class identity to gender and/or age. Beyond virtuality, researchers might correlate ethnographies of soap opera creation with the claims of the production and/or audience investigations performed here. Utilization and development of the concepts of affect and long-lived currency might enhance future examinations of gender, age, and empowerment in cultural texts and their interpretations and uses by fans. Pursuant to this study, future scholarship addressing questions of marginality, pleasure, and resistance might be increasingly sensitive to the subtleties and complexities involved. Does one marginal group's pleasure equal another's pain? Is the pleasure derived from resistance comparable in character and fulfillment to that obtained through preferred readings? What labor is demanded to acquire resistive pleasure?

To what extent does such labor mitigate any potentially subversive fall-out? Additionally, a multiperspectival approach based in articulation theory (Hall, 1986)—one that considers audience readings in light of specific text and/or production practices—has proved to be invaluable in addressing such issues.

Based on the present investigation, however, it is apparent that just because the age, race, gender, or class of cybersurfers might not be immediately obvious, it does not follow that there is equality of partici-pation or that such traits are not central to disagreements and differ-ences among fans on and offline, the commercial goals of the powers that be, the texts they offer, or to politics generally. Pretending otherwise does not change this. In fact it can aid those who reproduce hegemony while insisting, as AW's writers did, that it does not matter how old (or what color, gender, class, etc.) you are. The need for public fantasies that bolster the affective sense of long-lived currency underpinning political vigor is inequitably met, but the political character of that inequity remains unexposed. Ultimately, Mumford's (1995) judgment lingers: There are no politics, and there is therefore no feminism, in the soap opera cyberfan community" (p. 66). The soap opera cyberfan community appears to be no exception.

ENDNOTES

1.   This double standard can be further appreciated in reactions to the 1999 film *Entrapment*, in which Sean Connery co-stars with Catherine Zeta Jones, some 40 years his junior. On the *Siskel & Ebert* review program (May 1, 1999), *Washington Post* contributor Jane Horowitz downgraded the film due, in part, to the May/December romance. When Roger Ebert asked if she would rather do without Sean Connery, Horowitz respond-ed that she would prefer to see him coupled with Meryl Streep or some-one else closer to his age. Ebert then asked whether she could picture Streep doing stunts, as if it is not equally (or even more) preposterous to see Connery, a generation older than Streep, performing them. Horowitz answered that it was all make believe anyway, and Ebert's comments implied that older men, but not older women, should be flat-tered through and by film fantasy. On Usenet (rec.arts.movies.current-films), selective perception reigned once again when a poster responded to a comment questioning *Entrapment's* casting by alluding to *Harold and Maude*, a film in which a romance between a senior woman and a young male paramour was an issue in the story and by arguing, quite serious-ly, that because nobody objected to this and other older woman/younger man films there is clearly a double standard favoring such an arrangement.

2. Some believed that P&G's clout as a major sponsor would prevent the network from axing *AW*. Ironically, however, it was the advertisers' demographic preferences that ultimately led to *AW's* demise. Many fans planned rallies to protest *AW's* cancellation and bombarded other networks with requests to pick it up. As a fan, my reaction to the news, like that of many long-time viewers, was a mixture of nostalgic regret and shoulder-shrugging resignation, because the show had lately chosen to squander assets appealing to me and my generation.

3. Anna Stuart (Donna) seemed to modify her previous slights against the story by stating in an online interview that, although Michael was Donna's true love, she wished the romance with Matt had continued a bit longer and thought that Donna should have a fling with her ex-lover (Stuart, 1999).

4. One of Holly's suitors, ex-husband Roger, was recast and then dropped from the canvas after his long-time performer, Michael Zaslow, began exhibiting symptoms of a mysterious ailment later discovered to be ALS (Lou Gehrig's Disease). *GL* fans were angry that the show refused to write an illness into Roger's story so that the fifty-something Zaslow could return. Later, *OLTL* did just that, inviting Zaslow to resume a previous role while he was bound to a wheelchair and using a computer to deliver his lines. He succumbed to the disease late in 1998.

5. Interestingly, many fans of Matt and Vanessa increasingly attributed the marginalization of the story to rumored bad blood between Vanessa's portrayer and the program's executive producer rather than to demographic considerations.

6. For instance, a huge collection on the subject, *Writing on the Body* (Conboy, Medina, & Stanbury, 1997), barely mentions age as an aspect of gender and embodiment.

7. A fan did post a poll on an *AW* bulletin board asking participants to respond with their gender, age, and education. Of 50 respondents, only 3 had less than a baccalaureate, and a couple of these were still students. Eleven had advanced degrees, including two doctorates. Their ages ranged considerably older than those who answered a previous fan poll on the age issue alone. Although both polls were likely skewed in terms of who felt comfortable posting which information, the notion that online fans are probably better educated and, logically, of higher class strata than soap fans generally was supported (see Jacobson, 1996).

APPENDIX
METHODOLOGY

An overview of the preceding study's data sources, selection, collection, and analysis is presented here. Where germane, categories, issues, and guidelines discussed by Thomas Lindlof in his book, *Qualitative Communication Research Methods* (1995), his article with Shatzer, "Media Ethnography in Virtual Space" (1998), and other methodological literature are referenced. The primary study period, December 1993 to March 1999, covers purposeful investigation of production practices, various protocols for audience/fan inquiry, scrutiny of magazines and other meta-texts, and textual analyses of previous, recent, and ongoing soap opera narratives.

DATA SOURCES

Data sources for the production, textual, meta-textual, and audience analyses performed in this investigation included:

1. Soap Operas. The following soap operas were viewed and taped for periods not less than 1 year during the study period: *Another World* (NBC), *Days of Our Lives* (NBC), *General Hospital* (ABC), and *Guiding Light* (CBS). The following soap opera was viewed and occasionally taped for a short time during the study period: *One Life to Live* (ABC). The following soap operas were viewed by the author for periods not less than 2 years prior to the study period: *Another World*, *All My Children* (ABC), *Days of Our Lives*, *General Hospital*, and *Young and the Restless* (CBS). The viewing and taping of these soap operas formed the basis for the textual analyses performed in the study.

2.   Magazines and Meta-Textual TV. The following magazines were subscribed to and reviewed for periods not less than 1 year during the study period: *Soap Opera Update, Soap Opera Digest, Soap Opera Magazine, Soap Opera Weekly, Soap Opera Now!, TV Guide,* and *Entertainment Weekly.* When subscriptions were not in force during the study period, the magazines listed before, as well as *Soap Operas in Depth* and *Soap Opera News,* were reviewed and purchased if they contained especially relevant material. Meta-textual TV shows included, before their cancellations, E! Network's *Pure Soap* program and CNN's weekly call-in segment, *Soap Update,* featuring *Soap Opera Digest's* editor. The annual Daytime Emmy and *Soap Opera Digest* award telecasts for the years 1994 through 1998 were also taped and reviewed. Magazines and meta-textual TV shows contributed to the production investigation in terms of their coverage of commercial imperatives, demographic targeting, backstage decision making, and interviews with insiders. They provided direct meta-textual evidence and/or contributed to textual analyses in terms of their previews, plot summaries, highlights, and other commentary on soap opera stories. They contributed to the audience analyses in terms of their publication of viewer letters and comments.

3.   Official Online Sites. The following online sites established by networks, magazines, or other official entities, some of which may no longer be available or available through the service provider(s) indicated, were observed and/or engaged during the study period: *TV Guide* Online (http://www.tvguide .com/soaps), NBC Online (America Online, http://www.nbc .com), ABC Online (America Online; http://www.abc.com), CBS Online (Prodigy; http://www.cbs.com), *Soap Opera Digest* Online (America Online; http://www.soapdigest. com), Soap Opera Forum (CompuServe), TV Zone Forum (Compu Serve), Media Domain/Soaps (http://www.media-domain .com/aw; http://www.mediadomain.com/gl), TV Message Boards/Soaps (America Online), *Soap Opera Now!* Online (America Online), and TV Bulletin Boards/Soaps (Prodigy). These sites contributed variously to the production analysis in terms of their coverage of commercial imperatives, backstage decision-making, and insider chats and interviews; textual analyses in terms of previews, plot summaries, and other commentary on soap opera stories; and the audience analyses in terms of their fan bulletin boards and chats. The use of data from bulletin boards and chats was subject to institutional review.

4. Fan Web sites and Usenet Newsgroups. The following Internet Web sites and unmoderated Usenet newsgroups established and/or maintained primarily by fans were observed and/or engaged during the study period: Soap opera Usenet newsgroups (rec.arts.tv.soaps.abc; rec.arts.tv.soaps.cbs; rec.arts.tv.soaps.misc), their progenitor (rec.arts.tv.soaps), Alt.Days (http://io.com/~jlc/alt_days), Dustin's Another World Web site (http://www.soapoperafan.com/aw/), Another Take on *Another World* (http://members.aol.com/SnowDrift7), Eddie Drueding's *Another World* Home Page (http://www.igs.net/~awhp/awhp.html), Matt and Vanessa's Fan Page (http://www.geocities.com/TVCity/6574), and Folly World (http://hometown.aol.com/follyworld/). These sites and newsgroups, some of which may no longer be available, contributed variously to the textual analyses in terms of previews, historical data, plot summaries, and, in some cases, the audience analyses in terms of their express content, bulletin board discussions, fan fiction, and other forms of fan expression. The use of data from bulletin boards and chats was subject to institutional review.

5. Focus Group. A focus group comprised of fans of *Another World's* Matt and Donna story was conducted in September 1994. Participants were solicited through a newspaper ad and paid $40 each. The group's 2-hour session at Florida Atlantic University was audiotaped. The group was composed of one female in her 20s, one in her 30s, and two between 45 and 55. Because only four fans participated, data from this source have been used sparingly and corroboratively in the audience analysis portions of the study. Informed consent was given by participants in this aspect of the study, which was subject to institutional review.

6. E-mail Group. An e-mail group formed through e-mail invitation extended to bulletin board posters who had established themselves as fans of Matt and Donna's story on *Another World*. Over the group's existence, approximately 4 years, five people in addition to this researcher participated for staggered but significant periods of discussion that included at least one other member. Discussion of ongoing storylines proceeded normally. The readings, reactions, and interactions of these five fans are featured in the audience analysis contained in Chapter 6. Descriptions of the participants and caveats concerning group composition are provided at the beginning of

that chapter. Informed consent (via e-mail) was given by participants in this aspect of the study, which was subject to institutional review.

DATA SELECTION

Data selection loosely followed a snowball sampling method in which one data source—typically a human subject—leads to another (Lindlof, 1995). In virtual ethnography, such an approach is necessitated by multisited research in which an investigator might "start from a particular place, but would be encouraged to follow connections which were made meaningful from that setting" (Hine, 2000, p. 60). In this case, Usenet newsgroup posts were the initial data from which the selection of other sources—chat transcripts, magazine meta-text, online sites, and other bulletin boards—snowballed. However, because the study is multiperspectival, dealing with textual data as well as audience readings, the identification of stories, characters, and production information most relevant to its emphasis on age, gender, fantasy, and romance also served to guide data selection.

DATA COLLECTION

Virtual ethnography warrants modification of the standards and proclivities associated with the investigatory roles of participant observation, which Lindlof (1995) tailored from Gold's (1958) prototypical guidelines. With regard to several of the bulletin boards, a participant-as-observer role, in which the researcher observes while also engaged as a participant, was used. These boards are highly transient public spaces in which there is little presumption of privacy. My presence was authentic by virtue of simultaneous, nonacademic interest in the subject matter under discussion.

In addition, the slippery notion of community was at play (see Lindlof & Shatzer, 1998). Because I focused on the community of fans of American daytime soap operas—particularly of *Another World*—and the Internet generally, and not on a single online site, the associated transience, multiple identities, and various locales expanded the data array beyond that of a typical, narrowly constructed subject group. A periodic announcement of my dual role was made in the course of normal participation. I felt an ethical obligation to reveal my coexistent status as a researcher to those with whom I might be repeatedly interacting. Although none did, participants could then request that I not include their comments in the study.

With respect to bulletin boards briefly or intermittently visited, a "complete observer" (Lindlof, 1995, pp. 148–149) role was adopted. This involved lurking—that is, eavesdropping on normal conversation and behaviors without interacting. Eavesdropping by persons known and unknown is assumed by participants to occur on a regular basis.

As mentioned previously, the study's protocol(s) with respect to public bulletin boards and chats did undergo institutional review, although informed consent was neither required nor sought. There is much debate concerning the ethical and legal requirements of virtual ethnography with respect to bulletin boards and similar online communities, with Lindlof and Shatzer (1998) concurring with Waskul and Douglass (1996) that informed consent should be procured. However, I am inclined to agree with Jones' (1994) perspective that such consent is difficult, if not impossible, to obtain in the transient, anonymous, public environments of cyberspace and, especially, in terms of the broader conception of community governing this study. Moreover, the fact that the sites in which I participated are public distinguishes them from most face-to-face settings for fan/audience ethnography. In this respect, a virtual bulletin board in a public space is little different from a real bulletin board in a public space.

Increasingly, privacy is not a practical possibility or expectation in terms of most fan-oriented public bulletin boards and online chats to the extent that their interactive content is assumed to be available to anonymous insiders and outsiders as well as declared participants and is often published in the form of archives and/or files for downloading. For instance, Usenet newsgroup postings are archived by Google (http://www.groups.google.com) and can be accessed long after their origination. Similarly, many sites archive their bulletin board postings and chat transcripts for downloading. Even without such archival, messages remain on bulletin boards and are generally accessible to interested persons for extended periods after submission. As such these discourses exist as documents, much as letters to the editor submitted to and published in magazines are documents. There is even the question, then, of whether any institutional review is legally imperative when views are meant to be publicly accessible.

The legal and ethical questions are stickier, however, when it comes to the use of bulletin board posts involving sensitive, personal subject matter and/or those submitted to mailing lists or other forums in which there is the illusion of a restricted, finite audience. Such use, if possible, should be consensual.

Nevertheless, the names and/or Internet handles of posters and chat participants are not revealed in the study. Only their demographic characteristics, if known, are stated. In the case of the e-mail group, pseudonyms are employed. Additional, self-reflexive discussion of the perils and pitfalls encountered in the audience ethnography has been provided in the concluding chapter.

The study's assorted data were collected as follows:

1. Soap Operas and Meta-Textual TV. Tapes and other observations of soap opera stories and meta-textual programs airing during the study period were reviewed, annotated, edited, dated, and catalogued so they could be analyzed and linked to other data.

2. Bulletin Board Messages and Chats. Observations of recurrent tendencies in fan bulletin board conversations and chats were recorded. Hard copies were made of exemplary discourse through saving and/or downloading. Sources were noted, and each was dated and catalogued in notebooks according to relevant categories (see Data Analysis section).

3. Online Sites and Magazines. Exemplary content of online sites and magazines pertaining to production, textual, and audience analyses were saved, dated, annotated, and catalogued in notebooks according to relevant categories (see Data Analysis section).

4. Focus Group. Conversation developed out of several key questions posed to subjects: (a) whether and why they identified with Donna's character; (b) what their hopes and expectations were as to the disposition of the story; (c) whether they perceived and approved of any changes in Donna's character during the course of the story; (d) whether they had or would consider a relationship with a younger man; and (e) whether and how the story might have affected their attitudes toward aging and romantic agency. The group's 2-hour elaboration of these issues was audiotaped and summarized. Exemplary, representative statements pertaining to the concerns of the audience analysis portions of the study were transcribed and catalogued in notebooks according to relevant categories. Focus group data were used for corroborative purposes only.

5. E-mail Group. Hard copies of e-mail discussions were saved, dated, annotated, and catalogued according to relevant categories (see Data Analysis section). Exemplary, representative statements were highlighted.

DATA ANALYSIS

The data in the study were, in the initial stages, loosely categorized in terms of Glaser and Strauss' (1967) grounded theory, frequently referred to as the *constant comparative method* (see Lindlof, 1995). Grounded theory is designed to inhibit imposition of preexisting stances. Instead appropriate categories are formed and reformed as the data are encountered. These categories and their data then generate appropriate theories and concepts, whether vetted or newly emergent.

The study's implementation of grounded theory is consistent with its effort to refrain from adopting an *a priori* angle derived from political economy, British cultural studies, or U.S. Cultural Studies preferentially. Still a perspective based in critical media studies' customary foci was assumed. Because the multiperspectival approach requires primary and/or secondary data related to production, text, and audience to be amassed, the biases inherent in limiting inspection to only one or two pieces of the puzzle were minimized with its use. Moreover, employing multiple methods of audience analysis served as an additional hedge against prejudgment. With a body of variously sourced, interrelated data, answers to characteristic questions of hegemony and resistance cultivated organically.

However, as Jankowski and Wester (1991) noted: "Data of and by themselves . . . cannot generate theory. It is only through intervention by a researcher, operating within a theoretical perspective, that data can be examined and used to develop theory" (p. 69). Pivotal issues pertaining to the study's subject matter could not be ignored as the data were collected. In this case, hegemonic power relations of gender, lifespan, and romantic fantasy such as the gender/age double standard were key. Inasmuch as data were not selected in terms of any anticipated result, an emphasis on such general foci was reasonable. Thereafter, encoding/decoding positions, articulation, interpellation, storyline closure and enigmas, affect, and the emergent notion of currency were affiliated with notions of hegemony and/or resistance to formulate the conceptual and theoretical framework illustrating the data's significance.

The key categories manifested in the data in light of the study's focus and leading to selection and development of this framework are displayed in Table C.2 in the concluding chapter. They include: (a) age, beauty, & romance; (b) intergenerational couples; (c) politics & controversy; and (d) fantasy & reality. Corresponding results were also classified along production, text/meta-text, and audience/cyberfandom axes.

REFERENCES

Age-old question. (1994, July 19). *Soap Opera Digest*, p. 140.

Aging in Hollywood. (1998, May 20). *New York Times*, p. A22.

Allen, R. (1985). *Speaking of soap operas.* Chapel Hill: University of North Carolina Press.

Allen, R. (Ed.). (1995). *To be continued . . . Soap operas around the world.* New York: Routledge.

Allocca, A. (1994a, September 6). A natural transition. *Soap Opera Magazine*, p. 46.

Allocca, A. (1994b, December 27). He said/she said. *Soap Opera Magazine*, p. 55.

Allocca, A. (1995a, March 28). What's ahead for *AW*'s key characters. *Soap Opera Magazine*, p. 30.

Allocca, A. (1995b, October 17). Matt Crane's masterworks. *Soap Opera Magazine*, pp. 18–20.

Althusser, L. (1971). *Lenin and philosophy.* New York: Monthly Review Press.

Amy Carlson Chat. (1995, July 11). Retrieved July 11, 1995, from NBC Online (via America Online).

Andersen, R. (1995). *Consumer culture & TV programming.* Boulder, CO: Westview.

Ang, I. (1985). *Watching "Dallas": Soap opera and the melodramatic imagination.* London: Methuen.

Ang, I. (1996). *Living room wars: Rethinking media audiences for a postmodern world.* New York: Routledge.

Another look at *AW*. (1994, November 28). *Soap Opera Now!*, p. 2.

Another World synopsis. (1995, August 29). *Soap Opera Digest*, p. 118.

Another World tries a new tactic. (1995, February 20). *Soap Opera Now!*, p. 1.

Ask Logan. (1997, February 6). Retrieved February 6, 1997, from *TV Guide* Online: http://www. tvguide.com/tv/soapdish/al.

AW's Donna and Michael hit the hay. (1995, November 21). *Soap Opera Weekly*, p. 8.

Baldwin, K. (1997, January 10). A new spin on soaps. *Entertainment Weekly*, p. 31.

Banner, L. (1992). *In full flower: Aging women, power, and sexuality*. New York: Vintage.

Barbatsis, G. (1991). Analyzing meaning in form: Soap opera's compositional construction of realness. *Journal of Broadcasting and Electronic Media, 35*, 59-74.

Barker, C. (2000). *Cultural studies: Theory and practice*. Thousand Oaks, CA: Sage.

Barlow, L., & Krentz, J.A. (1992). Beneath the surface: The hidden codes of romance. In J.A. Krentz (Ed.), *Dangerous men and adventurous women of the romance* (pp. 15-29). Philadelphia: University of Pennsylvania Press.

Barthes, R. (1975). *The pleasure of the text*. New York: Hill & Wang.

Baym, N. (1993). Interpreting soap operas and creating community inside a computer-mediated fan culture. *Journal of Folklore Research, 30*, 143-176.

Baym, N. (1995). The emergence of community in computer-mediated communication. In S. Jones (Ed.), *Cybersociety: Computer-mediated communication and community* (pp. 138-163). Newbury Park, CA: Sage.

Baym, N. (2000). *Tune in, log on: Soaps, fandom, and online community*. Thousand Oaks, CA: Sage.

Bazzini, D., McIntosh, W., Smith, S., Cook, S., & Harris, C. (1997). The aging woman in popular film: Underrepresented, unattractive, unfriendly, and unintelligent. *Sex Roles, 36*, 531-543.

Beniger, J.R. (1995). Who shall control cyberspace? In L. Strate, R. Jacobson, & S. Gibson (Eds.), *Communication and cyberspace: Social interaction in an electronic environment* (pp. 49-58). Cresskill, NJ: Hampton.

Best trend: May/December romances. (1995, January 3). *Soap Opera Digest*, p. 40.

Bird, E. (1992). Travels in nowhere land: Ethnography and the "impossible" audience. *Critical Studies in Mass Communication, 9*, 250-260.

Blumenthal, D. (1997). *Women and soap opera: A cultural feminist perspective*. Westport, CT: Praeger.

Bonderoff, J. (1995a, June 6). We used to be the summer storyline (sigh!). *Soap Opera Digest*, pp. 30-33.

Bonderoff, J. (1995b, August 29). I'm still here. *Soap Opera Digest*, pp. 54-59.

Bowen, W. (1994). Divide and flatter: TV's stealth attack on the Woodstock generation. Retrieved November 10, 2002, from Citizens for Media Literacy: http://interact.uoregon.edu/medialit/mlr/readings/articles/Divide.html.

Brennan, T. (1999). Social physics inertia: Energy and aging. In K. Woodward (Ed.), *Figuring age: Women, bodies, generations* (pp. 131-148). Bloomington: Indiana University Press.

Brooks, P. (1976). *The melodramatic imagination: Balzac, Henry James, melodrama and the mode of excess.* New Haven, CT: Yale University Press.

Brown, M.E. (1990). Conclusion: Consumption and resistance—the problem of pleasure. In M.E. Brown (Ed.), *Television and women's culture: The politics of the popular* (pp. 201-210). Newbury Park, CA: Sage.

Brown, M.E. (1994). *Soap opera and women's talk: The pleasure of resistance.* Newbury Park, CA: Sage.

Brunsdon, C. (1981). Crossroads: Notes on a soap opera. *Screen, 22*(4), 32-37.

Brunsdon, C. (1995). The role of soap opera in the development of feminist television scholarship. In R. Allen (Ed.), *To be continued . . . Soap operas around the world* (pp. 49-65). New York: Routledge.

Brunsdon, C. (2000). *The feminist, the housewife, and the soap opera.* New York: Oxford University Press.

Buchanan, K., & Middleton, D.J. (1993). Discursively formulating the significance of reminiscence in later life. In N. Coupland & J.F. Nussbaum (Eds.), *Discourse and lifespan identity* (pp. 55-80). Newbury Park, CA: Sage.

Buckingham, D. (1987). *Public secrets: "EastEnders" and its audience.* London: BFI Press.

Buckman, P. (1984). *All for love: A study in soap opera.* Salem, NH: Salem House.

Cantor, M., & Cantor, J. (1983). Audience composition and television content: The mass audience revisited. In S. Ball-Rokeach & M. Cantor (Eds.), *Media, audience, and social structure* (pp. 214-225). Newbury Park, CA: Sage.

Cantor, M., & Pingree, S. (1983). *The soap opera.* Beverly Hills, CA: Sage.

Caploe, R. (1994, October 11). A woman's world. *Soap Opera Digest*, pp. 32-33.

Caploe, R. (1995, August 29). Still in the closet: Why is daytime so afraid of homosexuality? *Soap Opera Digest*, pp. 50-53.

Cassata, M., & Skill, T. (Eds.). (1983). *Life on daytime television.* Norwood, NJ: Ablex.

Champagne, C. (1994, December 6). Cybersoaps. *Soap Opera Digest*, pp. 44-46.

Cohen, J. (1991). The "relevance" of cultural identity in audiences' interpretations of mass media. *Critical Studies in Mass Communication, 8*, 442-453.

Conboy, K., Medina, N., & Stanbury, S. (Eds.). (1997). *Writing on the body: Female embodiment and feminist theory.* New York: Columbia University Press.

Condit, C. (1989). The rhetorical limits of polysemy. *Critical Studies in Mass Communication, 6,* 103-122.

Coons, J. (1995a, July 10). Young love: Is it the answer to daytime's problems? *Soap Opera Now!,* p. 5.

Coons, J. (1995b, July 31). *Guiding Light's* Kurt McKinney (Matt): Would you buy a car from this man? *Soap Opera Now!,* p. 5.

Coons, J. (1995c, September 4). *Another World's* Kale Browne: Michael Hudson isn't in Kansas anymore! *Soap Opera Now!,* p. 5.

Coontz, S. (1992). *The way we never were: American families and the nostalgia trap.* New York: Basic Books.

Cooper, B. (1999). The relevancy of gender identity in spectators' interpretations of *Thelma & Louise. Critical Studies in Mass Communication, 16,* 20-41.

Coward, R. (1985). *Female desires.* New York: Grove Press.

Cukor, M. (1994a, February 8). Sleepless in Bay City. *Soap Opera Update,* pp. 68-69.

Cukor, M. (1994b, September 6). When will they be lovers. *Soap Opera Update,* pp. 44-45.

Cukor, M. (1995, July 25). Seems like old times. *Soap Opera Update,* pp. 24-26.

Cukor, M. (1996, April 16). Older women, younger men. *Soap Opera Update,* pp. 30-31.

Cybergossip. (1995, April 11). *Soap Opera Digest,* p. 95.

D'Acci, J. (1994). *Defining women: Television and the case of "Cagney & Lacey."* Chapel Hill: University of North Carolina Press.

Damning Dinah. (1996, October 22). *Soap Opera Weekly,* p. 41.

Daytime's forbidden lovers. (1995, November 14). *Soap Opera Update,* pp. 34-35.

The debate begins. (1995, May 8). *Soap Opera Now!,* pp. 2 & 6.

DeCerteau, M. (1984). *The practice of everyday life.* Berkeley: University of California Press.

DeLacroix, M. (1994a, August 23). Older women/younger men. *Soap Opera Weekly,* p. 34.

DeLacroix, M. (1994b, August 30). 20 Intriguing midsummer questions. *Soap Opera Weekly,* p. 18.

DeLacroix, M. (1997a, July 1). Letters with a French twist. *Soap Opera Weekly,* p. 36.

DeLacroix, M. (1997b, October 7). Maytime in October letters. *Soap Opera Weekly,* p. 37.

DeLosh, L. (1994, December 13). Bay City blues. *Soap Opera Weekly,* pp. 2-3.

DeLosh, L. (1995, April 4). The changing face of Bay City. *Soap Opera Weekly,* p. 5.

DeLosh, L. (1998, June 2). Fan Brigade disbanded. *Soap Opera Weekly,* p. 9.

Deming, C. (1990). For television-centred television criticism: Lessons from feminism. In M.E. Brown (Ed.), *Television and women's culture: The politics of the popular* (pp. 37-60). Newbury Park, CA: Sage.

Derenski, A., & Landsburg, S. (1981). *The age taboo: Older women-younger men relationships.* Boston: Little Brown.

DiLauro, J. (1994, September 13). Hit: Donna's hot flashes on *AW*. *Soap Opera Weekly*, p. 14.

Does knowing too much ruin the fun? (1995, November 14). *Soap Opera Update,* pp. 42-43.

Dow, B. (1996). *Prime-time feminism: Television, media culture, and the women's movement since 1970.* Philadelphia: University of Pennsylvania Press.

DuPlessis, R. (1985). *Writing beyond the ending: Narrative strategies of 20th century women writers.* Bloomington: Indiana University Press.

Elaesser, T. (1987). Tales of sound and fury: Observations on the family melodrama. In C. Gledhill (Ed.), *Home is where the heart is: Studies in melodrama and the woman's film* (pp. 43-69). London: British Film Institute.

Fall preview. (1994, October 4). *Soap Opera Magazine*, pp. 8-13.

Ferguson, M. (1990). Images of power and the feminist fallacy. *Critical Studies in Mass Communication, 7*, 215-230.

Feuer, J. (1995). *Seeing through the eighties: Television and Reaganism.* Durham, NC: Duke University Press.

Feuer, J. (1997). Different soaps for different folks. In The Museum of Television and Radio (Eds.), *Worlds without end: The art and history of the soap opera* (pp. 89-97). New York: Harry N. Abrams, Inc.

Fielding, H. (1996). *Bridget Jones's diary.* New York: Viking.

Fishman, R. (1996, April 9). The rats pack: Internet newsgroups have soap fans glued to their (computer) screens. *Soap Opera Digest*, pp. 54-57.

Fiske, J. (1987). *Television culture.* London: Methuen.

Flitterman-Lewis, S. (1992). All's well that doesn't end. In L. Spigel & D. Mann (Eds.), *Private screenings: Television and the female consumer* (pp. 217-226). Minneapolis: University of Minnesota Press.

Frentz, S. (Ed.). (1992). *Staying tuned: Contemporary soap opera criticism.* Bowling Green, OH: Bowling Green State University Press.

Frerking, B. (1998, January 28). The power of sex. *Palm Beach Post*, pp. 1D-4D.

Fuqua, J. (1995). "There's a queer in my soap!" The homophobia/AIDS story-line of *One Life to Live*. In R. Allen (Ed.), *To be continued . . . Soap operas around the world* (pp. 199-212). New York: Routledge.

Gallop, J. (1988). *Thinking through the body.* New York: Columbia University Press.

Garnham, N. (1995). Political economy and cultural studies: Reconciliation or divorce? *Critical Studies in Mass Communication, 12,* 62-71.

Gauging the value of daytime data. (1997, March 22). *TV Guide,* p. 198.

General Hospital (1996, May). *Daytime TV Soap Opera Almanac,* p. 54.

Geraghty, C. (1991). *Women and soap opera: A study of prime time soaps.* Cambridge: Polity Press.

Gerbner, G. (1995). Casting and fate: Women and minorities on television drama, game shows, and news. In E. Hollander, C. van der Linden, & P. Rutten (Eds.), *Communication, culture, and community* (pp. 125-135). The Netherlands: Rohn Stafleu van Loghum.

Gergen, M.M., & Gergen, K.J. (1993). Autobiographies and the shaping of gendered lives. In N. Coupland & J.F. Nussbaum (Eds.), *Discourse and lifespan identity* (pp. 28-54). Newbury Park, CA: Sage.

Gibbs, M. (1996). Rec.arts.tv.soaps monthly FAQ: Inappropriate posts. Retrieved November 10, 2002, from http://www.faqs.org/faqs/tv/soaps/faq/part4/.

Gilchrist, E. (1997, September). In praise of the young man. *Vogue,* pp. 190-192, 207.

Gitlin, T. (1983). *Inside prime time.* New York: Pantheon.

Glaser, B., & Strauss, A. (1967). *The discovery of grounded theory: Strategies for qualitative research.* Chicago: Aldine.

GL to pair Matt and Dinah. (1996, July 23). *Soap Opera Update,* p. 21.

Gledhill, C. (1988). Pleasurable negotiations. In E.D. Pribram (Ed.), *Female spectators: Looking at film and television* (pp. 64-89). London: Verso.

Gold, R.L. (1958). Roles in sociological field observations. *Social Forces, 36,* 217-223.

Gramsci, A. (1971). *Selections from the prison notebooks.* London: Lawrence & Wishart.

Greenberg, B., & Busselle, R. (1996). Soap operas and sexual activity: A decade later. *Journal of Communication, 46*(4), 153-161.

Grossberg, L. (1992). *We gotta get out of this place: Popular conservatism and postmodern culture.* New York: Routledge.

Grossberg, L. (1995). Cultural studies vs. political economy: Is anyone else bored with this debate? *Critical Studies in Mass Communication, 12,* 72-81.

Gullette, M.M. (1999). The other end of the fashion cycle: Practicing loss, learning decline. In K. Woodward (Ed.), *Figuring age: Women, bodies, generations* (pp. 34-58). Bloomington: Indiana University Press.

Haines, C. (1996, August 27). *GL'*s Maeve Kincead on why she and Vanessa have to go. *Soap Opera Weekly,* p. 26.

Hall, S. (1980). Encoding/decoding. In S. Hall, D. Hobson, A. Lowe, & P. Willis (Eds.), *Culture, media, language* (pp. 128-139). London: Hutchinson.

Hall, S. (1986). On postmodernism and articulation: An interview with Stuart Hall. *Journal of Communication Inquiry, 10*(2), 45-60.

Harms, J., & Dickens, D. (1996). Postmodern media studies: Analysis or symptom? *Critical Studies in Mass Communication, 13*, 210-227.

Harrington, C.L., & Bielby, D.D. (1995). *Soap fans: Pursuing pleasure and making meaning in everyday life.* Philadelphia: University of Pennsylvania Press.

Haskell, M. (1987). *From reverence to rape: The treatment of women in the movies.* Chicago: University of Chicago Press.

Haskell, M. (1998, February 15). C'mon boys, will you please act your age? *Boca Raton Sun-Sentinel*, pp. 4D-5D.

Hayward, J. (1997). *Consuming pleasures: Active audiences and serial fictions from Dickens to soap opera.* Lexington, KY: University Press of Kentucky.

Heide, M.J. (1995). *Television culture and women's lives: "thirtysomething" and the contradictions of gender.* Philadelphia: University of Pennsylvania Press.

Henderson, K. (1997, June 24). Do the right thing. *Soap Opera Digest*, pp. 25-28.

Hine, C. (2000). *Virtual ethnography.* Thousand Oaks, CA: Sage.

Hinsey, C. (1995, July 4). The state of soaps. *Soap Opera Digest*, pp. 28-31.

Hobson, D. (1982). *Crossroads: The drama of a soap opera.* London: Methuen.

Hornblower, M. (1997, June 9). Great Xpectations. *Time*, pp. 58-69.

Huston, V. (1987). *Loving a younger man.* Chicago: Contemporary Books.

In praise of younger men. (1995, April 4). *Soap Opera Update*, p. 52.

Interrogate the Internet. (1996). Contradictions in cyberspace: Collective response. In R. Shields (Ed.), *Cultures of Internet: Virtual spaces, real histories, living bodies* (pp. 125-132). Thousand Oaks, CA: Sage.

Intintoli, M.J. (1984). *Taking soaps seriously: The world of "Guiding Light."* New York: Praeger.

Is America ready for controversial storytelling? (1995, November 28). *Soap Opera Update*, pp. 44-45.

Is the youth emphasis now over? (1997, August 15). *Soap Opera Now!* [Electronic version]. Retrieved August 15, 1997, from America Online.

Jacobson, R. (1996). "Are they building an off-ramp in my neighborhood?" and other questions concerning public interest in and access to the information superhighway. In L. Strate, R. Jacobson, & S. Gibson (Eds.), *Communication and cyberspace* (pp. 143-154). Cresskill, NJ: Hampton Press.

Jankowski, N., & Wester, F. (1991). The qualitative tradition in social science inquiry: Contributions to mass communication research. In K.B. Jensen & N. Jankowski (Eds.), *A handbook of qualitative methods for mass communication research* (pp. 44-74). New York: Routledge.

Jenkins, H. (1992). *Textual poachers: Television fans and participatory culture.* New York: Routledge.

Jewell, C. (1994, April 12). Heat wave. *Soap Opera Weekly*, p. 41.

Jones, R.A. (1994). The ethics of research in cyberspace. *Internet Research*, 4(3), 30-35.

Kape, M. (1995a, April 24). Have you noticed. . . . *Soap Opera Now!*, p. 4.

Kape, M. (1995b, August 14). Living in the past. *Soap Opera Now!*, p. 2.

Kape, M. (1995c, September 11). Double standard. *Soap Opera Now!*, pp. 2 & 6.

Kape, M. (1997, April 18). Youth overboard. *Soap Opera Now!* [Electronic version]. Retrieved April 18, 1997, from America Online.

Kaplan, E.A. (1988). Whose imaginary? The televisual apparatus, the female body, and textual strategies in select rock videos on MTV. In E.D. Pribam (Ed.), *Female spectators: Looking at film and television* (pp. 132-156). London: Verso.

Keene, G. (1993, April 26). Should actors use their fans to help get their storylines changed? *Soap Opera Now!*, p. 5.

Keep the love alive. (1995, April 11). *Soap Opera Digest*, p. 141.

Kelley, A. (1995, October 10). Group therapy. *Soap Opera Digest*, pp. 54-57.

Kelley, A. (1996, May 7). Golden fears. *Soap Opera Digest*, pp. 60-63.

Kellner, D. (1992a). *The Persian Gulf TV war.* Boulder, CO: Westview.

Kellner, D. (1992b). Toward a multiperspectival cultural studies. *Centennial Review, 26*, 5-41.

Kennedy, D. (1993, October 29). Soaps on the ropes. *Entertainment Weekly*, pp. 37-38.

Kuhn, A. (1982). *Women's pictures: Feminism and cinema.* London: Routledge.

Kuhn, A. (1996). Women's genres. In H. Baehr & A. Gray (Eds.), *Turning it on: A reader in women and media* (pp. 62-69). London: Arnold.

Lemay, H. (1981). *Eight years in another world.* New York: Atheneum.

Let love reign. (1996, March 19). *Soap Opera Update*, p. 48.

Lewis, J. (1991). *The ideological octopus: An exploration of television & its audience.* New York: Routledge.

Liccardo, L. (1996, April 30). Who really watches the daytime soaps? *Soap Opera Weekly*, pp. 36-38.

Liebes, T., & Katz, E. (1990). *The export of meaning: Cross-cultural readings of "Dallas."* New York: Oxford University Press.

Liebes, T., & Livingstone, S. (1994). The structure of family and romantic ties in the soap opera. *Communication Research, 21*, 717-741.

Lindlof, T. (1995). *Qualitative communication research methods.* Thousand Oaks, CA: Sage.

Lindlof, T., & Shatzer, M. (1998). Media ethnography in virtual space: Strategies, limits, and possibilities. *Journal of Broadcasting & Electronic Media, 42,* 170-189.

Logan, M. (1994, April 30). *World* enters taboo territory. *TV Guide,* p. 37.

Logan, M. (1995, November 18). Can a rapist be a romantic hero? *TV Guide,* p. 38.

Logan, M. (1996a, July 27). *Days*-ed and confused. *TV Guide,* p. 46.

Logan, M. (1996b, August 10). He's ba-ack. *TV Guide,* p. 42.

Logan, M. (1998a, January 3). The worst in soaps. *TV Guide,* p. 34.

Logan, M. (1998b, March 7). Dad's dirty little secret. *TV Guide,* p. 46.

Logan, M. (1998c, May 9). There's life in them yet. *TV Guide,* p. 78.

Logan, M. (1998d, May 16). Another whirl; Soap fans in a lather. *TV Guide,* p. 31.

Logan, M. (1998e, August 22). Life preserver. *TV Guide,* p. 38.

Logan, M. (1999, May 1). Logan rant. *TV Guide,* p. 48.

Logan, M. (2000, October 28). Erica's family outing. *TV Guide,* p. 58.

Longhurst, B. (1987). Realism, naturalism and television soap opera. *Theory, Culture & Society, 4,* 633-649.

Love is a many splendored thing for *Another World's* Matt and Donna. (1994, May 24). *Soap Opera Digest,* pp. 40-41.

Love it/hate it (1996, January 30). *Soap Opera Digest,* pp. 62-63.

Love it/hate it (1997, July 22). *Soap Opera Digest,* pp. 68-69.

Lovell, T. (1981). Ideology and *Coronation Street.* In R. Dyer, C. Geraghty, M. Jordan, T. Lovell, R. Paterson, & J. Stewart (Eds.), *Coronation street* (pp. 40-52). London: BFI Press.

Lovenheim, B. (1990, December 17). Older women, younger men. *New York,* pp. 46-56.

Loving Lucci. (1994, May 13). *Entertainment Weekly,* p. 8.

MacKinnon, R.C. (1995). Searching for Leviathan in Usenet. In S.G. Jones (Ed.), *Cybersociety: Computer-mediated communication and community* (pp. 112-137). Thousand Oaks, CA: Sage.

Maeve Kincead in Q&A with Logan. (1997, March 27). Retrieved March 27, 1997, from *TV Guide* Online: http://www.tvguide.com/tv/soapdish/qa.

Mail call. (1994, January 4). *Soap Opera Weekly,* p. 41.

Mail call. (1996, February 6). *Soap Opera Weekly,* p. 41.

Martin, D. (1995a, March 14). Rape and redemption: Why daytime turns its rapists into heroes. *Soap Opera Weekly,* pp. 12-14.

Martin, D. (1995b, May 9). You're not getting older, you're getting better. *Soap Opera Weekly,* pp. 32-33.

Martin, D. (1996, June 11). The age of romance: Why May/December romances are a daytime staple. *Soap Opera Weekly,* pp. 34-36.

Matelski, M. (1988). *The soap opera evolution: America's enduring romance with daytime drama.* Jefferson, NC: McFarland & Company.

A matter of degrees. (1995, March 24). *Soap Opera Digest,* pp. 76-78.

May/December love affairs. (1997, October 14). *Soap Opera Weekly,* p. 33.

McAllister, M. (1996). *The commercialization of American culture: New advertising, control and democracy.* Thousand Oaks, CA: Sage.

McEachern, C. (1994). Even-handed/multi-stranded: The problem of representation of women in a rural soap opera. *Australian Feminist Studies, 20*(3), 151-170.

McGuigan, J. (1992). *Cultural populism.* New York: Routledge.

McLaughlin, M.L., Osborne, K.K., & Smith, C.B. (1995). Standards of conduct on Usenet. In S.G. Jones (Ed.), *Cybersociety: Computer-mediated communication and community* (pp. 90-111). Thousand Oaks, CA: Sage.

McRobbie, A. (1981). Just like a *Jackie* story. In A. McRobbie & T. McCabe (Eds.), *Feminism for girls* (pp. 113-128). London: Routledge.

McRobbie, A. (1994). *Postmodernism and popular culture.* London: Routledge.

Michael Laibson Chat. (1996, June 13). Retrieved June 13, 1996, from *Soap Opera Digest* Online (via America Online).

Mitchell, S. (1995, October). The next baby boom. *American Demographics* [Electronic version]. Retrieved November 22, 1995: http://www.marketingtools.com/ad_current/ad813.

Modleski, T. (1982). *Loving with a vengeance: Mass-produced fantasies for women.* Hamden, CT: Archon.

Modleski, T. (1986). Introduction. In T. Modleski (Ed.), *Studies in entertainment: Critical approaches to mass culture* (pp. ix-xix). Bloomington/Indianapolis: Indiana University Press.

Moffitt, M.A. (1993). Articulating meaning: Reconceptions of the meaning process, fantasy/reality, and identity in leisure activities. *Communication Theory, 3,* 231-251.

Morley, D. (1980). *The nationwide audience.* London: BFI Press.

Mulvey, L. (1975). Visual pleasure and narrative cinema. *Screen, 16*(3), 6-18.

Mumford, L.S. (1995). *Love and ideology in the afternoon: Soap opera, women and television genre.* Bloomington: Indiana University Press.

NBC wants to be no. 1. (1996, June 11). *Soap Opera Weekly,* p. 8.

Networks are listening. (1994a, April 26). *Soap Opera Magazine,* pp. 28-29.

Networks are listening. (1994b, September 20). *Soap Opera Magazine,* pp. 28-29.

Networks are listening. (1995, September 19). *Soap Opera Magazine,* p. 41.

No status quo. (1994, March 15). *Soap Opera Digest,* pp. 141-142.

Nochimson, M. (1992). *No end to her: Soap opera and the female subject.* Berkeley: University of California Press.

Norment, L. (1994, November). Black men/white women: What's behind the new furor? *Ebony*, pp. 44-50.

Norris, T. (1994, March 8). About *Another World*'s Donna and Matt. *Soap Opera Update*, p. 16.

On the set with *Another World*. 1994, December). *Daytime TV - Soap Opera Super Special*, pp. 40-41.

The other survey says. (1995, February 14). *Soap Opera Digest*, p. 62.

Penley, C. (1991). Brownian motion: Women, tactics, and technology. In C. Penley & A. Ross (Eds.), *Technoculture* (pp. 135-161). Minneapolis: University of Minnesota Press.

Perry, J. (1993, November 30). May-December disaster. *Soap Opera Weekly*, p. 42.

Poll, J. (1999). *"Another World": 35th anniversary celebration*. New York: HarperCollins.

Porter, D. (1977). Soap time: Thoughts on a commodity art form. *College English, 38*(2), 782-788.

Press, A. (1991). *Women watching television: Gender, class, and generation in the American television experience*. Philadelphia: University of Pennsylvania Press.

Probyn, E. (1992). Theorizing through the body. In L. Rakow (Ed.), *Women making meaning: New feminist directions in communication* (pp. 83-99). New York: Routledge.

Radway, J. (1984). *Reading the romance: Women, patriarchy, and popular literature*. Chapel Hill: University of North Carolina Press.

Readers' notes. (1995, June 13). *Soap Opera Update*, p. 16.

Reep, D. (1992). The siren call of the super couple: Soap opera's destructive slide toward closure. In S. Frentz (Ed.), *Staying tuned: Contemporary soap opera criticism* (pp. 96-102). Bowling Green, OH: Bowling Green State University Press.

Reitz, R. (1977). *Menopause: A positive approach*. New York: Penguin.

Rich, F. (1998, October 22). Lie was felicitous while it lasted. *Palm Beach Post*, p. 20A.

Riding, A. (1998, March 8). When the tables are turned in adultery's secret rooms. *New York Times*, p. II-15.

Rogers, D. (1991). Daze of our lives: The soap opera as feminine text. *Journal of American Culture, 14*(4), 29-42.

Rouän, B. (Director). (1997). *Post coitum*. France: New Yorker Films.

Rouverol, J. (1984). *Writing for the soaps*. Cincinnati, OH: Writer's Digest Books.

Russo, M. (1999). Aging and the scandal of anachronism. In K. Woodward (Ed.), *Figuring age: Women, bodies, generations* (pp. 20-33). Bloomington: Indiana University Press.

Scodari, C. (1995). Possession, attraction, and the thrill of the chase: Gendered myth-making in film and television comedy of the sexes. *Critical Studies in Mass Communication, 12,* 23-29.

Scodari, C., & Felder, J.L. (2000). Creating a pocket universe: "Shippers," fan fiction, and *The X-Files* online. *Communication Studies, 51,* 238-257.

Secret rules of the Nielsen ratings game. (1994, August 28). *New York Times,* pp. H1, H29.

Segal, B. (Director). (1987). *Power of suggestion.* Berkeley, CA: Images of Men & Women.

Seiter, E. (1999). *Television and new media audiences.* New York: Oxford University Press.

Seiter, E., Borchers, H., Kreutzner, G., & Warth, E. (1989). "Don't treat us like we're so stupid and naive": Toward an ethnography of soap opera viewers. In E. Seiter, H. Borchers, G. Kreutzner, & E. Warth (Eds.), *Remote control: Television, audiences, and cultural power* (pp. 223-237). New York: Routledge.

Shugart, H., Waggoner, E., & Hallstein, D.L. (2001). Mediating third-wave feminism: Appropriation as postmodern media practice. *Critical Studies in Media Communication, 18,* 194-210.

Sloane, S. (1994, July 9). Having a ball. *Soap Opera Digest,* pp. 52-55.

Soaps enter cyberspace (1996, May 28). *Soap Opera Update,* pp. 20-21.

Sobchack, V. (1999). Scary women: Cinema, surgery, and special effects. In K. Woodward (Ed.), *Figuring age: Women, bodies, generations* (pp. 200-211). Bloomington: Indiana University Press.

Sontag, S. (1967). *Against interpretation.* London: Eyre & Spottiswode.

Spigel, L. (1992). *Make room for TV: Television and the family ideal in post-war America.* Chicago: University of Chicago Press.

Stoddard, K. (1983). *Saints and shrews: Women and aging in American popular film.* Westport, CT: Greenwood.

Stolley, C. (1993, December 28). May-December debate. *Soap Opera Weekly,* p. 41.

Strate, L., Jacobson, R., & Gibson, S. (1995). Surveying the electronic landscape: An introduction to communication and cyberspace. In L. Strate, R. Jacobson, & S. Gibson (Eds.), *Communication and cyberspace: Social interaction in an electronic environment* (pp. 1-22). Cresskill, NJ: Hampton Press.

Stuart, A. (1999). Chat. Retrieved November 22, 1999, from *Soap Opera Digest* Online: http://www.soapdigest.com/soap/article5.cfm?.d=1507.

Summer preview. (1994, July 7). *Soap Opera Magazine,* pp. 11-16.

Sunila, J. (1980). *The new lovers: Younger men/older women.* New York: Fawcett.

Susman, L. (1993, December 28). Straight talk from NBC's Susan Lee. *Soap Opera Weekly,* pp. 2-3.

Taking it to the Matt. (1996, February 20). *Soap Opera Update,* p. 54.

Ten things we're truly thankful for. (1994, November 22). *Soap Opera Digest,* pp. 60-62.

Terrific triangles. (1995, July 7). *Soap Opera Digest,* p. 142.

Thompsen, P.A. (1995). What's fueling the flames in cyberspace? A social influence model. In L. Strate, R. Jacobson, & S. Gibson (Eds.), *Communication and cyberspace: Social interaction in an electronic environment* (pp. 298-315). Cresskill, NJ: Hampton Press.

Thou shalt program. (1998, May 23). *TV Guide,* p. 40.

Thumbs down: Romance interruptus. (1995, January 31). *Soap Opera Digest,* p. 70.

Thumbs up/thumbs down (1997, September 2). *Soap Opera Digest,* pp. 74-75.

Torchin, M. (1994, November 22). Speaking my mind. *Soap Opera Weekly,* p. 4.

Torchin, M. (1995, May 9). Speaking my mind. *Soap Opera Weekly,* p. 4.

van Zoonen, L. (1994). *Feminist media studies.* Thousand Oaks, CA: Sage.

Viewers' voice. (1995, April 4). *Soap Opera Weekly,* p. 10.

Viewers' voice. (1996, January 30). *Soap Opera Weekly,* p. 10.

Wade-Gayle, G. (2000). Who says an older woman can't/shouldn't dance? In D.W. King (Ed.), *Body politics and the fictional double* (pp. 1-22). Bloomington: Indiana University Press.

Waggett, G. (1997). *The soap opera encyclopedia.* New York: Harper Paperbacks.

Wagner, D. (1998, March 4). Ask the experts. Retrieved March 4, 1998, from *TV Guide* Online: http://www.tvgen.com/soaps/al/1030498b.

Wakefield, D. (1976). *All her children.* Garden City, NY: Doubleday.

Walters, S. (1996). *Material girls: Making sense of feminist cultural theory.* Berkeley: University of California Press; New York: Routledge.

Ward, N. (1995, March 23). Actor turns artist. *Argus (Lakehead University),* p. 10.

Waskul, D., & Douglass, M. (1996). Considering the electronic participant: Some polemical observations on the ethics of on-line research. *The Information Society, 12,* 129-139.

Wells, R., & Wells, M. (1990). *Menopause and mid-life.* Wheaton, IL: Tyndale House.

Wendy Riche in Q&A with Logan. (1997, March 25). Retrieved March 25, 1997, from *TV Guide* Online: http://www.tvguide.com/soapdish/qa.

What's age got to do with it? (1998, August 10). *People,* pp. 90-99.

White, M. (1994). Women, memory and serial melodrama. *Screen, 35*(4), 336-353.

Who's getting the most letters. (1994, October 18). *Soap Opera Update,* p. 16.

Why *GL's* Vanessa went to the Matt (1994, October 25). *Soap Opera Digest,* p. 10.

Why soaps get no respect (1997, August 26). *Soap Opera Weekly,* p. 37.

Will Donna turn her back on that? (1995, November 7). *Soap Opera Magazine,* p. 20.

Williams, C.T. (1992). *"It's time for my story": Soap opera, sources, structure and response.* Westport, CT: Praeger.

Women's Health Books Collective. (1992). *New our bodies ourselves.* New York: Touchstone.

Woodward, K. (Ed.). (1999). *Figuring age: Women, bodies, generations.* Bloomington: Indiana University Press.

Y&R's interracial romance. (1998, June 23). *Soap Opera Digest,* p. 5.

You'll see some changes made. (1994, November 1). *Soap Opera Magazine,* p. 46.

Your turn: *AW.* (1994, November 22). *Soap Opera Magazine,* p. 32.

Youthful demographics (1995, May). *American Demographics,* p. 31.

Author Index

A

Allen, R., xvii, xx, xxi, 6, 7, 11, 16, 35, 70, 127, 128, 129, 143, *181*
Allocca, A., 82(*n*1), 90, 92, 139, *181*
Althusser, L., xviii, *181*
Andersen, R., 63, *181*
Ang, I., xxi, xxii, xvii, 1, 2, 3, 4, 5, 150, 156, *181*

B

Baldwin, K., 12, *182*
Banner, L., xviii, 68, 79, 157, *182*
Barbatsis, G., 136, *182*
Barker, C., 169, *182*
Barlow, L., 18, 85, *182*
Barthes, R., 5, *182*
Baym, N., xxiv, 15, 44, 51, 145, 146, 148, *182*
Bazzini, D., xvii, *182*
Beniger, J. R., 147, *182*
Bielby, D. D., xxi, xxv, 43, 138, 143, 156, *187*
Bird, E., 155, *182*
Blumenthal, D., xxi, xxv, 151, *182*
Bonderoff, J., 9, 66, 83, 129, *182*
Borchers, H., xxvii, 3, *192*
Bowen, W., 12, *182*
Brennan, T., 5, *183*
Brooks, P., xxi, *183*

Brown, M. E., xv, xxi, xxv, 1, 3, 7, 16, 55, 146, 167, *183*
Brunsdon, C., xx, xxii, 146, *183*
Buchanan, K., 134, *183*
Buckingham, D., xvii, xxi, 5, *183*
Buckman, P., xxii, *183*
Busselle, R., xvii, *186*

C

Cantor, J., 12, 66, 127, *183*
Cantor, M., xvii, 12, 66,127, *183*
Caploe, R., 48, 127, *183*
Cassata, M., xx, xvii, *183*
Champagne, C., 144, *183*
Cohen, J., xxviii, *183*
Conboy, K., 172, *183*
Condit, C., 42, 43, 58, 145, *184*
Cook, S., xvii, *182*
Coons, J., 135, 140, *184*
Coontz, S., 169, *184*
Cooper, B., xxviii, *184*
Coward, R., 2, *184*
Cukor, M., 69, 72, 94, 139,147,156, *184*

D

D'Acci, J., xvi, 46, 136, *184*
DeCerteau, M., 122, *184*
DeLacroix, M., 82(*n*1), 135, 140, 150, 156, *184*

DeLosh, L., 23, 57, 89, 92, 142, *184*

Deming, C., 17, *185*

Derenski, A., 62, *185*

Dickens, D., xv, 164, *187*

DiLauro, J., 82, (n1), *185*

Douglass, M., 177, *193*

Dow, B., xviii, 127, *185*

DuPlessis, R., 18, *185*

E

Elaesser, T., 147, *185*

F

Felder, J. L., 2, *192*

Ferguson, M., xvi, 127, *185*

Feuer, J., 3, 46, 96, *185*

Fielding, H., 130, *185*

Fishman, R., 144, *185*

Fiske, J., xv, 13, 16, 17, 55, 86, *185*

Flitterman-Lewis, S., xix, 16, *185*

Frentz, S., xxi, *185*

Frerking, B., 159, *185*

Fuqua, J., 48, *185*

G

Gallop, J., 6, *185*

Garnham, N., xiv, xxviii, *186*

Geraghty, C., xix, xx, 16, *186*

Gerbner, G., xvii, 186

Gergen, K. J., 6, 186

Gergen, M. M., 6, 186

Gibbs, M., 148, 186

Gibson, S., 147, 153(n6), 192

Gilchrist, E., 159, 186

Gitlin, T., 169, 186

Glaser, B., 179, 186

Gledhill, C., 136, 186

Gold, R. L., 176, 186

Gramsci, A., xiv, 186

Greenberg, B., xvii, 186

Grossberg, L., xv, xxiii, xxviii, 1, 4, 43, 165, *186*

Gullette, M. M., 51, *186*

H

Haines, C., 138, *186*

Hall, S., xix, xxii, 41, 42, 43, 171, *186*

Hallstein, D. L., 165, *192*

Harms, J., xv, 164, *187*

Harrington, C. L., xxi, xxv, 43, 138, 156, *187*

Harris, C., xvii, 182

Haskell, M., xviii, 61, 62, 63, 159, 170, *187*

Hayward, J., xxv, 19, 20, *187*

Heide, M. J., xxi, 136, *187*

Henderson, K., 27, *187*

Hine, C., xxv, xxvi, 176, *187*

Hinsey, C., 44, *187*

Hobson, D., xvii, xxi, 3, 5, *187*

Hornblower, M., 12, *187*

Huston, V., 62, *187*

I

Intintoli, M. J., xvii, xxi, 8, 12, 56, 151, *187*

J

Jacobson, R., xxvi, 147, 153(*n*6), *192*

Jankowski, N., 179, *188*

Jenkins, H., xv, xxiv, xxv, 2, 122, 143, *188*

Jewell, C., 77, *188*

Jones, R. A., 177, *188*

K

Kape, M., 132, 140, *188*

Kaplan, E. A., xviii, *188*

Katz, E., xxi, *188*

Keene, G., 138, *188*

Kelley, A., 132, 134, *188*

Kellner, D., xiv, xv, *188*

Kennedy, D., 131, *188*

Krentz, J. A., 18, 85, *182*

Kreutzner, G., xxvii, 3, *192*

Kuhn, A., xviii, 136, *188*

L

Landsburg, S., 62, *185*
Lemay, H., xxii, 12, 29, *188*
Lewis, J., xxii, 41, 42 70, 73, 89, *188*
Liccardo, L., xxvi, *188*
Liebes, T., xix, xxi, 28, *188*
Lindlof, T., 173, 176, *189*
Livingstone, S., xix, 15, 28, *188*
Logan, M., 19, 21, 23, 27, 36, 50, 51, 82(*n*1), 101, 105, 106, 161, *189*
Longhurst, B., 136, *189*
Lovell, T., 168, *189*
Lovenheim, B., 63, *189*

M

MacKinnon, R. C., 145, 148, *189*
Martin, D., 19, 20, 28, 156, *189*
Matelski, M., xx, *190*
McAllister, M., 8, *190*
McEachern, C., xvii, *190*
McGuigan, J., xv, *190*
McIntosh, W. xvii, 182
McLaughlin, M. L., 148, *190*
McRobbie, A., xiv, 46, *190*
Medina, N., 172, *183*
Middleton, D. J., 134, *183*
Mitchell, S., 12, *190*
Modleski, T., xviii, xix, xxi, xxii, 3, 4, 16, 64, 155, *190*
Moffitt, M. A., xxiii, 43, *190*
Morley, D., xiv, 167, *190*
Mulvey, L., xviii, *190*
Mumford, L. S., xix, xxiv, 16, 22, 76, 84, 146, 168, 171, *190*

N

Nochimson, M., xviii, xix, xxiv, 17, 18, 20, 31, *190*
Norment, L., 23, *191*
Norris, T., 71, *191*

O

Osborne, K. K., 148, *190*

P

Penley, C., 166, *191*
Perry, J., 70, *191*
Pingree, S., xvii, *183*
Poll, J., xxii, *191*
Porter, D., 84, *191*
Press, A., xxi, 3, *191*
Probyn, E., 6, *191*

R

Radway, J., xx, xxii, 18, 150, *191*
Reep, D., 30, 31, *191*
Reitz, R., 80, *191*
Rich, F., 153(*n*1), *191*
Riding, A., 153(*n*3), *191*
Rogers, D., xix, *191*
Roüan, B., 153(*n*3), *191*
Rouverol, J., xxii, 8, 9, 10, 36, *191*
Russo, M., 51, *191*

S

Scodari, C., 2, 17, 70, 76, 77, *192*
Segal, B., 19, *192*
Seiter, E., xxv, xxvii, 3, 166, *192*
Shatzer, M., 173, 176, *189*
Shugart, H., 165, *192*
Skill, T., xx, xvii, *183*
Sloane, S., 69, *192*
Smith, C. B., 148, *190*
Smith, S., xvii, 182
Sobchack, V., 51, *192*
Sontag, S., 46, *192*
Spigel, L., 8, *192*
Stanbury, S., 172, *183*
Stoddard, K., xviii, 9, 13, *192*
Stolley, C., 71, *192*
Strate, L., 147, 153(*n*6), *192*
Strauss, A., 179, *186*
Stuart, A., 172, *192*
Sunila, J., 62, *192*
Susman, L., 66, *193*

T

Thompsen, P. A., 148, *193*
Torchin, M., 132, *193*

V

van Zoonen, L., xvi, *193*

W

Wade-Gayle, G., 51, 63, *193*
Waggett, G., 19, 25, 29, 132, *193*
Waggoner, E., 165, *192*
Wagner, D., 140, *193*

Wakefield, D., xxii, *193*
Walters, S., xvi, xvii, xxviii, 19, *193*
Ward, N., 139, *193*
Warth, E., xxvii, 3, *192*
Waskul, D., 177, *193*
Wells, M., 80, *193*
Wells, R., 80, *193*
Wester, F., 179, *188*
White, M., 17, *194*
Williams, C. T., xix, xx, xxiv, *194*
Woodward, K., xviii, *194*

Subject Index

A

ABC, 48, 88, 132, 161-162
A Perfect Murder, 159
active audiences, xv
advertisers, 4, 8-9, 12-13, 54, 87,
  139, 147, 152, 160, 171-172, 166
affect (concept), 1, 4-6, 128, 152,
  167, 170-171, 179
All My Children (AMC), xxiii, 11,
  22, 27, 32, 33, 48-50, 54, 65, 88,
  164, 173
  Bianca, 49-50
  gay and lesbian storylines, 49-
  50
  Ellen, 65
  Erica, 11, 27, 32, 33, 49-50, 54
  Julia, 22
  Kendall, 11
  Mark, 65
  Michael, 48-49
  Noah, 22
All That Heaven Allows, 63, 84, 97
Ally McBeal, 159
  Judge Whipper, 159
  Richard, 159
America Online (AOL), 45, 55, 148-
  150, 153
ambiguity, 47, 71, 73, 86
  textual 20, 47, 70-76, 86

reduction of, 46-47, 72-76, 89
Another World (AW), xxii-xxiv, 7,
  10, 11, 12, 19, 23, 25, 26, 28-29,
  30-31, 32, 33, 34, 36, 44-46, 47,
  51-54, 56-57, 59, 61, 66-88, 89-
  110, 132, 135, 138-140, 141-144,
  149, 156-157, 159, 160-161, 165,
  171-172, 173, 175, 176
  Amanda, 33
  Angela, 84
  Blair, 100-103, 124
  Bridget, 80, 82, 88
  cancellation and, 56-57, 66, 100,
  160, 171-172
  Carl, 29, 54, 101, 104-107, 120
  Cass, 10, 105-107, 121, 160-161
  Clara, 92
  costuming, hairstyling, and
  makeup, 74, 97-99
  Donna, 32, 66-88, 89-110, 111-
  130, 132-135, 137-140, 141-143,
  147, 149, 156-157, 160-161, 165,
  167-168, 172, 175
  Etta Mae, 107
  Fan Brigade, 57
  Fan Club, 118
  fan response, 68-75, 78-79, 80-
  88, 89-94, 96-97, 100-104, 106-
  109, 111-130, 156-157

fan support, 56-57, 143-144, 172

Felicia, 23, 44-46, 59, 101, 106, 159

Frankie, 52-53, 103, 105-106, 110, 157

Gary, 47, 138, 149

Grant, 28-29, 107-108

Ian, 34

Jake, 19, 31, 34, 72, 94, 97, 107-108, 137, 141-143

John, 44-46, 59, 101, 105

Josie, 47, 68-74, 127, 138, 149

Justine, 92

Kathleen, 33

Lila, 105-107, 121, 160-161

Lorna, 47, 122-123

Lucas, 11

Mac, 29

Marley, 19, 23, 26-27, 66, 90, 104, 106-108

Matt, 32, 33, 61, 66-68, 89-110, 111-130, 132-135, 137-140, 141-144, 147, 149, 156-157, 160-161, 165, 167-168, 172, 175

menopause storyline (Donna), 79-83, 88

Michael, 11, 47-48, 53, 66-68, 78-79, 85, 90-107, 110, 113-115, 119-121, 124, 127-128, 132, 138, 140, 143, 147, 156-157, 160-161, 165, 167-168, 172

Morgan, 47

multigenerational family theme, 92

Nick, 10, 11, 25, 47-48, 93, 103-105, 110, 116

older woman/younger man storyline (Matt & Donna), 61, 66-68, 89-110, 111-130, 132, 134, 135, 137-140, 141-143, 156-157, 160-161

Paulina, 34, 137, 142-144, 154

Rachel, 29, 32, 54, 105-106, 120

Reginald, 90, 108

Ryan, 30-31, 33

screwball comedy style, 67, 70, 71, 75-77, 85, 113-114, 129-130

Shane, 53, 107, 109

Sharlene, 44-46, 59, 101, 105, 157

Sofia, 102-106, 110, 113, 116, 120, 123

tabloid triangle storyline (Sharlene, John, & Felicia), 59, 44-46, 101

Toni, 10

Tyrone, 23

Vicky, 23, 26-27, 28-29, 30-31, 32, 66, 89-90, 93, 104-105, 107-110, 121

youthification of, 44, 54, 100, 105-107, 160

articulation, xviii, xxii-xxiii, xxviii, 4-5, 15, 41, 46, 50, 59, 61, 64, 129, 150, 164-165, 167, 170-171, 179

As Good as It Gets, 159

As the World Turns (ATWT), 7, 9-10, 29, 48, 65, 88, 113, 164

Casey, 65, 113

Hank, 48

Holden, 29

Jeff, 9-10

Larry, 65, 88, 113

Lily, 29

Lyla, 65, 113

Penny, 9-10

Susan, 65, 88, 113

audience readings, xiv-xvii, xix-xxiv, 4, 15, 19, 41-43, 46-59, 68-72, 74, 80-81, 83, 89-94, 96-97, 101-102, 104, 108-109, 111-130, 145-152, 166-167, 179

aberrant, 129

counter-hegemonic, 42-45, 47, 53, 55, 71, 76, 81, 86, 104, 108, 118, 122, 136-137, 166-167 hegemonic, xvi, 42-43, 45-47, 49, 76, 86, 91, 96, 108, 113, 118, 167, 168, 170

labor involved in, 2, 58, 122, 127, 166-167

negotiated, xx-xxi, 41-43, 71, 167, 170

negotiation and, xiv, xvi, xvii, 42, 43, 45, 50-59, 91, 96, 108, 110, 126-127, 151, 170

oppositional, xiv, xx, 35, 41-43, 45-46, 53, 65, 68, 70-71, 74, 76, 86, 109-110, 145, 167

preferred/dominant, xiv, xx, 41-46, 55, 65, 68, 70, 86, 89, 108, 113, 165, 170

resistance and, xiv, xxii, xxiv, 1-2, 13, 23, 30, 41, 51, 58, 77, 96, 146, 155, 158, 166, 168, 170, 179

resistive, xv, 42, 45, 47, 59, 70, 71, 91, 158, 166-167

B

Baby Boomers, 11-13, 36, 54, 57, 103, 105, 132, 134, 157-158, 161-162

Bedelia, Bonnie, 159

Bell, Bill, 7-8

Beverly Hills, 90210, 160

Bold and the Beautiful (B&B), 7-8, 35, 54, 150, 160, 164

Brooke, 35

Eric, 150, 164

Ridge, 35

Sally, 54

Stephanie, 54, 150, 164

Taylor, 35

Brooks, Randy, 23

Browne, Kale, 105-106, 140, 161

Buchanan, Jensen, 26, 32

bulletin boards (Internet), xxi, xxv-xxvi, 44, 46, 70, 153,175-178

Bullworth, 159

C

CBS, 134, 164

CNN, 160

Cagney and Lacey, xvi, 46, 136

camp aesthetic, 33, 36, 46, 50, 132, 164

Carlson, Amy, 69, 138

Cheers, 17

Collins, Joan, 46

computer-mediated communication (CMC), xxiv-xxv, xxvii, 145-152, 156

acronyms, emoticons, and smileys, 15-16, 32, 53, 156

flaming, 148, 151

lurking, xxv, 157, 177

nettiquette, xxvii, 57, 59, 131, 145, 148-149, 151

trolls and, 148-149

Connery, Sean, 171

constant comparative method, 179

consumer culture, xxv-xxvii, 8, 1 52, 157, 165

content analysis, xvii

Corday, Ken, 8

Coronation Street, 136

Crane, Matt, 66, 70, 83, 104-105, 116, 138-139, 160

Crossroads, xvii, xx-xxi, 5

Culliton, Richard, 7, 106

cultivation hypothesis, xvii

cultural dopes/dupes, xv, 145, 168

cultural feminist perspective, xxi

cultural populism, xv

cultural studies, xiv, xv, xxi, xxiii, xiv, 150, 168

British, xiv, xxiii

feminist, xxi, 4, 16, 167

U.S., xv, xxi, xxiii, xxv, 43, 179

currency (concept), 1, 4-6, 50-59, 61, 97, 110, 112, 117, 126, 128-129, 152, 165-166, 167, 170-171, 179

cyberfandom, xxiv-xxvi, 2-3, 7, 29, 43-48, 50-59, 65, 69, 81, 90-91, 101-102, 104, 119, 126, 141-152, 156-157, 166, 170-171
  creator, actor, and/or press involvement in, 138-145, 153
  flame wars and, 44, 146
  age, gender, race, class and, 50-51, 81, 120, 145-152
cybergossip, 131, 141-145
cyberspace and community, 147, 176-177

D

Dallas, xxi, 3, 115
  Sue Ellen, 3, 115
Damon, Matt, 159
Dano, Linda, 159
Days of Our Lives (DOOL), xxiii-xxiv, 8, 17-18, 19, 22-23, 25, 26, 27, 28, 30, 33, 34, 36-39, 44, 46, 49, 51-54, 64-65, 88, 91, 94, 101, 105, 132, 134, 149, 154, 173
  Addie, 65
  Adrienne, 30
  Alice, 28
  Austin, 34, 38
  Bill, 19
  Billie, 34-35, 38, 91
  Bo, 30, 34-35, 91
  buried alive storyline, 27, 37, 44
  camp aesthetic in, 33, 36, 132, 164
  Carly, 27
  Caroline, 52
  Carrie, 34, 38
  demon possession storyline, 38
  Doug, 65
  embryo theft storyline, 27, 37
  fantasy orientation, 33, 36-38
  Hope, 30, 34-35, 38, 65, 91
  Jack, 18, 19, 22, 34
  Jennifer, 34, 38
  John, 34, 36-37, 54, 140

Julie, 65
Justin, 30
Kate, 27
Kayla, 17-18, 19, 22-23
Kimberly, 22
Kristin, 34, 38, 109
Laura, 19, 64-65
Lawrence, 27
Lucas, 25
Maggie, 52
Marcus, 22-23
Marlena, 27, 34, 36-37, 38, 46, 54, 140
Peter, 34
Roman, 36-37
Sami, 26, 34, 37, 52, 149, 154
Stefano, 28, 46, 101, 140
Steve, 17-18
supercouple storyline (Kayla & Steve), 17-18
supertriangle storylines, 34-35, 37-38
Tom, 28
Victor, 27
Vivian, 27, 101, 105
Dean, James, 25
DeGeneres, Ellen, 50
demogenic, 8
demographics, xxvi, 3, 6, 8-13, 28, 30, 34, 36, 38-39, 51, 53, 56-57, 66, 71, 113, 116-117, 127, 132, 147, 168, 170, 172
DePriest, Maggie, 7
Designing Women, 63
desire, xxvii, 1-14, 18, 24, 166
Diaz, Cameron, 43-44
DiCaprio, Leonardo, 159
Drueding, Eddie, 59
Dynasty, 46, 115, 160
  Alexis, 46, 115

E

ER, 3
EastEnders, xvii, xxi, 5

Ebert, Roger, 171
Echo Boomers, 12-13, 164
e-mail groups, xxv, 111, 142, 149, 175, 178
embodiment, 5-6, 129-130, 137, 158, 164-166, 172
Emmerdale Farm, xvii, 136
Emmy Awards (daytime), 174
encoding/decoding model, xix-xx, xxii, 41-43, 179
Entertainment Weekly, 160, 174
Entrapment, 171
essentialism, xix, 167
ethnography, xiv, xv, xx-xxi, xxiv-xxvii, 3, 4, 15, 43, 71, 111-112, 155-158, 170, 176, 178
    multi-sited, xxv, 176
    naturalistic, xxv, 111, 155-158, 170
    virtual, xxv-xxvii, 111-112, 156-158, 170, 176-178
Evans-Luciano, Judi, 154
everyday life, 2, 136-137, 149-150

F

fan fiction (fanfic), 122, 125, 166
fans (*see* soap opera audiences)
fantasy, xiv, xv, xvi, xxi, xxvii, 1-14, 17, 22-24, 41, 47, 61, 75, 77, 114-115, 122, 126, 128-129, 139, 150, 158, 164, 165, 168, 179
    public, 2, 24, 39, 59, 110, 122, 127, 134, 165-166, 171
    private, 2, 145
fanzines, 2
feminism/feminist research, xvi-xviii, xx-xxii, 127, 136, 146-147, 149, 158, 165, 167, 171
fetishism, xviii
Fili-Krushel, Pat, 132-133
focus groups, xv, xx, 80-81, 111, 126, 132, 175, 178
FOX (network), 134
Friends, 3

G

gap filling, 116, 122
Geary, Anthony, 21
gender/age double standard, xviii, 6, 9, 35, 45, 51, 61-65, 71-72, 78, 85, 95, 102, 112, 114, 134-135, 139-140, 159-160, 169-170, 179
General Hospital (GH), xxiii-xxiv, 3, 7, 10, 11-12, 17, 18-22, 28, 30, 35, 37, 143, 159,161, 173
    AIDS storyline (Robin & Stone), 37, 143-144
    A.J., 22
    Brenda, 35
    Edward, 28
    ice princess storyline (Luke & Laura), 37
    Jax, 35
    Keesha, 22
    Laura, 11-12, 17, 18-22, 30, 37
    Lila, 28
    Luke, 11-12, 17, 18-22, 30, 37
    Monica, 159
    rape redemption storyline (Luke & Laura), 18-22
    Robin, 10, 37, 143-144
    Sean, 13
    Simone, 22
    Sonny, 35
    Stone, 143-144
    Tiffany, 13
    Tom, 22
Generation X, 10-13, 69, 87, 102, 160, 164
genre, xvi, xviii-xx, xxii, 18, 23-24, 36, 70, 129, 147, 152, 168
good mother/bad mother dichotomy, 27
Graduate, The, 63
grounded theory (*see* constant comparative method)
Guarnieri, Terri, 127

Guiding Light (GL), xvii, xxi, xxiii-
  xxiv, 7, 10, 11, 19, 25-26, 27, 28,
  29, 31, 32, 38, 48, 55, 56, 65, 85,
  94, 122, 133-136, 138, 140, 144,
  153, 157, 158, 164, 172, 173
  Alan, 28
  Alexandra, 28
  Annie, 26
  Billy, 134
  Blake, 29, 32
  Buzz, 28, 29, 32
  clone storyline (Reva), 38
  Dinah, 55, 135, 140
  Ed, 28
  fan response, 133-135, 144
  Fletcher, 29, 122
  Frank, 32
  Holly, 19, 29, 32, 122, 157, 164,
    172
  Jenna, 29
  Jesse, 10, 25
  Kelly, 25-26
  Lillian, 28
  Lucy, 133, 144
  Matt, 29, 48, 55, 65, 85, 133-136,
    138-139, 158, 164, 172
  Michelle, 10, 25, 31
  Morgan, 25-26
  Nadine, 28
  Nola, 26
  older woman/younger man
    storyline (Matt & Vanessa), 48,
    55, 65, 85, 133-136, 138-139,
    158, 164
  Reva, 11, 27, 38, 164
  Roger, 19, 28, 29, 32, 140, 172
  Ross, 28, 29
  Vanessa, 29, 48, 55, 65, 85, 133-
    136, 138-139, 157, 158, 164, 172

H

Hall, Deidre, 27, 88
Harold and Maude, 171

Heche, Anne, 50
hegemony, xiv-xv, xxiv, 2, 41-43,
  51, 59, 67, 70, 86-87, 108, 110,
  118, 126, 145-146, 149, 158, 164-
  165, 167-168, 171, 179
Her Costly Affair, 159
Horowitz, Jane, 171
How Stella Got Her Groove Back,
  63, 160
Howarth, Roger, 19
Hudson, Rock, 97

I

ideal mother, xix, xxi, 3-4
identity, xiv-xix, xxi, xxvi-xxvii,
  xxviii, 3-4, 30, 50-57, 157, 164-
  165, 167
  age, xvii-xix, xxvi-xxvii, 4, 30,
    38, 41, 50-51, 58, 77, 157, 164-
    165, 167, 172, 179
  class, xv, xix, xxi, xxvi, 3, 30, 50-
    51, 77, 157, 164-165, 167
  gender, xv-xix, xxi, xxvi-xxvii,
    15-38, 41, 50-51, 157, 164-165,
    167, 179
  race, xv, xix, xxvi, 3, 30, 50-51,
    157, 164-165, 167
  sexuality, xv, xviii, 46-50, 165
ideology, xiv, xix-xx, xxiii-xxiv,
  5-6, 15-17, 19, 23, 38, 41-43, 67,
  96, 129, 137, 164-165
image of women (role modeling)
  approach, xvi, 3-5
interpellation (identification),
  xviii-xix, xxi, 3-4, 6, 25, 38, 45-
  46, 64, 77, 86, 102-103, 114-115,
  117, 120, 126, 127, 134, 136, 150,
  179
interviews, xv

J

Jekyll and Hyde, 100
Jerry Springer, 109
jouissance, 5

K

Kape, Michael, 140
Keating, Charles, 106, 109
Kincead, Maeve, 135, 138

L

Lady Killer, 159
Laiman, Leah, 7
Leahey, Lynn, 69
least objectionable programming, 128
Lemay, Harding, 12
Light, Judith, 159
Loving, 28
Lucci, Susan, 27, 88

M

male gaze, xviii
Malone, Michael, 105-106
Marland, Douglas, 25-26
Mary Tyler Moore Show, The, xviii
McCullough, Kimberly, 10
McKinney, Kurt, 135, 138
McLachlan, Sarah, 97
media literacy, 167
melodramatic identification, xxi, 1, 115
Melrose Place, 160
menopause, 79-83, 88
Monty, Gloria, 11-12
Moonlighting, 70
Moore, Demi, 159
multiperspectival analysis, xv, xxiii, 89, 171, 179
Murphy Brown, xviii, 63, 159
My Best Friend's Wedding, 43-44

N

NBC, 3, 51, 57, 66, 71, 104, 134, 144, 161
narrative, xiv, xvi-xix, xxiv, 15-18, 22, 30, 84, 119-120, 125, 146-147
    closure, xviii-xix, xxiv, 15-17, 18-19, 20-22, 31, 67, 76, 84, 96, 104, 125, 168, 179
    enigmas, 16-18, 22, 67, 84-87, 104, 125, 179
    seriality, xviii-xix, xxiv, 15-16, 18, 33
Nationwide, 167
Nixon, Agnes, xxii
Northern Exposure, 70
nostalgia, 5, 33, 89-92, 123, 132, 167-168

O

observation (research method), xv, xx, xxv-xxvii, 176-178
    complete observer role, 177
    participant, xxv-xxvii, 176-178
    participant-as-observer role, 176
Ohlmeyer, Don, 106
O.J. Simpson murder case, 83, 122, 152
older woman/younger man taboo, xviii, 61-64, 118, 135, 159-160
    Hollywood film, 62-63, 159-160, 171
    prime time television, 63-64, 159
One Day at a Time, xviii
One Life to Live (OLTL), xxiv, 7, 19, 20, 27, 48, 56, 65, 75-76, 88, 137, 153, 157, 159, 161, 172
    Billy, 48
    Bo, 161
    Carlotta, 56
    Dorian, 27, 56, 65
    gang rape storyline (Todd & Marty), 19-20, 137
    Hank, 56
    homophobia storyline (Billy), 48, 75-76
    Joey, 48, 65
    Marty, 19
    Nora, 88, 157, 161
    Rae, 159

Sam, 161
Téa, 137
Todd, 19, 20, 137, 153
Viki, 27, 65, 159
Oslin, K.T., 62

P

Passions, 160
pastiche, 145
patriarchy, xiv, xix, 2, 9, 16-18, 42,
  127-128, 147, 150, 165
Phelps, Jill Farren, 7, 52, 57, 94,
  101, 103, 135, 144, 161
plaisir, 5
pleasure (of audience), xiv, xviii,
  xxi-xxii, xxvii, 1-3, 13, 96, 145,
  150-151, 155, 158, 165, 167, 170
political correctness, 59, 91-92, 137
political economy, xiv, xv, 168
polysemy (pluri-signification),
  xxiv, 42-43, 45, 70, 84, 108, 127,
  146, 151, 167
polyvalence, 42-43, 45, 96, 108, 133,
  151, 167
Port Charles, 160
Post Coitum, 153
postmodern culture, xv, xviii, 37-
  38, 132, 159, 164-165
Princess Diana, 169
private sphere, 13, 146-147, 169-
  170
Procter & Gamble (P&G), 44, 65-
  66, 72, 79, 83, 94, 134, 144, 160,
  164, 171-172
psychoanalytical analysis, xvii, 18
public sphere, 13, 146-147, 169-170
Pure Soap, 66, 160

Q

qualitative research, xx, xxv

R

reader-oriented approach, xvii, xx
Reilly, James, 34, 36, 37-38, 109,
  132, 160

relevancy, xxviii
research methodology, xiv, xvi-
  xvii, xx-xxii, xxiv-xvii, 111-112,
  155-158, 173-179
  ethics, 112, 176-179
  informed consent, 177
  institutional review, 175-176,
    174
Ricki Lake, 45
Roberts, Julia, 43-44
romance novels, xx, xxii, 18, 150
Rowand, Nada, 28

S

Santa Barbara, 7, 30, 36, 94
  Cruz, 30
  Eden, 30
Sarandon, Susan, 159
Savitch, Charlotte, 7
scopophilia, xviii
Scott, Melody Thomas, 27
Seinfeld, 3, 82
semiotic democracy, xv
sexuality as problem paradigm,
  48-50, 75
Siskel & Ebert, 171
Sisters, 63-64
Six Days, Seven Nights, 159
Slezak, Erika, 159
Sloane, Peggy, 72, 75, 84
Smith, Hillary B., 88
Smith, Pat Falken, 20
snowball sampling, 176
  soap opera
  actors, 7, 33, 35-36, 138-141, 144
  age deletion syndrome
    (SOADS), 32-34, 165, 168
  age representation, 8-9, 13, 24,
    31-33, 51-54, 56, 100-102, 106-
    107, 120, 128, 132, 147, 150, 164,
    168-169, 172
  audiences (fans), xiv, xxi-xxii,
    xxiv-xxvii, 1-14, 34-35, 41-58,
    89-90, 93-94, 96-97, 101-102, 108-

109, 126, 132, 143-152, 166-167, 172

back burner characters and storylines in, 35-36, 52-53, 132, 159, 164

babes, 11, 25-27, 64, 87

catfighting, 43-45, 101, 167

character archetypes, 24-31

character aptonyms, 44-45, 96

class representation, 3, 13, 137, 152, 165, 168, 170

commercial imperatives, xiv, xxvii, 6, 24, 28, 41-42, 57-59, 71, 97, 126-127, 128-129, 146-147, 152, 174

contracts, 35-36, 104

core families and characters, 34

divas, 25-27, 88

DOOLification, 36-39, 43-46, 52, 92, 109, 161, 164

education of audience, 132, 172

escape and, 37, 118, 149-151, 165

executive producers, 7, 166

format, 15-17, 33, 168

friendship networks (fan groups), xxi, 43, 145, 151

front burner characters and storylines, 35-36, 69, 103

gay readings, 46-50

gay representation, 46-50, 165

gender representation, 13, 24, 51-54, 56, 101-102, 125, 165

genre hybridization, 69-70

harridans, 25-27, 35, 45, 65, 164

head writers, 7-8, 166

hunks, 11, 25-27

ideology, 16-17, 128, 129

Internet sites, 141, 174-175, 178

interracial romance, 22-24, 72

listening posts, 27-28, 52

lobbying of actors, 138-141

meta-text, xxvii, 138-145, 173-176, 178

older man/younger woman romances, 28, 118, 134, 136, 138, 140

older woman/younger man romances, 48, 55, 64-65, 61-88, 89-110, 111-130, 133-140, 158-159

online fans, xxi, xxiv-xxv, xxv-xxvi, 7, 54-56, 58, 81-83, 90-92, 101-102, 132, 141-152, 166, 172

political resistance and, 49, 59, 115, 125, 145-152, 165, 168, 170

press and pundits, 13, 19-20, 69, 132, 140-143, 150, 160

production processes, 6-14, 41-42, 120

race representation, 145-149, 165

rape redemption storylines, 18-22, 137

rapid aging syndrome (SORAS), 10-11, 31-33, 65, 103, 160

ratings, 36, 127, 131-132, 135

realism (sereality), 33, 37, 46, 72, 74-75, 86, 114-116, 126, 131, 136-137, 167

resurrection, 30, 33

satellites, 27-28, 35

serial monogamy, 31, 168

spoilers, 141

standards of appearance, 25, 149, 153-154, 165, 169

Summer storylines, 9-11

supercouples/couples, 12, 17, 19, 21-22, 29-31

supertriangles/triangles, 34-35, 103-104

supervillains, 27-29

tabloidization of, 43-46, 101, 109

time and, 31-34

tentpole characters, 34

vixens, 25-27, 35

youthification of, 8-13, 28, 36-
    37, 52-58, 106, 132, 153-154, 160
Soap Opera Digest, 55-56, 69, 140
    150, 160, 174
Soap Opera Magazine, 160, 174
Soap Opera News, 160
Soap Opera Now!, 69, 140, 174
Soap Opera Update, 174
Soap Opera Weekly, 174
Soap Operas in Depth, 160, 174
Soap Update, 69, 174
social inertia, xviii, 5
spamming, 153
spectatorship, xviii
Spelling, Aaron, 12
Star Trek, 2, 122, 130
Streep, Meryl, 171
Stuart, Anna, 32, 65, 70, 72, 88, 108-
    109, 119, 138-139, 164, 172
subjectivity, xvi, xviii, xx-xxi, xxvi-
    xxvii, 2-4, 15-38, 87, 117, 125,
    137-137, 166
Summer of '42, 63
Sunset Beach, 12, 159, 160
    Olivia, 159
Sunset Boulevard, 62
Sweeney, Alison, 154
sweeps, 29, 73

T

tabloid talk shows, 43-45
Tea and Sympathy, 63
textual analysis, xiv, xvii-xviii, xx,
    4, 19, 126, 173-174
textual poaching, 2, 122, 126,
    170
The City, 160
Thelma and Louise, 25
Thin Man, 70
thirtysomething, xxi, 63, 136

time-factored analysis, xxiv, 20,
    68-69
time-shifting, 126
TV Guide, 174

U

Usenet newsgroups, 56-57, 122,
    145-142, 1148-149, 151, 153, 171,
    177

V

Valente, John, 143-144
voyeurism, xviii

W

Wagner, Don, 140
Weston, Riley, 153
Wheeler, Ellen, 26
White Palace, 63
Will and Grace, 3
woman as image approach, xviii
Wyman, Jane, 97

X

X-Files, 2, 130

Y

Young and the Restless (Y&R),
    xxiii, 7, 23-24, 27, 28, 49, 64, 164,
    173
    Cole, 64
    Hope, 164
    Katherine, 28
    Neil, 23-24
    Nikki, 27, 64, 164
    Victor, 164
    Victoria, 23-24

Z

Zaslow, Michael, 172
Zeta-Jones, Catherine, 171
Zimmer, Kim, 27

Printed in the United States
15723LVS00004B/229-282